Fostering
Volunteer Programs
in the Public Sector

Jeffrey L. Brudney

Fostering
Volunteer Programs
in the Public Sector

Planning, Initiating,
and Managing
Voluntary Activities

 Jossey-Bass Publishers

San Francisco   •   Oxford   •   1990

FOSTERING VOLUNTEER PROGRAMS IN THE PUBLIC SECTOR
Planning, Initiating, and Managing Voluntary Activities
by Jeffrey L. Brudney

Copyright © 1990 by: Jossey-Bass Inc., Publishers
350 Sansome Street
San Francisco, California 94104
&
Jossey-Bass Limited
Headington Hill Hall
Oxford OX3 0BW

Library of Congress Cataloging-in-Publication Data
Brudney, Jeffrey L.
  Fostering volunteer programs in the public sector : planning,
initiating, and managing voluntary activities / Jeffrey L. Brudney.
    p.   cm. -- (A joint publication of the Jossey-Bass public
administration series and the Jossey-Bass nonprofit sector series)
  Includes bibliographical references (p. 217).
  ISBN 1-55542-242-X
  1. Voluntarism--United States--Management.   I. Title.
II. Series: Jossey-Bass public administration series.   III. Series:
Jossey-Bass nonprofit sector.
  HN90.V64B78 1990
350.007'8--dc20   90-4226
                                                                       CIP

Manufactured in the United States of America

The paper in this book meets the guidelines for
permanence and durability of the Committee on
Production Guidelines for Book Longevity of the
Council on Library Resources.

JACKET DESIGN BY WILLI BAUM

FIRST EDITION

Code 9045

A joint publication in
The Jossey-Bass Public Administration Series
and The Jossey-Bass Nonprofit Sector Series

Contents

For Nancy, Megan, and Philip Brudney

Preface

It would be easier to do it myself. Anonymous

How much could it be worth if it is free?
Anonymous

I had heard the preceding opinions expressed about volunteers long before I started this book. I had also heard that volunteers consume valuable staff time that could be better applied to other pursuits. Other common views are that public organizations have no quality control over volunteers, but an agency, especially one mired in fiscal stringency, can hardly turn down citizens who want to help out, regardless of their qualifications. Without the leverage of a paycheck, volunteers cannot be managed: They are unreliable, balk at paperwork, and resist supervision. Since volunteers give their time, an organization would be ungrateful to evaluate them or to hold them accountable for performance, much less to "fire" them for not meeting standards of conduct or quality.

As with most aphorisms, opposing ones seemed equally plausible. Volunteers can stretch public budgets. They can add a new dimension of "sharing and caring" to government services. They possess important linkages to the community. People volunteer for disparate reasons, but improvement—of themselves, public agencies, clients—is a salient motivation.

xiii

To meet their goals, volunteers expect, and will accept, direction. Volunteers are not selfless, but they do want to make a difference in some way. Perhaps the worst fate that could befall them would be to learn that their time has been wasted because an agency lacks a commitment to managing all of its human resources.

Based on original survey research and extensive fieldwork, as well as literature from several disciplines, this book evaluates competing claims regarding volunteers. Specifically, it examines how volunteers are involved in the delivery of government services and how volunteer programs can be initiated, bolstered, and sustained in the public sector.

Scope and Features

Most of the research on volunteers is not concerned with programs sponsored by government. Nonprofit organizations are the chief employers of voluntary assistance, and to the degree that public agencies have received attention, the coverage has been secondary. Even within the field of public administration, treatment has been rare. This book adopts a different perspective.

Here, government is the focus of inquiry. Volunteers have a lengthy and distinguished record of assistance to the public sector, and their participation continues to grow. Governments are turning away from the direct delivery of public goods and services toward reliance on third parties. Many public administrators already have responsibilities in volunteer management, and the trend is accelerating. This obligation is too important and too widespread to be left to past habit and convention.

Fostering Volunteer Programs in the Public Sector shows how volunteer involvement can be a coherent approach for providing and enhancing services, and for aiding government organizations in achieving policy goals. To that end, it explores methods for planning and designing the volunteer program, attracting and retaining capable volunteers, coordinating the efforts of paid staff and volunteers, and managing the program and strengthening accountability. It addresses attendant issues, including: possible resistance from paid staff, evaluation of volunteer performance, insurance coverage for volunteers, the monetary costs of a program, the need for support from the top of the organization, and steps that practitioners and scholars can take to encourage the approach in the public sector.

In addition to the focus on volunteer programs within government, other features make this book distinctive. First, it draws on a rich store of information from a public agency whose experience with volunteers spans a quarter of a century. Since 1964, volunteers from the Service Corps of Retired Executives, or the SCORE Association, have assisted the U.S. Small Business Administration (SBA) in counseling and training agency clients in techniques of business management. From the beginning, the SBA has played a very active role in organizing the volunteers and developing the association. SCORE receives all funding from the SBA and has no other functions or purpose than service to the agency. The volunteers might be considered "gratuitous employees" of the Office of Business Development. Extensive fieldwork and interviews conducted at SBA offices and at the SCORE national headquarters and chapters in the field illustrate the dynamics of a long-standing partnership.

Second, results from surveys administered to officials of the two groups add empirical grounding to the discussion. In 1985 and 1986, I mailed questionnaires to chairpersons of all SCORE chapters and to SBA business development personnel who work with the volunteers. Completed questionnaires are available from 333 chairpersons (85 percent response rate) and 103 of the business development officers (51 percent). Thus, the study combines systematic information from both principals to the volunteer-agency relationship.

Third, the text takes advantage of the broad literature on volunteerism, much of it the product of scholars outside the field of public administration. While examination of the SBA-SCORE collaboration in the delivery of government services lends depth and empirical assurance to the inquiry, the book is not a case study of a single organization or program. Instead, this example is used for purposes of supporting and amplifying general themes regarding volunteer involvement. The SBA and SCORE assume a greater role to the degree that the literature is ambivalent, or even silent, on matters crucial to volunteer programs in government.

Audience

This book is intended for two main groups. The first consists of public administrators at all levels of government whose jobs encompass working with volunteers in the provision of services. Although managers of volunteer programs in the public sector should find this book most useful, it will also help line employees who collaborate with volunteers to do so more constructively. In addition, the book can assist elected and appointed officials in agencies that do not have volunteers to assess the challenges and potential of the method. Should they decide to introduce volunteers, the book elaborates the measures and support necessary to establish and maintain a successful program.

The second major audience consists of students and academics with an abiding interest in the participation of volunteers in government services. As proposals for national public service and other volunteer-based initiatives gain visibility and momentum, this group is on the rise. It includes students and their mentors in graduate programs in public administration and related fields who want to learn more about volunteerism. It also embraces researchers studying alternative means to the direct production of services by government employees, particularly greater involvement by citizens.

Another group who should find this book useful are executives and managers of nonprofit organizations that have volunteers or contemplate their participation. Although the work environment differs from the public sector, volunteer programs sponsored by these organizations share basic concerns with government programs, such as satisfactory relations with paid staff and adequate control over performance. To a lesser degree, the book could also help managers of employee volunteer programs underwritten by civic-minded business firms. Although the context and thrust of these efforts are quite distinct from government, the managers face similar problems of volunteer program design, organization, recognition, and funding.

Overview of the Contents

Chapter One elaborates the scope of volunteer activity in the public sector that is intended to aid government organizations in producing goods and services and reaching other agency goals. It explains why volunteer involvement has increased in government and how this change affects public employees and managers. The chapter reviews research on volunteerism in public administration and suggests a reorientation toward greater attention to volunteer programs organized and sponsored by government.

The remainder of the book is organized into three major sections. Part One examines the effects of volunteers on the delivery of public services. Chapter Two shows that well-designed and well-managed volunteer programs are not "free," but that they more than justify expenditures in terms of service to clients and the organization. The chapter presents an inventory for costing volunteer programs and uses SCORE to illustrate a methodology for estimating the dollar value of volunteer efforts and calculating a ratio of cost-effectiveness for the program. The chapter exposes the legal, ethical, and practical dilemmas of displacing employees with volunteers.

Dollars alone are not an adequate standard for evaluating the burdens and benefits of a volunteer program. Chapter Three turns to the criterion of effectiveness. The chapter describes three ways in which volunteers can improve the quality and impact of government services. These dimensions consist of (1) the performance of volunteers in the jobs assigned to them, (2) their facilitation of the work of paid staff, and (3) their unique contributions and insights as citizens beyond simply filling job requirements.

Chapter Four examines the involvement of service volunteers in the public sector as part of a growing trend among jurisdictions in this country toward "government by proxy": the delivery of publicly funded goods and services by nongovernmental organizations and personnel. The chapter elaborates the challenges to public administrators arising from volunteer participation. It calls for appropriate methods to foster effective performance and ensure accountability when the producers of government services are not employees.

Part Two addresses issues of planning, design, and management of the volunteer program. Chapter Five shows how to design the volunteer operation to realize the full benefits of the approach. The chapter elucidates a framework for this purpose, consisting of five general elements: (1) organizing the program, (2) matching volunteers and organizational needs, (3) educating citizens for volunteer service in the public sector, (4) training employees in volunteer management and supervision, and (5) evaluating and recognizing the volunteer effort.

Experts concur that the most enduring obstacle to the implementation and operation of a productive volunteer program is the often antagonistic reaction from employees. Chapter Six presents a strategy to overcome this barrier. The strategy centers on the formulation of goals for the program; review and possible amendment of agency policy and pertinent legislation; support from top management; involvement of agency leadership, staff, and volunteers in program planning and decision making; and incentives to staff members for effective collaboration with volunteers.

All the advantages (and difficulties) of volunteer programs discussed thus far presume the willing availability of citizen participants to public agencies. As Chapter Seven shows, this truism should not obscure the reality that attracting and retaining volunteers has become an increasingly demanding task for government as well as for other organizations. The chapter assesses the size of the volunteering public potentially available to government, analyzes societal and economic trends that will affect its magnitude, and elaborates methods to meet the essential challenges of recruiting and retaining volunteers.

Part Three is concerned with fostering greater volunteer involvement in the public sector. Because this book is written for practitioners and scholars in public administration, Chapter Eight discusses actions that each group should consider to encourage a volunteer approach. For elected and appointed officials and public employees, priorities include appropriate legislation and organizational policies, insurance coverage for volunteers, volunteer demonstration projects, and measures to promote acquisition and sharing of knowledge on volunteerism. For academics, the research agenda should encompass firmer estimates of the magnitude and nature of volunteer involvement in public agencies, alternative techniques for sharing the workplace between employees and volunteers, improved methods for evaluating the volunteer program, and examination of volunteer activity outside of government-sponsored efforts.

The concluding chapter presents recommendations for strengthening existing government volunteer programs and guiding new voluntary initiatives. The recommendations focus on adequate funding for the volunteer program, arrangements for power sharing, orientation and training for employees and volunteers, increased access to volunteer opportunities, and promotion of feedback from the program.

A "Resource" section at the end of the book describes the procedures and details of the surveys administered to chapter chairpersons of the Service Corps of Retired Executives and the business development officers of the Small Business Administration. This section displays both questionnaires.

Athens, Georgia   Jeffrey L. Brudney
March 1990

Acknowledgments

Probably the most enjoyable aspect of preparing this book was the opportunity to meet a variety of interesting people. In one way or another, many individuals assisted in this project, and I am most grateful to them.

At the earliest stages of the project in 1984, Richard D. Lee, formerly a regional representative of the SCORE Association, took an interest in the research and helped in the development of survey questionnaires to be administered to SCORE officials. He was instrumental in convincing the SCORE board of directors of the merits of a survey. James Black, Kel Bamford, and John Titley, past presidents of the SCORE Association, also lent their support. The National SCORE Office (NSO), then headed by Paul Eiseman, facilitated the survey process and has proved a great resource as well as friend to the project. In particular, I wish to thank NSO Executive Director John Daniels and Office Administrator Priscilla McNeil for their graciousness in responding to my all-too-frequent requests for information.

My debt is also great to the U.S. Small Business Administration and numerous SBA officials. At the central office in Washington, D.C., Lawrence R. Rosenbaum, Arnold S. Rosenthal, Charles Thomas, and Carolyn Shackleford kindly supplied data on SBA personnel, finances, and activities. Thomas A. Gray of the SBA Office of Advocacy provided additional data. Several officials discussed with me at length the operations of the Office of Business Development and SCORE: Patricia Czerwonky, Christopher Kobler, Grant C. Moon, Harriet P. Soll, John R. Cox, and George Solomon.

Individuals at field offices of the SBA were equally accommodating. When the project was just beginning, I took advantage of my proximity to the Atlanta SBA office to talk frequently with John Jones, Burton Scott, Clarence Barnes, John L. Brown, II, and John P. Latimer. Throughout the research, I benefited from Philip Mahoney's experience and perceptiveness. James N. Thomson opened many doors for me. Craig S. Rice of the Omaha SBA office offered good advice. I also learned from interviews with SCORE members, especially Joseph Lommer and John Gaines of the Atlanta chapter.

I want to express my gratitude to the Small Business Development Center (SBDC) at the University of Georgia. William C. Flewellen, Jr., founder of the Georgia SBDC, and Frank Hoy, former director, provided encouragement, support, and access. These individuals, as well as Jennifer Horton and Eugene W. Griner, gave me a better understanding of the SBDC and its relationship to the Small Business Administration.

Other people at the University of Georgia have earned my appreciation. James R. Kuhlman, head librarian for the social sciences, was extremely helpful in directing me to relevant sources and acquiring a great number that were not in the collection. Several graduate students assisted me at various stages of the research: Jong-Soon Kim, Clifford Mulder, Soo-Geun Song, and Samuel Bellin. Catherine Getzen Willoughby and Yew-Mei Yao did a superior job in coding the data from the surveys and preparing them for analysis. A grant from the University of Georgia Office of the Vice President for Research provided funding for the surveys and some of the field work.

I wish to thank Thomas G. Powers, chief counsel to the Committee on Small Business, U.S. House of Representatives, and C. Randall Nuckolls, who worked as chief counsel and legislative director to Senator Sam Nunn, for their assistance. Ruth March, of Involvement Corps, kept me apprised of the status of resolutions in the Congress to recognize the importance of volunteerism. Joseph Bass, of the ACTION agency, and Billie Ann Myers, Director of the Arkansas Office of Volunteerism, provided useful information on State Offices of Volunteerism.

Many of the themes and conclusions developed in the pages that follow are based on findings from the surveys administered to chapter chairpersons of SCORE and business development personnel at the SBA. I am grateful to participants for their time and interest. Their responses greatly aided in refining, and often revising, my ideas concerning volunteer programs in the public sector.

At Jossey-Bass, Lynn D. W. Luckow helped to transform initial impressions and hypotheses, fieldwork observations, and survey findings into a viable book plan. Alan Shrader has been an able successor as editor. I have appreciated their constant support and encouragement. Vivian Koenig, Stacey C. Sawyer, and Elizabeth Judd provided excellent editorial assistance.

Finally, I want to thank the reviewers for observations and insights that have strengthened this book. Ivan Scheier read early drafts of two chapters and offered useful comments and suggestions. Delwyn A. Dyer, Kenneth B. Perkins, and Jon Van Til reviewed the entire manuscript and provided constructive critiques that helped me to avoid errors and improve the study. I bear final responsibility for the contents.

Most of these individuals received no direct compensation for their assistance, although I would hope that they take some measure of satisfaction in seeing the end product to which they contributed. In that sense, they were volunteers. This project would not have been easier—or, perhaps, even possible—if I had had to do it myself. It surely would not have been as rewarding. And because these people gave their help freely, it was worth all the more to me.

J.L.B.

The Author

Jeffrey L. Brudney is an associate professor of public administration in the department of political science at the University of Georgia. He received his B.A. degree (1972) in political science from the University of California at Berkeley and his M.A. (1974) and Ph.D. (1978) degrees, also in political science, from the University of Michigan at Ann Arbor.

Brudney's main research activities have centered on citizen participation in the delivery of public services. Some of this research has appeared in *Public Administration Review, Journal of Voluntary Action Research* and its successor *Nonprofit and Voluntary Sector Quarterly, Administration and Society, Public Productivity Review, Policy Studies Journal,* and *Urban Affairs Quarterly.* He has been a member of the Association of Voluntary Action Scholars since 1985, and in 1989 he was elected to its board of directors.

Brudney maintains a strong interest in public administration education. He is chair-elect of the Section on Public Administration Education of the American Society for Public Administration (ASPA). He is a contributor to the *Handbook of Public Administration* (edited by J. L. Perry, 1989) and the author, of *Applied Statistics for Public Administration* (with K. J. Meier, 1987).

Fostering
Volunteer Programs
in the Public Sector

1

The Growth of Volunteerism
in the Public Sector

Ask not what your country can do for you—ask what you can do for your country. President John F. Kennedy, 1961

The old ideas are new again because they're not old, they are timeless: duty, sacrifice, commitment and a patriotism that finds its expression in taking part and pitching in. President George H. Bush, 1989

Nearly three decades separated the inaugurations of Presidents Kennedy and Bush, but on one issue at least they expressed remarkable continuity: the need for greater involvement of citizens in the delivery of public services. The encouragement of volunteerism by recent presidential administrations, including those of Lyndon Johnson, Richard Nixon, Jimmy Carter, and Ronald Reagan, forms part of a venerable tradition in America, dating back to the seminal observations of Alexis de Tocqueville in the early 1800s, if not to "the days of the Mayflower" (Ellis, 1985b, p. 11). As their appeals indicate, volunteerism is not the exclusive province of one political party or the other; expansion of volunteering has been a goal of public policy since the 1960s (Chambré, 1989). Nor despite current interest in the approach should it be considered only

1

as a stopgap measure to deal with harsh economic realities, or a cynical ploy for governments to offload responsibilities. Volunteers have been active in providing public services in periods of munificence as well as scarcity, usually preceding the formal introduction of government. Indeed, many consider volunteerism interwoven with the very fabric of American democracy and culture (see Park, 1983; Kramer, 1981).

An approach to government services emphasizing the participation of volunteers might build on an impressive foundation. According to the most recent survey on volunteerism conducted by the Gallup Organization, in 1988, nearly half (45.3 percent) of the adult, noninstitutional population of the United States—some 80 million people—donated time to an organization. They contributed a total of 14.9 billion hours, the equivalent of 8.8 million full-time employees. If recipient organizations had to pay for this labor, the estimated dollar value would have reached 149.8 billion (Hodgkinson and Weitzman, 1988b, p. 8).

Volunteers are usually considered in the context of the voluntary, nonprofit sector. National surveys consistently find that the great majority of volunteers report working for nonprofit organizations (for example, Hodgkinson and Weitzman, 1988b; Gallup Organization, 1986, 1981). Yet a significant amount of volunteer labor is directed to public agencies: U.S. government agencies operate as many as 20 to 30 percent of all organized volunteer programs, and perhaps another 20 to 30 percent of these programs are associated with the public sector (Rydberg and Peterson, 1980, pp. 19-20). In 1985, just over one in five volunteers contributed time to government (Gallup Organization, 1986, p. 5). In that year, 13.2 percent of the American populace—about 23 million people—volunteered to a public agency at the local, state, or federal level (Sundeen, 1989, p. 558). As Ivan H. Scheier, an authority in the field of volunteerism, states, "A substantial proportion of volunteer efforts in this country today are government-sponsored in some significant sense" (in Rydberg and Peterson, 1980, p. 20).

This book follows from a simple premise: Scholars and practitioners of public administration need to know more about working with volunteers to deliver government services. While volunteerism has a long, even "ancient" history (Newland, 1984, p. 162), only recently have students of public administration begun to consider the participation of volunteers as a systematic approach to providing services. What follows is intended to advance that discussion. This first chapter elaborates the magnitude of volunteer involvement in the public sector, the reasons for the renewed emphasis on volunteerism, the state of research within public administration on the approach, and its importance for public management.

Service Volunteers in the Public Sector

Volunteerism and *volunteer* are not easy terms to define. This book focuses on service-oriented or "operations" volunteering occurring under the auspices of a government agency. In a key article, David Horton Smith (1972) defines service volunteers as individuals who donate their time to help other people directly, in the realms of health, welfare, housing, education, recreation, rehabilitation, and so forth. Their activities are "widely perceived as the heart of volunteerism . . . the countless individual acts of commitment encompassing an endless variety of volunteer tasks" (Park, 1983, p. 118). The hallmark of the volunteer concept is that these individuals are not compensated monetarily for their labor, but Smith (and other scholars) allow that they may receive partial, subsistence remuneration and/or reimbursement for out-of-pocket expenses.

In this study, volunteers work in an organizational setting, in programs sponsored by government. Although the emphasis remains on their involvement in delivering public services, the study considers associated functions performed by volunteers, particularly organizational maintenance, and fund raising and advocacy on behalf of government agencies. Here, the approach is limited to volunteers who work directly for an institution in the public sector, rather than for a private (for example, charitable or nonprofit) organization.

Service Volunteers in Government. At all levels of government, volunteers are prevalent in the delivery of services. A 1982 survey of cities and counties conducted by the International City Management Association (ICMA) documented high levels of volunteer involvement, especially in the human and social services. The most common area of volunteer assistance was in cultural and arts programs (in 32 percent of local governments), followed by museum operations (21 percent), recreation services (20 percent), programs for the elderly (18 percent), fire prevention and fire fighting (18 percent), emergency medical services (16 percent), and ambulance service (15 percent) (Valente and Manchester, 1984, p. xv).

A replication of the ICMA local government survey in 1988 demonstrates strong growth over the decade in the participation of volunteers in delivering services (Morley, 1989). At least one-quarter of the cities and counties that responded to the more recent survey relied on volunteers in the areas of culture and the arts (41 percent of local governments), museum operations (34 percent), recreation services (26 percent), and programs for the elderly (25 percent). In addition, between 1982 and 1988, the percentages of localities with volunteers assisting in drug/alcohol treatment (6 percent versus 10 percent), child welfare programs (6 percent versus 11 percent), and crime prevention (9 percent versus 16 percent) nearly doubled. While the rates of volunteer involvement in fire prevention and fire fighting (19 percent), emergency medical services (18 percent), and ambulance service (17 percent) showed minimal increases, by 1988 volunteers had emerged as a principal means for many cities and counties to combat problems of homelessness. Of local governments with such initiatives, 37 percent employed volunteers in food programs for the homeless, and 26 percent had them at homeless shelters.

Although comparable data do not exist pertaining to other levels of government, the participation of service volunteers in federal agencies and among the states also appears substantial. With respect to the latter, since 1974, ACTION— the "Federal Domestic Volunteer Agency"—has sponsored a grant program to assist in the establishment of "State Offices of Volunteerism" (SOV). Over the course of the program, ACTION has awarded grants totaling approximately $3 million; nearly all states have participated. The SOVs promote and coordinate existing volunteer programs within state government and aid in the design and development of additional offices and programs. They also facilitate and support federal volunteer efforts, as well as the activities of private voluntary organizations (Schwartz, 1989). As of 1989, thirty-two states maintained offices to foster volunteerism, and another seven had a contact person or representative with this responsibility.

The State Offices of Volunteerism are a complex federal-state interaction. Volunteers are also active in state-operated functions, such as human services, corrections, parks and recreation, public health, education, and tourism (Allen and others, 1989). For example, 60 percent of state park systems employ volunteers to provide visitor services (Myers and Reid, 1986).

At the federal level, ACTION and the Peace Corps are the agencies best known for enlisting volunteers. ACTION resulted from President Nixon's Reorganization Plan Number 1 of 1971, which attempted to consolidate federal volunteer programs into a single organization responsible for promoting citizen volunteerism. With a volunteer complement that numbers in the hundreds of thousands, ACTION houses most of these programs, including Volunteers in Service to America (VISTA), citizen participation and volunteer demonstration programs, and Older American volunteer programs (Retired Senior Volunteer program, Foster Grandparents, and Senior Companion program). Once a part of ACTION but autonomous since 1981, the Peace Corps places over 5,000 Americans in voluntary service in over sixty countries worldwide. In general, ACTION and Peace Corps volunteers receive a minimal stipend.

Federal volunteer programs are not limited to these agencies. The national government also sponsors 4-H clubs and extension programs of the Cooperative Extension Service of the Department of Agriculture; the Volunteers in the Parks of the National Park Service of the Department of the Interior; the Tax Counseling for the Elderly (TCE) and Volunteer Income Tax Assistance (VITA) programs of the Internal Revenue Service of the Department of the Treasury; and the Service Corps of Retired Executives (SCORE) volunteers of the Small Business Administration. Additional federal agencies that support volunteer programs include the Department of Housing and Urban Development, the Department of Health and Human Services, the Department of Justice, the Department of Transportation, the Environmental Protection Agency, the Forest Service, and the Veterans Administration.

Aside from studies of city and county governments, systematic data on the participation of service volunteers in the public sector are limited. Nevertheless, the evidence available suggests that volunteers assist large numbers of government offices at all levels, and that this practice is increasing (see below).

Volunteers and Public-Private Partnerships. Public administrators and their mentors in academia need to learn more about the involvement of volunteers in service delivery, not only because of the prevalence of this approach in government but also because of its importance to nonprofit organizations. Lester M. Salamon (1987, p. 116) has documented the extensive interdependence between the public and voluntary, nonprofit sectors: "For better or worse, cooperation between government and the voluntary sector is the approach this nation has chosen to deal with its human service problems. Though largely overlooked both in treatments of the voluntary sector and in analyses of the American welfare state, this pattern of cooperation has grown into a massive system of action that accounts for at least as large a share of government-funded human services as are delivered by government agencies themselves and that constitutes the largest single source of nonprofit-sector income." Through public-private partnerships, nonprofit organizations actually deliver a larger share of the health and human services financed by government than do public agencies themselves—and they depend heavily on volunteers to do so. Thus, even if their agency does not have volunteers, public employees may well find that their job requires them to work with a nonprofit organization in which volunteers play an integral role in providing government-sponsored services.

Partnership agreements between the public and the nonprofit sectors, moreover, are on the rise. According to a 1987 report prepared for the National Association of Schools of Public Affairs and Administration (NASPAA), "the public sector involvement of nonprofits has been increasing over time and this trend promises to continue, no matter what the political stripe of future administrations" (Young, 1987, pp. 6-7). As partnerships become ever more common, and the nonprofit sector assumes greater significance for public management, the need for education regarding volunteerism grows apace.

Volunteerism: A Renewal of Interest

The involvement of volunteers in the production of public services is not a new phenomenon. Historically, volunteer personnel have been the backbone of a variety of government services (Valente and Manchester, 1984). In the late 1970s and throughout the 1980s, however, several forces combined not only to increase reliance on volunteers but also to change the way in which scholars and practitioners conceive of this practice. These forces are likely to continue, and with them, the significance of the volunteer option in the public sector.

The Fiscal Climate. The primary catalyst to increased governmental interest in volunteer involvement is a serious, long-term erosion in fiscal capability. At the federal level, the unprecedented budget deficits accumulated during the administration of President Ronald Reagan and the cutback measures taken to arrest them, such as the 1985 Balanced Budget and Emergency Deficit Control Act (Gramm-Rudman-Hollings), offer the most compelling evidence. But even before the deficits commanded political attention and action, the administration had exacted deep cuts in federal appropriations for social welfare, health, housing, education, the environment, and culture and the arts. President Reagan's "New Federalism" policies aimed at devolving service-delivery responsibilities to the states and localities, yet the cuts impaired the capacity of these governments to assume additional obligations. The reductions also began at a time when the states had largely depleted their current and prospective fiscal reserves, thus making it especially difficult for them to replace lost federal funds or to take over new programs (Peterson, 1982). The cessation of federal revenue sharing funds in 1986 has exacerbated these conditions. A number of scholars attribute the rise in citizen involvement in public service provision to the financial stress faced by communities suffering from a declining local economic base and heavy decreases in federal funding (for example, Ferris, 1988; Manser, 1987; Warren, 1987; Duncombe, 1985; Valente, 1985; Brown, 1983; Farr, 1983).

Particularly during the late 1970s and early 1980s, citizen opposition to tax increases foreclosed this traditional remedy for fiscal imbalance. In June 1978, Californians overwhelmingly approved Proposition 13, slashing property taxes and setting off a flurry of initiatives across states and cities to cut or cap revenues—perhaps the best known among them being Proposition 2½, passed by Massachusetts voters in 1980. Before 1978, only three states had state tax limitations; ten years later, twenty limited either taxes or spending. As evidenced by the adamant public stance of Presidents Reagan and Bush, the resounding defeat in the 1984 presidential campaign suffered by Walter Mondale (who had promised to raise taxes) and in 1988 by Michael Dukakis (who refused to dismiss this possibility), and the recourse to automatic spending cuts (rather than increased taxes) in the Gramm-Rudman-Hollings legislation, this movement extends to the federal level as well. Although voters may have moderated antitaxation views somewhat as the decade wore on (Peirce, 1988), consensus exists that the economic, social, psychological, and political maladies besetting the nation cannot be dealt with by massive growth in government along the lines of the 1950s and 1960s (Glazer, 1983, p. 90).

At the same time, the populace seems unwilling to tolerate major retrenchment in the provision of government goods and services as the "answer" to fiscal problems. Skeptical of a connection between reductions in taxing and spending authority and diminished services, the public has shown little inclination to temper demands on government to satisfy basic human needs and to combat enduring social and economic problems. As substantiated by many studies, the impetus behind the citizen "tax revolt" was not necessarily a desire for lower service levels, but the belief that local governments could attain greater technical efficiency, that is, produce the same level of services with fewer resources (Ferris, 1988). In fact, the demands of the public for government services continue to escalate (Beck, Rainey, Nicholls, and Traut, 1987).

In addition to the service expectations of citizens, the nation must address critical unmet needs in the fields of education, health care (including care of the elderly and the infirm), child care, conservation and the environment, and a number of other social services, such as criminal justice and public safety, libraries and museums, food distribution, and urban parks and recreation (Danzig and Szanton, 1986). Demographic changes in the composition of the population as well as decay in essential infrastructure systems (streets, highways, bridges, water treatment and distribution, airports and other public facilities) will put enormous pressure on governments for at least the next two decades (Democratic Leadership Council, 1988; David, 1987; Choate and Walter, 1983).

Volunteers and Alternative Service Approaches. The combined forces of fiscal stress, revenue restrictions, and rising popular demand have led many government officials to rethink traditional modes for the delivery of services. A report prepared by the Task Force on Critical Problems (1982, p. i) for the New York State Senate emphasized the challenge to state and local governments posed by these developments: "Will the State and its localities be able to continue to offer the wide variety of high quality human services that their citizens have come to expect and rely upon?"

The broad parameters of an approach began to appear as early as 1980. Warning of the need to "get by modestly," an ICMA-assembled Committee on Future Horizons advised local governments to effect greater involvement by citizens, as well as use of private firms in delivering services (Rutter, 1980, pp. 93–97). The results of a 1987 national survey of city governments of more than 5,000 population and counties above 25,000 attest to the viability of this strategy (Touche Ross, 1987). Citing citizens' demands, popular opposition to tax hikes, and the elimination of federal revenue sharing funds most often as reasons, nearly 80 percent of the 1,086 respondents stated that in the last five years their governments had moved toward greater reliance on the private sector. And a study of 714 cities and counties with a population of at least 25,000 found that governments that imposed a high tax burden on residents were more likely to enlist volunteers in the production of public goods and services (Ferris, 1988).

The consideration of alternative methods for the delivery of public services reflects a growing spirit of entrepreneurship and innovativeness among local officials (Cigler, 1989). Volunteer personnel are an important element of this approach (Morgan and England, 1988; Savas, 1987; Valente and Manchester, 1984; Hatry, 1983; Shulman, 1982). While contracting out has attracted most attention as an alternative to the standard model of service provision through public employees, volunteers offer a highly potent means to limit the size yet increase the effectiveness of government. Indeed, the New York State Legislature Task Force Report (1982) urged states and municipalities to facilitate and support volunteerism as the key to maintaining programs and services in an era of fiscal decline.

An increase in volunteer involvement during the 1980s suggests that many governments have accepted that judgment. Economist Burton A. Weisbrod (1988, p. 202) estimates that the number of full-time equivalent volunteers to government (calculated on the basis of 1,700 hours per year) grew by 50 percent from 1977 to 1985, from 0.8 million to 1.2 million. The trend is most evident among localities. Based on the survey results discussed above, the ICMA estimated that in 1982, 56.5 percent of cities over 4,500 population employed volunteers in at least one service domain (Shulman, 1982). By 1985, the number had swelled to 72.6 percent (Duncombe, 1985). According to the second ICMA survey, in 1988 the extent of volunteer participation reported by cities and counties ranked second only to use of contracting with respect to both the number of services where the method is applied and the percentage of local governments that have adopted it. Elaine Morley (1989, p. 44), the author of that study, concludes that the volunteer option has become "well entrenched" as a service delivery approach across a wide range of services. "It seems reasonable to expect . . . continuation or potential growth in the future."

The "Push" and the "Pull" of Volunteerism. The search for greater cost-effectiveness in the delivery of public services has fueled much of this expansion. An editorial in the January 1983 issue of the *National Civic Review* put the case for government volunteers most forcefully: "When an increase in people's needs for public services . . . occurs at the same time that governments find it necessary to reduce services due to fiscal constraints, the absolute necessity of volunteer service becomes obvious" (1983, p. 4). In a similar manner, a Virginia legislator summarized one of the chief merits of the state's office for volunteerism: "We're not talking about saving money—we're talking about providing services with money we do not have" (in Millard, 1983, p. 263). Although this view overlooks the monetary costs of volunteer programs, the underlying logic seems persuasive: As a relatively inexpensive form of labor, volunteers offer governments the potential to maintain or even enhance the amount and quality of services with a minimal investment of public resources. Thus, citizen participation in the delivery of services has emerged as an attractive option for financially strapped governments to augment capacity and reduce dependence on paid employees (for example, Ferris, 1988; Strickler, 1987; Allen, 1987; Agranoff and Pattakos, 1984; DeHoog, 1984). Chapters Two and Three examine the extent to which volunteers can assist public organizations in providing services efficiently and with greater effectiveness.

For many governments, these anticipated advantages constitute the primary "pull" or attraction of volunteers. Two other developments provided the "push" to heighten awareness of the approach and to confront "the traditional inclination of public administrators to keep the *participation* of citizens in agency operations at arm's length" (Levine, 1984, p. 185, emphasis in original; compare Walter, 1987; Haeuser and Schwartz, 1984; Kweit and Kweit, 1981). First, President Reagan's pledge to restore private, voluntary initiative as a meaningful component of domestic affairs deserves much of the credit. Though the approach was not defined in any precise way, the president repeatedly called on voluntary and civic associations, nonprofit and community organizations, corporate and individual philanthropy, and volunteers themselves to contribute to the achievement of public purposes. "Voluntarism is an essential part of our plan to give the government back to the people," the president declared in a speech typical of pronouncements of his administration. He designated the year May 1, 1983 until April 30, 1984 as the "National Year of Voluntarism" and established a Task Force on Private Sector Initiatives to publicize successful voluntary efforts, encourage new ones, and carry forward this work among the states. By 1983, task forces in forty-two states were spreading the message.

Scholars have legitimately questioned whether President Reagan fully understood the nature and parameters of the voluntary sector, and whether his administration took appropriate actions to strengthen rather than weaken it (for example, O'Connell, 1989; Hall, 1987; Musselwhite, 1986). No one questions the impact of his endorsement, however. Even in a sharp critique of administration policy, Brian O'Connell (1989, p. 489), founding president of Independent Sector, a national coalition of 650 foundations, corporations, and national voluntary organizations, allows that President Reagan's attention to private sector initiatives was "very helpful, and will have lasting benefits."

David Adams (1987) credits Reagan with reviving voluntarism as a "civil religion." A content analysis of the president's eight State of the Union addresses shows that in the area of domestic social affairs, the emphasis placed on voluntarism was second only to that accorded moral issues (Moen, 1988). His championing of private initiatives raised all forms of voluntary action into unaccustomed prominence on the public agenda (Salamon, 1984). Robert Agranoff and Alex N. Pattakos (1984, p. 81) agree that the "changes by the Reagan administration clearly have brought volunteerism as an alternative service strategy to center stage." The Democratic Party has contributed to this development through legislative proposals to enact a range of volunteer programs (Kuntz, 1989; Democratic Leadership Council, 1988).

Second, a gradual warming in adversarial relationships between public administrators and citizen participants at the local level has been equally important in encouraging volunteerism in government. Despite contentious roots in federal policies such as the Community Action Program of the Economic Opportunity Act of 1964, some twenty years of experience with citizen involvement came to fruition in the 1980s with a degree of softening of attitudes and behaviors on both sides. In a comprehensive study of this relationship in Cincinnati, John Clayton Thomas (1986, pp. 89–105) found that not only had citizen participation shifted away from petitioning elected officials and institutions to contacting city administrators and the service bureaucracy, but also that these interactions had become decidedly more amicable. Most of the time, residents and public managers collaborated in exchanging information and negotiating over agency plans, programs, and services. These changes may be associated with the onset of fiscal stress: Some research suggests that financial difficulties prompted officials in a number of cities to establish mechanisms for incorporating greater citizen involvement (for example, Pecorella, 1984).

While the scope of such initiatives cannot be determined across all local governments, citizen participation has refocused on the delivery of services through neighborhood groups and community organizations, normally in concert with public agencies (Nalbandian, 1987). The advantages to governments of an increase in involvement notwithstanding, the movement toward "empowerment" is largely citizen-driven. It springs from frustration with past modes of participation to provide genuine channels for influence in policy making, and from a concomitant desire of citizens to play a larger role in determining the quantity and quality of services they receive and the policies that affect them (for example, Brudney, 1989b; Sharp, 1980). Many local governments have abetted the movement by assisting neighborhoods in forming associations and organizing the groups on a citywide basis. Citizen participation in the production of services has become more common, and more accepted.

During the decade of the 1980s, diminished fiscal capacity in the face of unyielding public demands led many government agencies to consider alternative methods for the delivery of services. The involvement of volunteers is one of these approaches. As public managers sought to improve operating efficiencies, President Reagan's insistence on private initiatives elevated the profile of volunteerism. At the same time, citizen participation at the local level evinced a new phase of greater cooperation with service bureaucracies. The result has been a rejuvenation of interest in the effective involvement of volunteers in public service.

Public Administration and the Study of Volunteers

The Coproduction Model.   Practicing public managers are not the only group with an interest in volunteers. Public administration scholars have coined the term *coproduction* to describe the active involvement of citizens, including volunteers in government agencies, in the creation and especially the delivery of public goods and/or services (Ferris, 1984; Percy, 1984; Brudney and England, 1983; Parks and others,

1981). Coproduction entails cooperative efforts between public officials on the one hand, and citizens, neighborhood associations, community organizations, or client groups on the other, in the provision of government services.

The coproduction literature points to two primary benefits of the approach. First, by combining the labor of citizens and employees in public endeavors, coproduction has the potential to expand government capability to meet human needs while holding the line on budget (Thomas, 1987; Percy, 1987, 1983; Brudney, 1984; Ferris, 1984; Bjur and Siegel, 1977). Second, by offering alternatives to conventional modes for citizen participation in public affairs, coproduction holds promise for a resurgence in citizenship and an enhanced role conception for government officials (Levine, 1984; Redburn and Cho, 1984; Sharp, 1980; Whitaker, 1980). These powerful ideas have stimulated a torrent of research on coproduction, including several symposia (*Journal of Voluntary Action Research*, July–September 1987; *Public Productivity Review*, Winter 1986–Spring 1987; and *Urban Affairs Quarterly*, June 1984). While this literature illustrates the valuable part that citizens can play in the delivery of services, three factors limit its contribution to the study and practice of volunteer involvement in government agencies.

First, very little of the research on coproduction is empirically based. In a 1984 study of the implications of the model for municipal productivity, Brudney (1984, p. 481) acknowledged that "the analysis has been hampered by a paucity of available data regarding coproduction." Although empirical analyses have begun to appear (Sundeen, 1988; Ferris, 1988; Schneider, 1987), researchers continue to note "the limited evidence available on the actual extent and effects of coproduction" (Thomas, 1987, p. 95). The lack of empirically validated findings undermines the possible application of much of the coproduction research to volunteer programs in government and elsewhere.

Second, most of the empirical research that has been undertaken focuses on the community safety and security policy domain. Percy (1987, 1978) has ably documented the kinds of coproductive behaviors that citizens engage in to protect themselves from crime and victimization, such as the installation of dead-bolt locks and the formation of neighborhood associations (compare Schneider, 1987). Warren, Rosentraub, and Harlow (1984, 1983; see also Rosentraub and Warren, 1987) have performed similar analyses as well as investigated the attitudes of police officers toward coproduction. As valuable as these studies might be for other purposes, they do not examine the impact of volunteers on law enforcement. Moreover, the data emanate from an area of unusually high visibility and citizen concern, yet as Sharp (1980, p. 113) argues, coproduction pertains to the "less spectacular forms of participation in the creation of urban services." Volunteers in government organizations offer a prime example: Most labor in the relative obscurity of the human and social services, well insulated from the type of controversy and stimulation generated by law enforcement. The coproduction literature has not adequately addressed issues of motivation and recruitment in these generally less salient policy arenas.

Third, although coproduction encompasses a wide range of citizen activities in the delivery of government services, the great bulk of this research concentrates on a single type: "consumer production," or the participation of individuals or groups in the provision of services that benefit them directly (compare Ferris, 1984). So prevalent is this understanding of the concept that some scholars describe coproduction as the "involvement by the formally stated beneficiaries of a program in its implementation" (Plant and Thompson, 1986, p. 155). The archetypical example is the neighborhood association, whose patrol and watch functions are intended to yield members ("consumer-producers") increased safety and security. Citizen actions taken in the home or vicinity to improve the level of fire protection or refuse collection are other instances. The model applies as well to recent initiatives in publicly assisted housing in which residents participate in the rehabilitation, conversion, and management of low-income units (Bratt, 1987; Forrister, 1987). Because participants reap the immediate benefits of these activities, discussions of alternative arrangements for the delivery of government services refer to consumer production as "self-help" (for example, Morley, 1989; Savas, 1987; Valente and Manchester, 1984; Hatry, 1983; Shulman, 1982).

Coproduction and Government Volunteer Programs. The consumer-producer perspective has illuminated both prosaic and novel means by which citizens can affect the level and quality of services they receive. Coproduction is not limited to this mode, however. The concept and its application are much richer (for example, Van Til, 1988, pp. 156–159; Warren, 1987, pp. 5–7). The productive involvement of citizens in the delivery of services encompasses as well government volunteer programs in which those donating time and labor to public agencies are not the primary beneficiaries of the goods and/or services they help to create (Sundeen, 1988; Ferris, 1984; Brudney and England, 1983; Sharp, 1980). Because the direct benefits accrue instead to the larger community, Brudney and England (1983, p. 64) identify these activities as "collective coproduction."

Only rarely have public administration scholars explored such programs, in a smattering of case studies of volunteer involvement in fields such as libraries (Walter, 1987), personnel agencies (Siegel, 1983), and police departments (Sundeen and Siegel, 1987, 1986; Siegel and Sundeen, 1986). Some survey research canvasses volunteer participation in local government (Ferris, 1988; Sundeen, 1988; Duncombe, 1986, 1985).

This literature suggests that government volunteer programs differ significantly from self-help efforts. First, consider the motivations and rewards for citizen involvement. Self-help offers the intrinsic motivation of possible service improvements to be realized by participants. Although such advantages may not be the sole motivation for participation in a neighborhood association or day-care cooperative, they are a powerful and predictable incentive. Tenant management of public housing projects offers an apt illustration (Butler, 1989, p. 3-D): "How can resident managers . . . succeed where trained professionals have failed? Simple, according to the tenants. When poor people are given a stake in their own community, and have the power to make decisions about that community, they have the incentive to join together to tackle its problems. That spurs them to rid the streets of crime. And it also gives them a good reason to provide residents with quality services, a rarity in most projects."

In contrast to self-help, volunteering aims at assisting other people, although this activity need not be self-sacrificial or contrary to an individual's own interest. Volunteers surely gain social, psychic, and personal development benefits from donating their time. "Most people," writes Harriet H. Naylor (in Wilson, 1976, p. 4), "have altruistic reasons for volunteering with a healthy streak of self-interest." A more accurate term to describe their behavior is "prosocial": actions intended to help others, but without restriction on the additional types of benefits that the volunteer may realize (Pearce, 1987). Jon Van Til (1988, pp. 1–9) similarly conceives of volunteering as helping behavior deemed beneficial by participants, even though this action "may contribute to individual goals of career exploration and development, sociability, and other forms of personal enhancement."

Appealing to this breadth of motivations presents an essential challenge to government (and other) volunteer programs. In comparison to self-help initiatives, these programs must cope with far greater diversity in incentives and must develop effective methods for recruiting and sustaining the contributions of volunteers to public organizations.

A second important distinction concerns the role of government. As the term implies, self-help can occur in the absence of collaboration or support from public officials, although an organized program might contribute to its success. Residential beautification or clean-up campaigns, for example, can proceed independently of government sponsorship or promotion. In the coproduction literature, in fact, the extent of service activities undertaken by citizens without any apparent connection to a public agency (so-called "parallel production") is a significant research question in itself

(Schneider, 1987; Warren, Rosentraub, and Harlow, 1984, 1983). By satisfying some of the service needs of participants, self-help programs may result in a lessening of citizen demands on government (Hatry, 1983). Yet, if various groups in the community lack the time, money, and organizational skills to engage in consumer production, this approach may jeopardize an equitable distribution of services.

As opposed to self-help, the participation of volunteers in government is a supply-oriented strategy intended to increase the amount and/or effectiveness of services enjoyed by the larger community. Because the immediate benefits of these activities are targeted not to the volunteers but to service recipients, the programs often aim at ameliorating societal inequities. And they involve citizen volunteers directly with public administrators in the work of government agencies. Consequently, they must resolve pivotal questions of organization design centering on the integration of volunteers into public bureaucracies. A successful volunteer program requires procedures and structures for the primary functions of recruitment, orientation, training, supervision, evaluation, and so on.

The burgeoning research on coproduction has brought needed attention to a set of innovative options open to governments for the delivery of goods and services. Only infrequently, however, has this scholarship fixed on the challenges and opportunities raised by the involvement of service volunteers in the public sector. In sum, while the coproduction literature reflects renewed awareness and appreciation of citizen participation among public administration researchers, it has not proven as helpful for understanding and informing government volunteer programs as its roots might suggest.

Beyond Coproduction Research.   To what other literatures might public administration students and practitioners turn to supplement their knowledge of volunteerism? Discussions of alternative approaches for the delivery of government services are one source of guidance (Morley, 1989; Savas, 1987; Valente and Manchester, 1984; Hatry, 1983; Shulman, 1982).

By evaluating the advantages and disadvantages of volunteers against other common service arrangements, these treatments place the method in useful comparative context. Perhaps their greatest contribution is to present government support of volunteer personnel as a legitimate service option, meriting the critical scrutiny of the public administration community.

Outside of public administration, volunteerism is a much more robust subject of inquiry. Scholars in a variety of disciplines, including sociology, social work, gerontology, criminal justice, public health, recreation, education, and economics, have greatly enriched understanding in this area. In addition, the field has spawned journals of its own, such as *Nonprofit and Voluntary Sector Quarterly* (formerly the *Journal of Voluntary Action Research*), *Journal of Volunteer Administration*, and *Voluntary Action Leadership*. This body of knowledge, as well as that accumulated on alternative service delivery, informs the present study.

The Importance of Volunteer Management

Although volunteers have a lengthy history in the public sector, the current interest in them reflects an important departure from the traditional outlook. In the past, volunteer involvement in domains such as recreation, libraries, and other social services derived more from habit and reflex than any desire or plan of public officials to affect the level and quality of services. Governments enlisted volunteers, but without a sense that this practice constituted a viable approach for the delivery of services that could be managed, refined, and improved. During the late 1970s and throughout the 1980s, the older perspective eroded before the combined onslaught of fiscal stress, tax limitations, and rising service demands. As governments have struggled to find ways to achieve more with less, the conception of volunteers has changed from nonessential frill to valuable human resource. And the idea of a volunteer program has evolved from haphazard initiative to systematic strategy for providing services.

Despite the enormous growth in the functions performed by the public sector over the past twenty-five years, the level of civilian federal employment has remained constant since 1967. As Donald F. Kettl (1988a, 1988b) explains, governments have chosen to meet their increased obligations not with employees, but through "proxies," third parties such as contractors and grantees, private firms and nonprofit organizations, which are ultimately responsible for the quality and responsiveness of public goods and services. The role of public administrators is changing from one of delivering services to managing the third parties who actually provide them (Salamon, 1989, 1981). Their success, accordingly, will be measured in the ability to work with these groups to accomplish public purposes. Volunteers who assist government agencies have emerged as one of the proxies. (See Chapter Four for a full discussion.)

Although precise estimates remain elusive, for a great many public administrators, volunteer personnel are a fact of organizational life. At all levels of government, substantial numbers of agencies include volunteers, as do the nonprofit organizations with which they regularly interact in public-private partnerships. In cities and counties, only contracting surpasses volunteer involvement as a service approach. Once a dispensable talent, skills in working with volunteers are becoming a vital tool for the public manager.

To assist officials in building these competencies, the chapters to follow take advantage of not only the literature on volunteerism but also an extensive empirically based study of the U.S. Small Business Administration (SBA). Since 1964 the SBA has relied on large numbers of volunteers from the Service Corps of Retired Executives—the SCORE Association—to provide counseling and training on the principles of business management to agency clients. Analysis of survey data collected from employees and volunteers, as well as other information documenting the SBA-SCORE experience over the past quarter-century, can help other public organizations that have volunteers or that are weighing their introduction. The following chapter turns to one of the most pressing issues to public administrators: the potential of volunteers to increase the cost-effectiveness of government service delivery.

Part One

Understanding Public Sector
Volunteer Programs:
Costs, Benefits, and Pitfalls

2

Evaluating the
Cost-Effectiveness of
Volunteer Programs

*There is evidence . . . that the number of
volunteer workers in public agencies is increasing
as local governmental units try to maintain
adequate service levels in the face of budget
reductions and restrictions.* Gordon Manser,
1987, p. 843

*Foremost among the issues that social work
education must address in order to elevate
volunteerism to an area of expertise is the
myth that volunteers represent cheap labor and
may, therefore, be used to replace or decrease
professional staff. Many professionals, like the
general public, believe that the use of volunteers
costs nothing, but, in fact, an effective volunteer
program is not necessarily cheap. A good
volunteer program requires the services of a
paid volunteer coordinator, and its purpose
is to extend and enrich human services, not to
replace professionals.* Adrienne A. Haeuser
and Florence S. Schwartz, 1984, p. 28

Perhaps no other issue has galvanized interest in the involvement of volunteers in the public sector to the degree that the

possibility for cost savings has. Implicitly or explicitly, nearly every discussion of volunteers in the delivery of government services alludes to this potential. Gordon Manser's remarks from the *Encyclopedia of Social Work* are typical. More often than not, however, the potential for volunteer assistance to result in cost savings has been accepted, rather than demonstrated. Adrienne A. Haeuser and Florence S. Schwartz present an apparent—though frequently overlooked—caveat to this presumption: Although the notion of costs for apparently "free" labor may seem anomalous, government agencies must commit funds to a volunteer program.

As with any service delivery arrangement, the question of whether volunteer involvement warrants the expenses incurred rests on weighing the costs of the program against the level and quality of services and other advantages yielded to the sponsoring organization. For a variety of reasons, systematic examination of this type has rarely been undertaken: Only recently have scholars and practitioners come to view volunteers as an approach to the delivery of public services; the requisite data are difficult to obtain; citizen participation is normally viewed as worthwhile in itself, quite apart from its implications for service delivery; to many, analysis seems to impugn the intrinsic nature of volunteering as a gift of time and service; in the minds of still others, it broaches the controversial issue of comparison with paid staff.

These objections notwithstanding, government managers responsible for a volunteer program must be prepared to determine its value to the organization. Increasingly, funding authorities require them to justify requests for monetary support in the budgeting process, and hold them accountable for the expenditure of public dollars and a return on this investment (Karn, 1983, 1982–83; Ilsley and Niemi, 1981; Moore, 1978; Wilson, 1976). The discussion in this chapter will help program managers to meet these obligations. The chapter elaborates common expenses in volunteer programs; examines the issue of cost savings in relation to volunteers and paid personnel; and describes the economic benefits public agencies have realized through the participation of service volunteers. Finally, it presents a methodology that officials can utilize for evaluating the cost-effectiveness of a volunteer program.

Common Expenses in Volunteer Programs

Although a few volunteer programs sponsored by government agencies pay a modest stipend to participants (for example, Peace Corps, ACTION, and some volunteer fire departments), normally organizations are spared the expense of directly compensating volunteers. Given the remuneration that would be necessary for paid employees to perform the same tasks, the costs avoided can be substantial—a calculus that helps to account for the interest this method has aroused among public officials. Yet programs that enlist volunteer time and talents require other monetary obligations. These consist of indirect and direct costs (Valente and Manchester, 1984, p. 63; Farr, 1983, p. 23).

Indirect costs cannot be distinguished clearly from other sources but have an immediate relationship to the volunteer program. For instance, when volunteers occupy the same facilities as the sponsoring agency, the cost of office space, utilities, and furnishings used by the program are indirect expenses. Other indirect costs include organizational support services, such as legal, accounting, auditing, and computing costs. Because estimation of these costs can be difficult and imprecise, they are frequently overlooked in the volunteer budget. Nevertheless, they are actual expenses and should be applied to the program.

Direct costs are those that can be attributed directly to volunteer services. The contributed labor of volunteers may be free, yet paid staff are usually essential to support and manage the program. Virtually all programs require a volunteer coordinator or director of volunteer services, usually paid, with overall responsibility for administration and oversight. In addition, Susan J. Ellis (1986, p. 54) advises that from its inception, the program needs the help of a secretary, again paid, to lend consistency and continuity to the volunteer effort. As the number of volunteers increases, the demand for management and supervision may call for more personnel to be assigned to the program.

If the program is highly centralized so that volunteers are managed and supervised entirely from within, no further labor costs are incurred. However, the most common arrangement for incorporating volunteers into the organization is to deploy them in agency departments that need assistance. In that case, program personnel may be responsible for recruitment, training, and administration of volunteers, but departmental staff provide day-to-day supervision. The frequency and intensity of the supervisory relationship can vary tremendously across organizations (Holme and Maizels, 1978), but the time allocated to the volunteers by line staff is a genuine program expense. So is the cost of training in volunteer management and associated activities in support of the program, such as travel and per diem.

Staff may serve the volunteer contingent on a full-time or part-time basis. Given their other work demands, departmental personnel can be expected to devote a relatively small fraction of their time to the volunteers. Often, program coordinators have work responsibilities beyond the volunteers; they are frequently housed in departments of public relations or personnel. As a result, they, too, may spend surprisingly little of their time on the program: In one study, just one-third of a sample of volunteer coordinators were able to devote full-time to this obligation, and almost 40 percent gave it less than one-half of their time (Appel, Jimmerson, Macduff, and Long, 1988, p. 4). Job titles notwithstanding, only the fraction of employees' time actually dedicated to the volunteers should be evaluated as a program cost.

If the volunteers occupy a different facility than the parent organization, for instance, to extend public outreach capability, office space and utilities are direct, rather than indirect, expenses of the program. The SCORE Association offers a pertinent illustration. In 1985, fewer than one-quarter (23.7 percent) of the SCORE chapters that maintained an office were housed with the SBA. The remainder were located in Chambers of Commerce (38.8 percent), other government agencies (18.2 percent), or alternative facilities (19.3 percent). In some of these cases, the organizations donated the office space to the volunteers; in the remainder, the SBA paid rent and associated expenses.

The major components of a volunteer program add to the direct costs. Recruitment and promotional efforts aim to bring volunteers into the agency. Orientation and training sessions prepare them for public sector work responsibilities. Recognition events and awards ceremonies reinforce volunteers' sense of purpose and contribution to the organization. Each of these activities constitutes an expenditure of time and funds to the organization, for example, for facilities, advertisement, travel, materials, meals, and so forth.

Government volunteer programs can result in several other categories of direct cost. A standard feature of many programs is reimbursement for volunteers' out-of-pocket expenses. These can range from the mundane (parking and transportation while on the job) to the novel (meals and day care) and can quickly escalate with the number of volunteers. Many larger programs, including the state offices of volunteerism discussed in Chapter One, publish a newsletter intended to foster volunteer education, motivation, and cohesion. The goals are laudable, but their attainment is not without cost. Normal operating expenses, such as those required for printing and reproduction, materials and supplies, uniforms and identification badges (if necessary), equipment, telephone, and postage add to the list of direct outlays for the program.

To protect the agency and its volunteers from exposure to liability, insurance is a necessary expenditure. Surveys of volunteer administrators leave little doubt that legal issues pertaining to liability and insurance are very much on their minds (Kahn, 1985–86). Although the cost and availability of insurance coverage are matters of controversy, Cheryl A. Farr (1983, p. 21) reports that "most local governments have found that volunteers can be used without dramatically increasing the liability risk, provided proper insurance coverage is included in the regular policies. In some cases, adding volunteers to insurance policies doesn't increase premiums significantly, if at all." As Chapter Eight discusses, many public and nonprofit agencies have not been as fortunate. Historically, the U.S. Small Business Administration has been vigorous in according legal protections to the SCORE volunteers: The Small Business Act formally recognizes volunteers as nonpaid employees and thus provides not only liability coverage but also worker's compensation in the event of injury or death on the job.

In sum, volunteers are not a free resource to government agencies. Their participation entails a variety of indirect and direct expenditures, most notably for office facilities, management and support from paid personnel, critical program functions, reimbursement practices, liability coverage, and routine administration. These costs are a natural outgrowth of dramatically increasing the number of workers serving the organization.

Limiting Volunteer Program Costs. All of these items are important, but are some more optional than others? The issue is a delicate one, for it has overtones of exploitation. No director of volunteer services or other public administrator should countenance any less support for a volunteer program than would be required for paid staff to carry out the same obligations. Volunteers should not go begging for operating funds, nor should they be relegated to inadequate facilities. Regrettably, this commitment is violated at least as often as it is observed. The reason is not always cynical organizations. The failure of a volunteer coordinator to prepare a "no-apologies budget" that fully explains and justifies essential costs is sometimes responsible (Karn, 1984). Yet, just as for any public endeavor, to the degree that volunteer expenses can be pared without jeopardizing program effectiveness, further resources become available to an agency to meet rising service demands. Cutback may also force hard budgetary choices, including the sacrifice of some elements of volunteer support.

One area that may weather cuts with less adverse effect

than others is reimbursement for the out-of-pocket costs of volunteering. In a study of the Cooperative Extension Service 4-H program in Minnesota, a statewide sample of volunteers ranked reimbursement thirteenth in a field of fourteen possible motivators for participation (Byrne and Caskey, 1985). Only one-third of the respondents bothered to keep records and claim volunteer expenses as a federal income tax deduction. According to the authors, reimbursement was not important regardless of income or length of service. The fact that many of the volunteers had children in 4-H weakens the generalizability of results, but other studies offer complementary findings.

For example, Ann DeWitt Watts and Patricia Klobus Edwards (1983) conducted a survey of administrators of 124 human service agencies in Virginia. Fewer than one-quarter of them (24.4 percent) considered reimbursement an effective method for retaining volunteers, and agencies that provided reimbursement were no more likely to gain (or lose) volunteers over time than agencies which did not. In 1987, the J.C. Penney Company sponsored a national survey on volunteerism (VOLUNTEER-The National Center, 1988). In response to a question that asked nonvolunteers to evaluate incentives that would be most important in getting them to volunteer, reimbursement of expenses ranked eighth in a listing of nine. On another item, just 7 percent referred to the costs of volunteering as their reason for not engaging in this activity.

While reimbursement for the out-of-pocket expenses of volunteering is a candidate for reductions, it should not be eliminated completely. If a policy of complete reimbursement is not feasible, these funds should go to volunteers on the basis of economic need, so that participation remains open to all citizens. Alternatively, some organizations may authorize reimbursement only when costs surpass a threshold amount. Officials should bear in mind that volunteers can deduct some nonreimbursed expenses on federal income tax returns and strive to provide for those that are exceptions, such as the cost of child care. In any case, volunteer administrators have the responsibility to share information on the tax implications of volunteering so that participants can take full advantage of existing statutes.

A second technique to control costs is to increase the involvement of volunteers in program management and oversight, in lieu of paid employees. Although the position of director of volunteer services is imperative to bring structure and coherence to the program, volunteers can assume a greater role in key activities, such as recruitment, orientation, placement, and training of other volunteers (Caldwell, 1988; Navaratnam, 1986; Hart, 1986). Moreover, as programs expand, it is not at all unusual for volunteers to act as mid-level supervisors for other volunteers. Training is necessary to take on these tasks, but experienced volunteers may have immediate knowledge as well as rapport that lends a special validity and effectiveness to their efforts. Some volunteers may find the expanded responsibilities satisfying and motivating, particularly if they carry professional development opportunities—for example, the chance to attend special conferences or training. As a by-product, their actions help to ease apprehensions of paid staff that volunteers will occupy too much of their time. Eventually, program growth may require the addition of paid staff to assist the coordinator, but volunteer involvement in program management is an attractive option.

A third possibility is to solicit donations to the volunteer program that defray a portion of start-up or operating expenses. Donations should be construed broadly to include not only gifts of money but also in-kind contributions of facilities, materials, equipment, labor, and services. Assistance to voluntary organizations carries tax advantages and community relations value that can have definite appeal to private firms and individual donors (Corporate Volunteer Coordinators Council, 1984). Volunteer managers can also augment budgets through traditional fund-raising and grant-seeking activities, as well as by instituting minimal fees for services, hopefully on a sliding scale of clients' ability to pay. In 1985, seven out of ten SCORE chapters (70.3 percent) reported that they had earned funds. Public administrators should realize, however, that self-generated resources have another dimension: Support gained by volunteers outside normal channels reduces dependence on the agency and "buys" a degree of autonomy that may lessen official control over the program. Chapter Four returns to this issue.

Volunteers, Cost Savings, and Paid Personnel

Depending on the size of the program and the extent of agency sponsorship, expenditures for volunteer services can vary substantially across government organizations. Nevertheless, because costs are unavoidable, these programs will not yield monetary savings unless cutbacks are enacted elsewhere in the agency budget. Given the differential in labor costs between volunteers and staff, some government officials (and members of the general public) have no doubt eyed paid positions as the target for reductions, with the idea that volunteers might step into them. No matter how tempting this policy might be from a fiscal perspective, for several reasons it is most ill-advised.

First, public law and contracts with employee unions prohibit many government organizations from substituting volunteers for paid staff. For example, the Department of Agriculture, which enlists huge numbers of volunteers through the Cooperative Extension Service, is enjoined from using them to displace any employee of the department, whether at the local, county, state, or federal level (U.S. Code 7, Section 2272). Such policies may be common, but public employee unions fear that they are not always observed. Since volunteerism is certainly preferable to elected officials than less popular alternatives, such as tax increases or service declines, they may promote volunteer involvement with little regard for the welfare of government personnel.

For example, when the New York City budget crisis of the mid-1970s precipitated a loss of 40,000 municipal jobs, Mayor Beame announced that the city would enlarge its volunteer contingent as one way of dealing with the shortfall. Although the mayor pledged that volunteers would not substitute for public employees, union officials claim that they had to invoke the labor contract with the city to stop a few overly zealous agencies (Gotbaum and Barr, 1976). In Canada, the Union of Public Employees charges that employers misused volunteers to take away jobs of paid personnel, despite contract provisions barring this action (Graff, 1984). Incidents like these can do little to reassure public employees that volunteers pose no threat to their livelihood.

The effects on paid staff of actual labor substitution— or its anticipation, whether well founded or groundless—are evident and offer the second reason why government organizations must resist this practice. Without question, the most serious impediment to a successful volunteer program is the likely indifference or, worse, outright opposition of regular personnel to volunteers. Perceived threats to job security fuel the natural apprehensions of employees and give rise to feelings of demoralization and hostility. The National Forum on Volunteerism offers a sobering estimate of the magnitude of the problem (Rydberg and Peterson, 1980, p. 54): "The resistance of helping professionals to volunteer involvement is so pervasive that it is unquestioned by the vast majority of volunteer leaders and administrators in the United States. In field after field—education, social services, museums and libraries, health care—the major barrier to effective volunteer involvement lies in the inability or unwillingness of paid helping professionals to accept volunteers as legitimate partners in the helping process."

Perhaps the most unfortunate ramification of such attitudes is that they can engender a self-fulfilling prophecy. When paid staff resent and suspect volunteers and, consistent with this appraisal, fail to support them, volunteer programs are likely to founder, suffering breakdowns in retention, morale, and performance. These outcomes would then appear not only to confirm employees' original suspicions but also to discredit volunteerism further. Antagonisms between staff and volunteers impair the ability of both parties to perform their jobs and distract them from pursuing organizational missions (Mausner, 1988, pp. 7-9). They jeopardize central purposes of the volunteer approach and must be ameliorated.

Chapter Six elaborates an overall strategy to forge mutually satisfying and productive working relationships between paid employees and volunteers.

Third, a strong ethic pervades the field of voluntarism that volunteers should not be involved to the detriment of regular staff. That volunteers can and should augment and enrich the work of employees, but not substitute for them, is a guiding principle that unites scholars and practitioners. Among this community, the primary rationale for the donation of time and energy lies not in relieving strain on public budgets but in enhancing the lives of those who receive as well as those who give voluntary assistance. One need look no farther for an illustration than the passage from Haeuser and Schwartz (1984, p. 28) with which this chapter began. Should volunteer efforts lead to increased operating efficiencies in government agencies, they are a worthwhile by-product, of secondary importance to improvements in the quality and scope of services. While fiscal stress, understandably, renders possible cost savings of far greater concern to elected officials and public administrators, displacement of salaried employees violates fundamental precepts of the field.

For their part, citizens seem no more enamored with the idea of substituting for government personnel than are volunteer scholars and practitioners, or the employees whose jobs might be at stake. Volunteers have always embraced the tenet that they not fill the positions of paid staff as a moral issue (Manser, 1987, p. 848). For the great majority of citizens, volunteering does not appear to be motivated by a desire to cut back or limit government spending. National surveys conducted by the Gallup Organization in 1981 and 1985 indicate that just two to five percent of volunteers donate their time with the intent to "help keep taxes down" (Gallup Organization, 1986, pp. 37–41). Moreover, in communities that have enacted limitations on the taxing authority of local governments in line with the "tax revolt" of the late 1970s, volunteers are actually less likely to be involved in delivering services than in other cities (Ferris, 1988).

Reductions in agency staff strain volunteers' commitment to principle, however. On the one hand, if budgetary cutbacks make the loss of positions inevitable, volunteers may be a last resort to maintain some level of essential service to clients. On the other hand, by meeting gaps arising from withdrawal of public support, volunteers mask real needs and may make it more difficult to obtain adequate funding in the future. Most volunteers have accepted the first option: As fiscal stress took its toll on government agencies during the 1980s, the involvement of volunteers in the public sector increased (see Chapter One). The desire to help others is a primary stimulus to volunteering, and one of its great strengths. Government organizations can benefit from this impulse so long as they introduce volunteers with the clear understanding of all parties that the goal is to attain service levels and quality that would not otherwise be possible, rather than to displace paid staff. Given this foundation, volunteers can be a tremendous asset to the public sector in times not only of fiscal stringency but also relative health.

The technical nature of government services imposes a final constraint on the potential of citizen volunteers to replace paid employees. Many public officials have acquired education, experience, and skills critical to effective service performance that are not shared by the general populace. For this reason, service arrangements based on wholesale substitution of citizens for public administrators cannot be expected to maintain prevailing levels of service quality or amount. Ambitious plans of this type make a sham of the system of professional education, certification, and advancement in public employment (Brudney, 1984, p. 477). Successful volunteer programs must offer training to participants, but the broad education that would be required in most cases would not only be expensive but also a poor substitute for degree programs in public administration and allied disciplines already in place.

Although no one should denigrate the huge pool of talents and skills among the public, a second aspect of this issue is reliability. Government officials fear that turning over primary responsibilities to volunteers would threaten service continuity and, thus, balk at the prospect. Research undertaken by Roger S. Ahlbrandt, Jr., and Howard J. Sumka (1983, p. 219) shows that cities enter into partnership agreements with community-based organizations, which rely heavily on volunteers, most commonly for the delivery of peripheral or supplementary services, as opposed to core public good services. Similarly, government organizations have been quite willing to employ volunteers to augment the work of police officers, teachers, social workers, medical specialists, sanitation personnel, and the like, but officials typically manifest no serious interest in replacing service agents at the heart of the delivery process.

To some extent, these limitations on volunteer involvement may stem from the efforts of public employees to protect their livelihood and to combat intrusions on their prerogatives. Yet they also arise from the apprehension that citizens with necessary professional expertise will not consistently give their time to the provision of government services (Thomas, 1986, p. 150). While paying a salary to employed personnel is the traditional method to ensure service continuity, well-designed and well-operated volunteer programs do not suffer from reliability problems (see Part Two).

The achievement of cost savings is a legitimate priority in the public sector. However, the displacement of paid personnel for volunteers is a dubious means toward this objective. The legal, ethical, and practical dilemmas raised by this plan offer convincing evidence that the strategy would undercut the very effectiveness of volunteer participation.

Economic Benefits of Government Volunteer Programs

Volunteers are not the remedy for cutting government payrolls. Instead, their true value lies in supplementing and broadening the services provided to clients by regular staff. The participation of volunteers in public agencies to assist in the delivery of services will not lead to budgetary reductions and may, in fact, produce some slight growth in expenditures. But public officials should not be deterred: The approach possesses significant economic advantages.

Chief among them is the potential to increase the cost-effectiveness of services (Karn, 1983, 1982–83; Moore, 1978). That is, while the benefits possible to clients through volunteer involvement in government programs elude precise statistical calculation, the method can help public agencies to hold costs down in achieving a given level of service, or to increase services for a fixed level of expenditure. An impressive body of published research bears out this conclusion. In area after area of governmental activity—public safety (Bocklet, 1988; Sundeen and Siegel, 1986), assistance to small business (Brudney, 1986), general city services (Valente, 1985; Brown, 1983; Martin, 1982), parks and recreation (Hart, 1986; Marando, 1986), libraries (Walter, 1987), health and human services (Lotz, 1982), natural resources (Sloan, 1986; Greer, 1985), programs for the elderly (Diana, Lawrence, and Draine, 1985; McCroskey, Brown, and Greene, 1983), rape prevention (Landau, 1980), education (Tierce and Seelbach, 1987; Goetter, 1987), personnel services (Siegel, 1983), and so forth—volunteers have greatly assisted public organizations in extending the reach and scope of public services at minimal cost. The annual reports of government organizations with volunteer programs add further weight to this judgment. Typically, the number of volunteers involved, the amount of hours they contribute, the economic valuation of their labor, and the types of activities they perform overwhelm the obligation of public dollars.

The reason is not hard to find: The approach spares the expense of financially compensating individuals whose donations of time can markedly expand the capability of public agencies to deliver services. Since labor and fringe benefit costs comprise a substantial portion of government spending (at the municipal level as much as half or more of city budgets), volunteers promise a healthy return to participating organizations. In this sense, funding for the volunteer component is "leverage money," because it can finance services valued at several multiples of the original expenditure (Ellis, 1986, p. 25). As detailed above, the method surely requires monetary costs, but its economic hallmark, the provision of labor without the necessity for remuneration, means that volunteers can stretch the resources available to the public sector. Although systematic data have not been assembled on this issue, evidence from agencies that sponsor volunteer programs is as dramatic as it is plentiful. For some governments, volunteers appear to make the difference between providing services and not providing them. In Marin County, California, volunteers help departments to deliver services "that they could not maintain . . . with the imposed budget cuts" (Brown, 1983, p. 9). Without the services of its volunteer reserve officers, the Arizona Highway Patrol "would be unable to meet its growing service need" (Deitch and Thompson, 1985, p. 60). In Arvada, Colorado, an army of over 400 volunteers offers services "which might not be possible otherwise," according to the city director of human resources (Martin, 1982, p. 13). Half this number work in the city center for the arts and humanities, a "department that could not have functioned without its volunteer staff." Like many rural towns, Bangor, Wisconsin, was not able to provide ambulance service throughout the community until citizen "First Responders" became involved. As a result of the work of the volunteers, "the outputs of the overall system have been increased in a way that is more responsive to many of the basic and everyday health needs of the citizenry" (Anderson and Clary, 1987, p. 37).

Other public organizations realize sizable gains in the cost-effectiveness of services. In Richmond, Virginia, the Cooperative Extension Service estimates a cost of $85 per month to supply a volunteer companion to a homebound elderly or disabled person; the monthly cost of maintaining the client in an institutional setting, the usual alternative, is $1,650, and far less preferable to most individuals (Diana, Lawrence, and Draine, 1985, p. 16). A study of volunteers in one school system found that volunteers were able to provide an average of over fifteen hours of interaction with each student per year; had the budget been spent on paid aides instead, only two hours of help for students would have been forthcoming (Tierce and Seelbach, 1987, p. 34).

Volunteers can significantly increase existing government capacity. For example, the Virginia Department of Volunteerism reports that in fiscal year 1988, volunteers contributed approximately 1.2 million hours, valued at well over $11 million, to agencies of state government. The involvement of volunteers in California personnel departments also extends public resources, in several offices by over $1 million per year (Siegel, 1983). The U.S. Forest Service estimates the value of services performed by volunteers in 1982 at $15 million, accounted for by 1,238 person-years of labor from 42,570 participants; in the same year, the National Park Service benefited from 600,000 hours of time donated by 12,000 volunteers, with a value of $4 million (Tedrick, Davis, and Coutant, 1984, p. 56).

Probably the most comprehensive assessment of this kind is a massive, five-year study of volunteerism in the U.S. Department of Agriculture Cooperative Extension Service (1988). Based on data provided by volunteers, clientele, community observers, and Extension agents in a random sample of 800 U.S. counties, the research documents impressive results. More than 2.9 million volunteers, in conjunction with about 11,200 agents, use Cooperative Extension information to help more than 48 million adults and youth annually. In 1983, the volunteers contributed 51 days for every day an employee spent working with them. In all, the estimated dollar value of volunteer service is five times the size of the total Extension budget.

As these examples attest, the monetary valuation of the work donated to an agency by volunteers can be substantial. Although such estimates are sometimes proffered as cost savings, the claim is misleading. Funds were not obligated to support governmental activity at the levels attained, nor would they be expended to employ the labor at its economically valued rate, particularly under conditions of fiscal stringency that often are the catalyst to public sector volunteerism. At best, costs are "avoided," rather than "saved." A more accurate and persuasive frame for interpreting the economic worth of volunteer time focuses not on expenditures forgone but on the gain in productive capability realized by an organization. The comments of the director of the department of human resources in a Florida county illustrate the point (Lotz, 1982, p. 10): "During the last fiscal year, volunteers provided over $930,000 worth of services. True, we didn't save that amount in taxes, but financially strapped programs used volunteers creatively to enhance objectives and to get more bang for the buck. Volunteers in several programs meant the difference between a caretaker program and a program able to provide quality care."

Evaluating the Cost-Effectiveness of Volunteer Programs

How do public administrators and researchers arrive at estimates of the economic worth of volunteer services, such as those highlighted above? How do they measure the cost-effectiveness of volunteer programs? To justify continued or increased funding for the program, the director of volunteer services needs to apply the appropriate technique.

      G. Neil Karn (1983, 1982–83) has developed the methodology most often used to assess cost-effectiveness. His approach is elaborated below, with special reference to the SCORE Association, a large volunteer effort underwritten by the U.S. Small Business Administration (SBA).

Assessing the Cost-Effectiveness of SCORE. In fiscal year 1987, SCORE counted 12,644 members, an amount over three times larger than the entire SBA staff and almost forty times the number of personnel assigned to the area in which the volunteers lend assistance, business development. SCORE performs two primary functions: individual counseling of SBA clients concerning issues pertinent to their businesses, and group training sessions directed to general business management. In 1987, SCORE members counseled 172,317 clients who sought help with business problems. They conducted a total of 3,380 workshops attended by 112,367 prospective or established entrepreneurs. About 85 percent were "prebusiness" workshops that focused on starting and operating a business; the remainder dealt with special interest topics, international trade and women's business ownership. In all, through counseling and workshops, SCORE served 284,684 SBA clients during the year (SCORE Association, 1988).

If the volunteer coordinator or researcher can derive monetary estimates of the value of the services provided to clients by volunteers, he or she could weigh them against the expenditures of the program, as in a typical cost-benefit analysis. In most cases, however, volunteers work in the human or social services, where the difficulty of placing a dollar value on the benefits received usually precludes such assessment. This obstacle is a consequence not of volunteer participation but of the service arenas involved. Estimation of benefits realized through paid personnel would be just as tenuous, but it is hazarded even less often for volunteers, on the presumption that the latter "cost" little or nothing. The SCORE Association is no exception to this rule. The SBA has not attempted to assess systematically the monetary value of SCORE activities—or, for that matter, of its Office of Business Development. Partly for this reason, in the mid-1980s, President Reagan proposed to dismantle the office but to transfer SCORE to the Department of Commerce.

Because the method does not require monetary estimates of the benefits achieved by public programs, evaluators can apply cost-effectiveness analysis (rather than cost-benefit analysis) to assess volunteer efforts (Karn, 1983, 1982–83; Moore, 1978). The key to the method is the substitution of the dollar value of volunteer time for program benefits; the former quantity is then compared with the costs of the program. The procedure consists of six steps.

Step 1.   Based on the agency's job classification schedule, determine the annual compensation that would be extended to volunteers if they were paid employees.

In order to value volunteer time, officials must prepare (or have available) job descriptions for volunteer positions parallel to those for paid employees. This task requires a careful job analysis of the work performed by volunteers, a considerable undertaking in itself (for examples, see Karn, 1983; Wilson, 1976; Naylor, 1973). As will be explicated more fully in Chapters Five and Six, job descriptions for nonpaid positions facilitate volunteer recruitment, program organization, and protection of staff prerogatives. Here, their purpose is to establish the equivalent job classification or category in the agency pay schedule. If none exists, several proxies are viable, such as a comparable paid position within other governmental or nonprofit organizations, or as a final recourse, in the private sector.

Karn's (1982–83, p. 4) equivalency model "proposes that the true value of volunteering be fixed at the fair market value or purchase price of parallel paid services." To begin the economic assessment of volunteer labor, the market value of a nonpaid position is set at the annual salary for the beginning level of the equivalent job classification grade. If volunteers fill several different agency jobs, a parallel paid position must be established for each one.

As mentioned above, the SCORE volunteers primarily counsel individual entrepreneurs and offer group training for clientele of the Small Business Administration. The commensurate paid position would be an entry-level business development officer or perhaps assistant. Most business development officers, whose job responsibilities encompass coordination and oversight of SCORE volunteers as well as other SBA counseling and training personnel, have attained the grade classification of GS-12. Section 8(b)(1)(C)(i) of the Small Business Act, as amended, stipulates that for purposes of determining compensation benefits for disability or death, "the monthly pay of a volunteer shall be deemed that received under the entrance salary for a grade GS-11 employee," an annual salary of $27,172 in 1987. This amount seems a fair appraisal of the annual monetary value of SCORE volunteering. It represents the minimum compensation that equivalent paid work would command in the federal general schedule.

To determine the total economic worth of volunteer services, Karn (1982–83) advises that the value of the associated benefits package (retirement, worker's compensation insurance, life insurance, and health or hospitalization insurance) should be added to the amount of compensation. Yet, volunteers work part-time schedules, for which the benefits package is often meager and sometimes nonexistent. Hence, although the sum of compensation plus benefits for the equivalent paid position may give a more accurate reading of how much it would cost to "replace" volunteers with paid employees, this adjustment is often forgone (for example, Sundeen and Siegel, 1986). It is in the present instance as well: The equivalent annual compensation for a SCORE volunteer remains the beginning salary for a federal GS-11 position ($27,172 in 1987). Since the benefits package is omitted, the resulting estimates of the economic worth of the volunteer program may be undervalued.

Step 2. Convert the annual compensation for the equivalent position to an hourly wage.

The compensation established in step 1 corresponds to the yearly remuneration that would be received by full-time, paid personnel for the jobs held by volunteers. Because volunteers are part-time employees, however, salary must be converted to an hourly wage. For this conversion, the evaluator requires a standard number of work hours in a year.

Many public agencies set the standard at 2,080 hours (40 hours for 52 weeks). In most cases, analysts can use this figure as a reasonable approximation for annual hours. Alternatively, the evaluator might correct this standard for the number of hours actually worked by agency employees by subtracting the amount of hours of paid holidays and annual leave (Karn, 1982-83, pp. 5-7). For instance, if the agency observes 12 holidays (96 hours), and the occupant of the position typically earns 10 days of leave (80 hours), total hours would be decreased by 176, yielding a basis of 1,904 hours of labor per year.

The federal government injects a new wrinkle into the calculation. According to the Office of Personnel Management (personal communication, 1988), as a means to reduce the national budget deficit, the 1986 Omnibus Budget and

Reconciliation Act established the standard of 2,087 hours for purposes of ascertaining hourly pay. Dividing the equivalent annual compensation for SCORE volunteering ($27,172 from step 1) by this standard yields an hourly wage of $13.02. Were total hours decreased to reflect paid holidays and annual leave, the wage would be higher. For example, if employees worked 1,904 hours annually as in the hypothetical case above, the resulting wage would be $14.27. As was true in step 1, the effect of not applying a correction is to undervalue the volunteer product.

Step 3. Estimate the number of hours worked by volunteers for the agency in the period under review (usually one year).

The accounting of hours is the least precise element in the assessment of the economic worth of volunteers to an organization (Karn, 1983, p. 4). For several reasons, the under- and even nonreporting of hours worked is a notorious problem for volunteer programs. Unlike most full-time and some part-time employees who are automatically credited for their hours on the job, volunteers must record their time. To some of them, this procedure smacks of the bureaucracy and "red tape" of a paid position, which they seek to escape through volunteering. For others, it is an inconvenience without discernable connection to client service or, worse, an act seemingly inimical to freely giving of oneself. Many volunteers, too, apparently misunderstand the nature of their time commitment: They tend to restrict the hours reported to those spent in direct contact with clients but ignore the other facets of the job. Much less often do they count the time consumed in meetings, job preparation, work-related travel, paperwork, and the like.

For fiscal year 1987, the SCORE Association estimates that its volunteers contributed a total of 814,000 hours of service to the U.S. Small Business Administration. SCORE has clearly absorbed the message on underreporting. According to the 1987 annual report of the Association, just 55 percent of this time was devoted to counseling cases and holding workshops, with the remainder spent in support activities (SCORE Association, 1988). Nevertheless, hours of direct service to clients, let alone those allocated to support functions, are likely underestimated. In 1985, the author conducted a survey of SCORE chapter chairpersons. According to them, on the average nearly 20 percent of the time (19.6 percent) chapter members fail to "complete the appropriate paperwork to record the progress of a case."

The estimate of total volunteer hours is crucial not only to the assessment of economic value but also to the justification for continued or more generous program funding. Hence, public administrators must impress on the volunteer contingent the importance of accurate record keeping and institute procedures to facilitate their cooperation. Although work remains to be done, SCORE has used member log-in sheets as well as monthly and annual reports summarizing chapter activity to good effect.

Step 4.   Compute the total economic worth of volunteer activities to the agency.

Since the equivalent hourly wage for volunteering (steps 1 and 2) and the number of hours contributed by citizens (step 3) are now available, this computation is straightforward: Multiplication of the two quantities yields a fair market assessment or "purchase price" of the time donated by volunteers to an organization. Most volunteer coordinators and the agencies they serve cite this figure as the dollar value of program activities, that is, the amount by which they add to public resources. For example, the studies of economic benefits of government volunteer programs discussed earlier in the chapter apply this method or a close variant.

In the case of SCORE, the equivalent hourly wage for volunteer activities was $13.02, and the total number of hours contributed 814,000. Multiplication of these quantities reveals that in 1987, SCORE provided services to the SBA worth $10,598,280. For the reasons discussed above, this estimate almost certainly undervalues the annual economic contribution of the volunteer program to the agency.

Step 5. Calculate the costs of the volunteer program.

Many assessments of volunteer efforts go no further than the previous step. No competent evaluator would be content, however, to look only at the services side of the equation and ignore the attendant costs. At this point, the direct and indirect expenses of the volunteer program must be brought to bear. These categories were discussed at the outset of the chapter.

In fiscal year 1987, the SBA obligated $2,181,000 directly to SCORE. The amount covered travel reimbursement (61 percent), paid clerical assistance (23 percent), operation of a National SCORE Office (15 percent), and insurance (1 percent). Although the SCORE Association prepares analyses that employ this figure as the total cost to the federal government, it ignores the expenses incurred by the SBA in overseeing the operation. The last year for which the SBA has completed a thorough examination of these expenses is 1983. According to the Office of the Comptroller (personal communication, 1988), they have changed little since that time and can be applied here.

In 1983, the SBA charged $3,521,000 in additional direct costs to SCORE for the agency portion of management and coordination of the volunteers, more than doubling the total to $5,702,000 (U.S. Small Business Administration, 1984). This amount went to the salaries and expenses of the business development staff for the fraction of their time devoted to SCORE responsibilities. The SBA charged another $3,804,000 in indirect expenses to SCORE. Most of this sum appears to represent the volunteer program's share of agency overhead expenses (for example, for financial management, legislative, and investigative services), rather than the costs it actually incurred for necessary support services. Some of the charges for the latter also seem dubious. The single largest pertained to administrative and computer services, for $1,454,000. In 1987, the SBA transferred this function to SCORE—with a grant of $30,000 to the volunteers.

The total of the direct ($5,702,000) and indirect ($3,804,000) expenses for the operation of SCORE come to

$9,506,000. While the costs seem inflated, the SBA charged this amount to the volunteer program for fiscal 1983, the most recent year for which complete data are available (U.S. Small Business Administration, 1984).

Step 6. Compute the cost-effectiveness ratio for the volunteer program.

Although the elusiveness of impacts in the human and social services precludes the assignment of a dollar value to the benefits realized by clients in most volunteer programs, steps 1 through 4 derive the aggregate worth of donated time. Step 5, in turn, determines the costs borne by an organization in sponsoring the volunteer effort. The cost-effectiveness ratio results from dividing the first of these quantities by the second: It expresses the value of volunteer time returned for every dollar invested in support of the program (Karn, 1983, p. 13). The ratio should be calculated in two ways, based first on total program costs and second on direct costs alone.

The estimate of monetary value of SCORE time contributed to the SBA in 1987 was $10,598,280 (step 4); total program costs were $9,506,000, and direct costs $5,702,000 (step 5). The attendant ratios of cost-effectiveness are 1.11 (based on total costs) and 1.86 (direct costs), respectively. These results indicate that for every dollar invested in the program, whether direct or indirect, SCORE returned $1.11 worth of services. For every dollar that went for direct program support, SCORE generated $1.86. Figure 2.1 summarizes the six-step procedure for the analysis of cost-effectiveness of volunteer programs, and its application to SCORE.

Placing the Analysis in Context. Program officials must interpret the cost-effectiveness analysis for agency leadership and funding authorities and place it in the appropriate context. By the analysis above, for example, SCORE is a bargain to U.S. taxpayers and the SBA: The dollar value of its activities on behalf of agency clientele exceeds total program obligations by 11 percent, and direct expenditures by 86 percent. Officials should use these results to make a persuasive case for funding.

Figure 2.1. Evaluation of Cost-Effectiveness for Volunteer Programs with Application to SCORE and the Small Business Administration.

Step 1. Based on the agency's job classification schedule, determine the annual compensation that would be extended to volunteers if they were paid employees.

For the SCORE volunteers, this amount is $27,172 for 1987 (GS-11).

Step 2. Convert the annual compensation for the equivalent position to an hourly wage.

For SCORE, the standard number of hours is 2,087 per annum. Dividing annual compensation ($27,172) by this figure yields an equivalent hourly wage of $13.02.

Step 3. Estimate the number of hours worked by volunteers for the agency in the period under review (usually one year).

The SCORE Association estimates that its members contributed a total of 814,000 hours to the SBA in 1987.

Step 4. Compute the total economic worth of volunteer activities to the agency.

Based on the hourly equivalent compensation determined in step 2 and the estimate of hours from step 3, the fair market value or "purchase price" of SCORE activities to the SBA is $10,598,280 ($13.02 × 814,000).

Step 5. Calculate the costs of the volunteer program.

In 1987, the SBA charged $5,702,000 in direct expenses to SCORE and another $3,804,000 in indirect expenses, for a total of $9,506,000.

Step 6. Compute the cost-effectiveness ratio for the volunteer program.

The estimate of economic value of the time donated by SCORE members to the SBA is $10,598, 280 (step 4); total program costs came to $9,506,000, and direct costs to $5,702,000 (step 5). Thus, for every dollar invested in the program, whether for direct or indirect expenses, SCORE generated $1.11 worth of service. For every dollar that went for direct support, the program returned $1.86.

Analyses of cost-effectiveness undertaken for other volunteer programs in the public sector also demonstrate enviable returns. Moreover, these estimates likely fail to reflect full program worth. Too often, assessments undervalue volunteer efforts by inputing the minimum wage to nonpaid labor, instead of the equivalent wage based on the agency classification schedule; incorporating the most stringent definition of this wage, rather than the actual market value or cost of hiring paid personnel; and accepting at face value organizational estimates of expenses. To the degree that the director of volunteer services is able to surmount these problems with better information, the analysis will prove both more accurate and more favorable to the program. Alternatively, the director needs to understand and elaborate how data limitations affect the results.

Program officials must combat a final undervaluation of volunteer effort that emanates, ironically, from the very ability to calculate ratios tapping cost-effectiveness. Many government administrators and funding authorities evidently believe that the benchmark of program success is a return of at least one dollar in services for every dollar of public funding (that is, a ratio of 1.0). In Karn's (1983, p. 13) judgment, expectations of much higher ratios from the volunteer component "are commonplace, and any volunteer program hovering around the 1.0 ratio is suspect." The director of volunteer services should point out the fallacy inherent in the assumption that if volunteers do not produce at least as much in services as it costs to support them, then paid services could be provided just as economically. At best, salaried employees can achieve a cost-effectiveness ratio of one-to-one, for their remuneration would appear in both the services component and the expenses component of the ratio (see above). Furthermore, when the costs of indirect and overhead support for staff are taken into account, the maximum will be attained very rarely, if ever.

As a more valid context for interpreting cost-effectiveness, the director of volunteer services might recommend that the ratio obtained for the volunteer program be compared with the ratios calculated for paid staff as well as for other feasible arrangements, such as contracting or vouchers. Undoubtedly, this comparison would demonstrate the true value of volunteers in applying government resources to meet pressing needs for services.

Summary and Implications

To determine the cost-effectiveness of a volunteer program, public managers must estimate the cumulative dollar value of the time donated to an organization, and weigh this quantity against the expenses incurred by the program. The assessment can be very helpful to organizational decision makers for both internal and external purposes. Internally, data pertaining to the actual economic worth of contributed labor and the attendant costs can assist program managers in providing appropriate recognition to participants and building support for the program. Externally, officials can use this information to convince sometimes dubious funding authorities that the organization is receiving its "money's worth" from its investment in volunteers. To facilitate interpretation, the director of volunteer services should place the cost-effectiveness ratio in comparative context.

Economic evaluation of the volunteer program begins with a job analysis of the positions held by volunteers. Developing job descriptions for nonpaid positions is fundamental not only to appraising the monetary value of donated time, but also establishing the goals underlying volunteer participation. This process is crucial to the success of the program and should involve organizational leadership, employees, and volunteers (see Chapters Five and Six).

The methodology for estimating cost-effectiveness can produce results no more reliable than the data available. Program officials must strive to develop accurate record-keeping systems. In particular, they must ensure that volunteers understand the importance of registering hours of service correctly, and that procedures are in place to assist them in doing so. The director of volunteer services must also maintain an accounting of the indirect and direct costs of the program.

Based on an examination of costs, the director should press for full monetary backing for the volunteer effort in a "no-apologies budget" that elucidates and justifies necessary expenditures. If agency funding precludes meeting the budget request, possible means for making up the difference include:

more stringent policies governing reimbursement of volunteer expenses, greater citizen involvement in positions of program management and supervision, and solicitation of external monetary and nonmonetary support for the program.

As the analysis of cost-effectiveness shows, volunteer programs are not "free" to government organizations. Nor should the introduction of volunteers be used as a cost-saving measure to displace paid personnel; this action is detrimental to the spirit and benefits of the approach. Instead, from an economic perspective, the main advantage offered by a volunteer program is the capability to limit expenditures and expand services in the public sector. Chapter Three turns to the quality and impact of the services provided by volunteers.

3

How Volunteers Can Improve Service Quality and Impact

One of the most uncreative—and unhelpful—questions posed to volunteer program leaders is: 'how many volunteers do we have and how many hours did they give us this year?' Unfortunately, this is too often the extent of program 'evaluation' for the volunteer component. A tally of hours served without analysis of what was accomplished and how well it was done is not worth compiling. It is a left-handed compliment to assume that somehow the importance of volunteer involvement is self-evident. Susan J. Ellis, 1986, p. 127

The focus in national service must always be on the services provided. If a national-service program cannot provide services more effectively or more cheaply than private enterprise or employees of public agencies, then there is no basis for it. Charles C. Moskos, 1988, p. 146

The previous chapter demonstrated the economic benefits that volunteers can extend government agencies in delivering services. The "dollar value" of contributed time, especially in relation to the support costs to the organization, can be a very persuasive statistic. Yet, as Susan J. Ellis points out, the number of volunteers retained by an organization and the amount of hours they donate do not tap the quality and impact of their activities, nor how they affect the achievement of organizational goals. A strong advocate of voluntary national service, Charles C. Moskos insists that evaluation of his proposal center on the services provided. Public managers should be just as concerned with the accomplishments of a volunteer program as with its economics.

This chapter examines the impact of volunteer participation on the effectiveness of government organizations. In three major ways, volunteers can influence the quality and impact of public services. First, volunteer programs assign to participants specific jobs in an agency. How well they discharge the attendant responsibilities has clear relevance for organizational effectiveness. Second, volunteers affect the performance of paid staff. If volunteer programs are designed and implemented with care, they can support and facilitate the work of salaried employees. If not, they can lead to rancorous conflict and wasted effort that detract from the effectiveness of both parties and diminish the stature of volunteers as a service resource.

Finally, volunteers are not the same as employees. Because they maintain closer ties to the community and relative freedom from bureaucratic mores, volunteers bring a unique status and fresh insight that can improve performance in organizations willing to listen. Without avenues for expression, however, these qualities represent missed opportunities. The chapter discusses each of the mechanisms by which volunteers can heighten effectiveness in public agencies.

Volunteer Job Performance

Given the importance of the issue to organizations that include them and employees who work with them, it is not surprising that the job performance of volunteers is the subject of controversy. In an article that questioned the health of volunteerism in the United States, Benjamin DeMott (1978,

p. 24) contended that good intentions are not enough: "Untrained amateurs tend to be disasters on the job." Training, of course, might improve performance, but DeMott felt that it would lure participants into paid employment. Although the article provoked a sharp response from the National Center for Voluntary Action (Allen and Schindler, 1978), the reply did not address the effectiveness issue directly.

Certainly, a pessimistic assessment of volunteers is not unusual. "The idea of volunteerism must be 'cleaned up,' " write Victor Gotbaum and Elinor Barr (1976, p. 51); "its preprofessional middle-class aura must be lifted, its noblesse oblige history must be reopened, and its danger as a cheap labor source must be entirely removed." In personal interviews conducted by the author with a variety of officials from the Small Business Administration, other government agencies, Congressional staff, business associations, and lobby groups, several respondents were openly skeptical of the quality of advice rendered SBA clients by SCORE volunteers. In a like manner, Aimée L. Morner (1977, p. 214) laid inadequacies in SBA management assistance programs at the feet of its volunteers, alleging that "some of them are sadly out of touch with how business is run today, and god only knows how to value their services." In a society that typically correlates the importance of work with income, such denigration of volunteer labor is to be expected (Scheier, 1988b; Clary, 1987; Park, 1983). At one time or another, most directors of volunteer services have probably heard the comment ventured to me by one SBA official: "It can't be worth much if it's free."

Are these opinions merely stereotype, or do they have some basis in fact? A national study of volunteer fire departments concluded that even though volunteer forces in small towns required less public revenue, they sustained greater losses due to fire, which contributed to considerably higher total costs borne by citizens (Hoetmer and Paul, 1981, p. 178). A review of literature in the area of fire fighting led Stephen McCurley (1981), hardly an opponent of volunteerism (he was an employee of VOLUNTEER–The National Center at the time), to inquire, "Should Paid Staff Replace Volunteers?" In some communities, the quality of library services aided by volunteers has also come under question (Valente and Manchester, 1984, p. 64). The success of volunteers in the Food Stamp program has been mixed, at best (Durant, 1985). Shortly after the passage of Proposition 13 in California in 1978, which ushered in an era of increased reliance on volunteerism as well as other service arrangements, public opinion polls and other indicators reveal a pronounced drop in service effectiveness. While alternative interpretations are plausible, Brudney (1984) suggests that citizens' reservations over the impact of voluntary efforts were responsible, at least in part, for the decline and for the defeat of a second tax limitation at the polls two years later (Proposition 9).

These accounts notwithstanding, far more systematic and convincing evidence shows that volunteers can contribute to organizational effectiveness. Stuart Langton (1988b) conducted a survey of government agencies and nonprofit organizations in eastern Massachusetts. Not only did large majorities of both samples involve volunteers in assisting clients directly and wish to recruit more in the next year for this purpose, but respondents also indicated that the primary result of attracting all the volunteers they wanted would be to boost effectiveness: Fully 83 percent from the nonprofit organizations and 70 percent from the government agencies felt that the quality of services would improve. Consistent with the analysis of the previous chapter, 85 percent and 64 percent of the two groups, respectively, anticipated that the level of services and activities would also increase. Although question wording makes those responses speculative, in a survey of a national sample of U.S. cities with over 4,500 population, just 6.2 percent of localities that had volunteers cited "poor work" as a liability of the method (Duncombe, 1985). A follow-up study of forty cities with extensive volunteer participation corroborated this finding (Duncombe, 1986).

A major study of the involvement of volunteers by social workers and probation officers in Great Britain offers further support (Holme and Maizels, 1978). That large proportions of these professionals, 51 percent and 70 percent, respectively, enlisted voluntary help gives a preliminary indication of its effectiveness (pp. 66–68). In fact, over half the social workers (55 percent) and probation officers (67 percent) who involved volunteers gave as their rationale the benefits reaped by clients (pp. 81–83). While 14 percent of the social workers and 18 percent of the probation officers assisted by volunteers said that participants lacked skill and experience, nearly one-half perceived no disadvantages whatsoever with the approach (pp. 104–106). The reasons expressed for not involving volunteers among their counterparts were sometimes ambiguous, but few of these employees seemed to doubt volunteer performance (pp. 109–112).

Investigation by the U.S. Department of Agriculture Cooperative Extension Service (1988) attests to the performance of volunteers. The mission of Extension is informal education. In a sample of 600 clientele, 93 percent said that volunteers helped them acquire information, and 87 percent indicated that volunteers helped them develop new skills. Large majorities (70 percent or more) reported benefits from the volunteer activities in a variety of domains, including management of economic resources, enhancement of self-esteem, and improvement of homes, health, safety, and family life.

Evidence from additional research is also persuasive. A comprehensive review of volunteer programs to treat offenders in criminal justice determined that "all evaluations that have been conducted have shown positive results. . . . The studies that have demonstrated methodological competence indicate that volunteers are indeed effective with criminal justice clients" (Sigler and Leenhouts, 1985, p. 102). In the area of public health, case studies validate the effectiveness of volunteers across diverse settings, including hospitals, nursing homes, and community hypertension programs (for example, Nagel, Cimbolic, and Newlin, 1988; Parkum, 1985; Caraway and Van Gilder, 1985). For instance, based on a survey of a stratified sample of patients in six hospitals, Kurt H. Parkum (1985, p. 131) concludes that "volunteering in hospitals is worthwhile and effective for the patients concerned. Voluntary patient support services compare very favorably with related formal organizational efforts." Across a wide variety of other policy arenas—the human and social services (Gamm and Kassab, 1983), recreation (Marando, 1986), national forests (Greer, 1985), state parks (Allen and others, 1989; Myers and Reid, 1986), education (Goetter, 1987; Tierce and Seelbach, 1987), emergency medical services (Anderson and Clary, 1987; Gora and Nemerowicz, 1985), and so on—volunteers have proven able partners in governmental activity.

Assessing SCORE Effectiveness. While instructive, much of this research lacks a comparison group against which the performance of volunteers could be evaluated. In some cases data that would constitute a benchmark are neglected. In others, work responsibilities have evolved to the point that volunteers and staff have unique roles so that no obvious point of comparison exists. Nevertheless, without some basis for comparison, it is difficult to assess volunteer accomplishment.

The context in which the U.S. Small Business Administration draws on its SCORE volunteers is quite different. The agency relies on several resources in addition to SCORE to provide management counseling, either individually or in workshops and courses, for aspiring and established business owners. To examine the relative effectiveness of the resources, the author surveyed SBA business development staff, who are responsible for working with the groups and integrating their activities into SBA operations. The groups encompass: Small Business Development Centers (SBDC), which employ university faculty, graduate students, and other staff to counsel small businesses; Small Business Institutes (SBI), a university-based program in which small teams of business administration students under the direction of a faculty member carry out in-depth projects to aid agency clients; and trade associations, such as those formed by realtors, bankers, and other professionals, which offer a limited amount of counseling and training assistance to the SBA. Finally, at the time of the survey administration (1986), business development officers also did a modicum of client counseling, although this aspect of their job had been declining over time and was phased out completely in 1987.

As shown in Table 3.1, on a scale of one to ten business development staff were asked to rate the quality of work performed by SCORE, SBDC, SBI, and trade associations in three areas: short-term client counseling (generally defined as less than twelve contact hours), long-term counseling (more than twelve hours), and the presentation of business workshops, seminars, and courses. Because the SBI program is dedicated exclusively to helping SBA clients for an academic term or more, data for this resource are restricted to long-term counseling. The table displays the mean evaluations given by the business development staff to each resource in the three areas; for comparative purposes, tests of statistical significance evaluate the difference in means between SCORE and each group.

Table 3.1 Mean Ratings of SBA Business Development Staff of Quality of Work Performed by SCORE, SBDC, SBI, and Trade Associations.*

Dimension	SCORE	SBDC	SBI†	Trade Associations
Quality of short-term counseling	7.8	6.6‡		5.8‡
Quality of long-term counseling	6.8	7.1	7.7‡	5.4§
Quality of workshops, seminars, and courses conducted	8.4	7.7§		7.2‡
Average N for mean comparison with SCORE+		74	93	54

* Question: "Using the scale where *10 = Greatest or Highest* and *1 = Lowest or Least*, would you please rate the resources in your District on each of the Dimensions listed below?"

† The SBI conducts only long-term counseling.

‡ Difference in means between SCORE and this resource is statistically significant at $p < .001$.

§ Difference in means between SCORE and this resource is statistically significant at $p < .01$.

+ N's differ because the resources are not available in all SBA geographical districts.

The results confirm the high quality work of the SCORE volunteers. With respect to short-term counseling, SCORE earned the highest average rating (7.8), surpassing the mean for SBDC (6.6) by more than one point and the mean for trade associations (5.8) by two points. Business development staff also awarded SCORE (8.4) the highest mean appraisal on the quality of workshops, seminars, and courses conducted; the mean is 0.7 greater than the mean for SBDC (7.7) and 1.2 larger than that for trade associations (7.2). (From a statistical standpoint, the probability is very small that differences in means of this magnitude could occur by chance.) Finally, staff gave the SBI the top mean rating on the quality of long-term counseling of SBA clients (7.7). The means for SBDC (7.1) and SCORE (6.8) were quite close, the difference between them indistinguishable from zero in a statistical test. Trade associations again garnered the lowest mean rating (5.4).

The SBI is a small, special purpose program for long-term counseling of SBA clients. Business development officers carefully screen the cases to determine those most suitable for student involvement and authorize only about 5,000 per year, less than 3 percent of all clients counseled; the SBA also allots participating schools a subsidy to cover expenses. SCORE and the SBDC counsel the great bulk of SBA clients, 67 percent by SCORE (127,185) and 30 percent by SBDC (56,859) in the 1987 fiscal year, and these units are charged with additional responsibilities as well. Given these circumstances, it should not be surprising that the SBI appears to do a better job of long-term counseling.

Nevertheless, in the two remaining functions (short-term counseling and the conduct of workshops, seminars, and courses), business development staff evaluated the quality of work of SCORE as superior to that of the other resources. In fact, on an item that will be discussed further in Chapter Five, half the respondents rated the ability of the volunteers to counsel clients as better than their own, and another 36 percent judged their ability as comparable to SBA staff (see Table 5.1).

Matching Volunteers and Positions. In sum, volunteers can perform effectively in service-delivery roles in public agencies. In light of available evidence, undifferentiated cynicism toward their individual achievements or organizational contributions cannot be substantiated. Yet this conclusion does not mean that everywhere they have been tried volunteers have met success, anymore than it means that their efforts have been universally futile. Even within the same city, volunteer-supported services can vary enormously in quality and reliability (Thomas, 1986; Pearce, 1978).

Crucial to the accomplishment of volunteers is the fit between their background and experience, as well as the training an agency is prepared to provide, and the jobs given to them. The principal reason that the analysis above reflects favorably on SCORE, as have evaluations based on different research methodologies (see Brudney, 1986), is that the program attends carefully to matching volunteers with work assignments. Qualifications for membership in SCORE include business expertise on the part of either retirees or those still employed; approximately one in five of the volunteers belongs to the Active Corps of Executives or ACE, a group that has been subsumed by SCORE. SCORE bylaws call for a probationary period for prospective volunteers, and the great majority of chapters supply preservice and in-service training to members. In addition, leadership in the SCORE chapters around the country strive to assign to clients seeking managerial counseling volunteers who command the skills requested and/or experience in the same industry; virtually all chapters (97 percent) use a skills inventory of chapter members in making case assignments. The outcome, in most instances, is an appropriate matching to satisfy client needs.

This result is not confined to SCORE, but applies more generally to volunteer programs. Based on case studies in criminal justice, mental health, and drug abuse treatment, Larry Gamm and Cathy Kassab (1983, p. 28) conclude that "overall organizational effectiveness in relation to desired outcomes might be improved and overall organizational productivity heightened through selective assignment of volunteers to those activities which they might perform as well as or better than paid professionals." Harry P. Hatry (1983, p. 51) agrees that "if volunteers are not wisely chosen, trained, and fitted to their tasks, service quality could suffer." For example, volunteers can help public libraries to maintain hours during a time of fiscal cutback, but without background in the field or requisite training, they cannot be expected to duplicate the skills of professional librarians. The tasks delegated to them in relation to their competencies will be the primary determinant of the quality and impact of volunteer activities.

For most purposes, public managers should discover that volunteers possess a foundation of desired attributes. Although the range of jobs for which governments enlist volunteers is constantly changing and expanding, public agencies continue to rely on them for assistance primarily in labor-intensive areas of the human and social services, such as safety and security, programs for youth and elderly, recreation, and culture and the arts (Valente and Manchester, 1984). According to Langton's (1988b) survey (see above), the skills and qualities of volunteers most sought after by government and nonprofit agencies are communication, listening, reliability, friendliness, honesty, organizational commitment, and a caring attitude. Volunteer jobs will frequently require more specific competencies as well, for which more intensive recruitment or specialized training will likely prove necessary. Yet the attributes identified in the survey are shared by a large segment of the population, or can be acquired relatively easily and quickly by motivated individuals. To the degree that the listing accurately reflects the demands of volunteer positions, public organizations are likely to be rewarded with effective performance.

By contrast, government agencies increasingly solicit voluntary help for more specialized and technical functions, in computer applications, tax administration, public finance, legal services, economic development, and so on. In these areas, the pool of volunteers with the requisite skills is much smaller. Vigorous but discerning recruitment consistent with organizational needs is the key to securing effectiveness in these positions (see Chapter Seven).

Contributing to the Effectiveness of Paid Staff

A common rationale for the introduction of volunteers into government agencies is to ease the burden on paid staff. By assuming a portion of their work activities, volunteers can relieve the pressure on beleaguered employees. The opportunity to allocate organizational responsibilities between staff and volunteers is one of the most constructive aspects of these programs. Not only can it lead to a serious rethinking of the tasks that public employees—and volunteers—might best carry out, but it can also enhance the attainment of organizational goals. As discussed above, direct service volunteers are most likely to achieve success when assigned to positions for which they possess the necessary competencies. In an analogous manner, when volunteer involvement allows staff to devote greater attention to the tasks for which professional training and expertise qualify them, their performance should also improve, with agency clients the chief beneficiaries. Conversely, volunteers might handle assignments for which employees lack requisite skills or experience, again to the advantage of clients.

Thus, it is not only through their own efforts that volunteers promote organizational effectiveness; they can also facilitate the work of paid staff. Perhaps no other area of public service better illustrates the possibilities of collaboration than law enforcement. Under the auspices of police departments, volunteers join reserve and auxiliary units, provide essential bilingual skills, assist with accident and crime scene work, and conduct community meetings on crime prevention. These activities appear to contribute to greater community safety and security (Bocklet, 1988; Sundeen and Siegel, 1986). In addition, "the use of volunteers enables police departments to free up sworn officers to devote greater time to activities considered more essential to crime prevention or reduction" (Sundeen and Siegel, 1986, p. 49). Police officers have greater opportunity for investigation and apprehension duties, as well as contact with their "beats," when volunteers assist in the great variety of supportive functions inherent in law enforcement. These tasks include telephone answering, record keeping, management of recovered property, finger-printing of noncriminals, photography, inventory control, monitoring of parking, security inspections of homes and businesses, public relations, and consumer services (Bocklet, 1988, pp. 180-181).

In their study of British social workers and probation officers, Anthea Holme and Joan Maizels (1978, pp. 74-76) uncovered a similar pattern. Both groups most often assigned volunteers to highly labor-intensive interactions with clients, such as befriending, visiting, shopping, and transportation. In light of the heavy demands on them, employees were not in a position to undertake these activities. Again, the involve-ment of volunteers contributed to the effectiveness of paid staff, "through the saving of their time, thus releasing them for what are judged to be more complex tasks" (Holme and Maizels, 1978, p. 88). In an evaluation of a community mental health center volunteer program, Jim Utterback and Steven R. Heyman (1984, pp. 231-232) determined that the value of time contributed by volunteers "multiplies," since their assis-tance increased the time available to clinical staff for im-portant functions. "Indeed the human costs of summarily eliminating the volunteer program might be quite high, stem-ming from a simultaneous decline in the quality and diversity of available services."

The participation of volunteers can yield comparable benefits to employees (and clients) of public libraries, muse-ums, schools, hospitals, nursing homes, senior citizens cen-ters, and recreational facilities. For example, teachers in a junior high school that engaged volunteers were grateful to them for help with routine, repetitious work and found, as one commented, that "they have helped me to be a more effec-tive teacher" (Powell, 1986, p. 33). In a national survey of local governments conducted by Sydney Duncombe (1985), officials in 45.3 percent of cities that had volunteers listed as an advantage that "volunteers can give detailed attention to people which city employees do not always have time to give." Nearly as many (40.1 percent) agreed that "volunteers provide specialized types of skills which city employees do not always have." In a follow-up survey of volunteer supervisors in local governments, who were more familiar with the programs, the numbers attributing these benefits to the approach rose to 64 percent and 67 percent, respectively (Duncombe, 1986).

Volunteer Supervision and Staff Effectiveness. As encouraging as these findings may be, increases in the effectiveness of paid employees resulting from the involvement of volunteers cannot be taken for granted. While gains have been achieved in many instances, they are contingent on the enthusiasm of staff for volunteer programs, their willingness to allow volunteers to shoulder a portion of their duties, and their acceptance of these workers as partners in the delivery of public services. As Chapter Two demonstrated, given the apprehension that often surrounds the introduction of volunteers into government organizations, none of these conditions should be assumed. Even when they are met, moreover, increases in the overall effectiveness of staff rest on attaining a critical balance: On the one hand, delegation of tasks to volunteers should allow employees greater time to pursue job components viewed as more complex and demanding. On the other, while the director of volunteer services is usually charged with final responsibility for the program, typically volunteers are deployed in operational departments of an agency, where they require oversight. Thus, these workers add to the supervisory burden.

Some public administrators complain that volunteers can consume more staff time and effort in the form of orientation, training, and supervision than the help they provide might warrant. The benefits of the approach do not come without cost: Working with volunteers can create special problems for employees. Nearly one-third (31 percent) of the social workers and probation officers in the British study mentioned as disadvantages the extra trouble, effort, and work involved with volunteers; the additional time taken up in supervising nonpaid personnel and in keeping a check on clients; and the difficulty of maintaining adequate feedback and liaison with part-time workers on variable schedules (Holme and Maizels, 1978, pp. 104-105). In Duncombe's (1985, pp. 362-363) survey of local governments, too, almost 40 percent (37.8 percent) of the officials who involved volunteers considered supervision of nonpaid personnel a problem. At the SBA and other public institutions with volunteers, employees can recount instances of time lost due to unreliable and uneven performance, lack of professional skills and in-service training, lapses in screening of candidates and in commitment to the organization.

While they acknowledged obstacles to effective collaboration, on balance, officials considered volunteer involvement a positive influence. Fully 98 percent of a sample of public sector volunteer supervisors agreed that "on the whole, the benefits of using volunteers outweigh the costs" (Duncombe, 1986, p. 294). Most of the British social workers and probation officers were also quite satisfied with volunteer participation (see above). The author's survey of SBA business development staff offers additional support. Over eight in ten (83 percent) of the respondents rejected the statement that "SCORE takes up too much of my time for the assistance it provides to small business." Using the same question format as that displayed in Table 3.1, business development staff rated their ability to work effectively with the counseling resources, SBDC, SBI, trade associations, and SCORE. Given the putative liabilities of volunteers, one might have anticipated that they would have ranked worst on this standard. In fact, SCORE earned the highest rating (a mean of 9.1 on a 10-point scale).

Volunteer programs have the potential to improve the effectiveness of paid staff—and of government agencies. At the same time, they raise new challenges for public employees to accommodate a nontraditional workforce and to exercise needed supervision and oversight. Part Two of this book addresses volunteer administration and management, but at this juncture it is well to point out that these hurdles can be surmounted.

The Volunteer Intangible

Volunteers are different than paid staff members. Though a truism, this idea is often overlooked in discussions of government volunteer programs. The potential of volunteers extends beyond increasing the workload of public agencies, facilitating the productivity of other organizational members, and performing admirably in the jobs assigned to them. These criteria could apply equally well to the evaluation of regular employees. The importance of the functions notwithstanding, they ignore the unique contributions that volunteers can make to public organizations. These contributions might be labeled the "volunteer intangible."

Volunteers may bring different and special qualities to government agencies. By definition, volunteers do not work for monetary compensation, but they have chosen to give their time to an organization for some reason(s): They may possess a resolute dedication to improving government services, an enduring concern for meeting clients' needs, a stubborn determination to better the lot of those who have fallen between the "cracks" of public assistance, or an especially strong interest or knowledge in a chosen policy domain—all of which may be reflected in their performance. In a study that examined job attitude and motivation differences between volunteers and employees in a matched sample of organizations, Jone L. Pearce (1983a) confirms that the volunteers had greater social and service motivations. Commitment to the goals of the organization is a crucial factor in deciding where to donate one's time (Park, 1983, pp. 184–185; Pearce, 1978, pp. 186, 275).

The reasons for volunteering are multiple and complex, but in national surveys the purpose expressed most frequently remains the desire to help others (for example, VOLUNTEER–The National Center, 1988; Hodgkinson and Weitzman, 1988b; Gallup Organization, 1986). Based on a comprehensive review of research published over a twelve-year period in the *Journal of Voluntary Action Research*, the major international journal in its field, Jon Van Til (1988,

p. 29) concludes that "concern for others, while not always purely altruistic, remains an important motivating force for much voluntary action." While instrumental rewards (career development, sociability, and the like) are also inducements for volunteering, as Chapter One elaborated, behavior aimed at helping other people does not preclude their attainment.

E. Gil Clary (1987, p. 67) writes that "in the area of emotional support the non-experts are the experts." He shows that more readily than professionals, volunteers are able to build relationships with clients characterized by acceptance, approval, empathy, care, regard, respect, understanding, and trust. Through direct contact with service recipients, volunteers can help to "humanize" the delivery of governmental services, lending them a more personalized and informal quality (Wineburg and Wineburg, 1987; Naylor, 1985; Schwartz, 1977). Not only does the provision of emotional support carry benefits of its own, for example by raising clients' self-esteem and self-confidence, but it is also likely to increase the motivation to accept and profit from the tangible forms of assistance offered by volunteers or government service agents.

In no way could one assess the price or monetary equivalent of the empathy, caring, and regard that committed volunteers routinely show clients. Nor would it be conceivable or genuine to pay employees to assume so many of the functions that volunteers undertake, such as friendly visiting, simple companionship, active listening, and social and emotional support. On the contrary, remuneration would spoil what is special and distinctive about volunteer activity: the gift of time and service free of overtones of a professional or authority relationship.

The status of volunteers in public organizations has decided advantages for acting on the helping impulse and reassuring clients of its authenticity. Since they are not tied to the organizational career and reward structure, volunteers enjoy relatively great latitude to place the needs of the client before those of the organization. As opposed to paid staff, who labor under a very different set of incentives and constraints, volunteers need not see the environment or mission of the organization in the prescribed fashion. Thus, they may more frequently choose to bypass cumbersome agency routines, test bureaucratic procedures, act as advocates of client interests, raise conflicting points of view, and experiment with innovations. An intangible benefit of volunteers seldom recognized is that they present the organization with an internal constituency with fresh perspectives for evaluating existing practices and identifying promising alternatives—and a position that facilitates expression of those judgments.

The relationship of volunteers to government agencies reinforces their capacity to secure the trust and confidence of clients. Whereas the public naturally associates employees with the fortunes of an agency, and therefore views them as bearing a degree of vested interest in its programs and operations, volunteers are seen as autonomous actors, lacking a parallel investment in the organization. Regardless of the accuracy of this perception, clients tend to view them as more credible and trustworthy, with no ax to grind or to sell. Volunteers are not strangers to this realization: As one SCORE volunteer related, "I tell them [business counselees] what works, not what is best for the SBA or what will look good on the monthly reports." It is also easy—albeit unfair—for clients to dismiss the dedicated efforts of staff to assist them. After all, employees have no choice in the matter; they are paid to do a job. Volunteers, in contrast, decide whether and where to donate their time, and from the client's perspective, harbor no other apparent incentive than service. The gift of self on the part of the volunteer may enhance the sense of personal worth and competence of clients (Salmon, 1985, pp. 219-220). One need not disparage employees in any way to appreciate that volunteers can be a unique asset to public organizations in helping people.

In general, volunteers possess closer ties to the community served and greater knowledge about it than do paid employees. More often, volunteers live in the community in which the agency is situated and are familiar with local resources and formal and informal helping networks. These attributes, too, can promote more effective services for clients, especially outreach and case finding.

For example, when a public program to teach proper breast self-examination techniques could attract only 13 percent and 19 percent of the women in two rural towns, staff decided to enlist the help of local women volunteers in recruitment. As a result of their familiarity with social networks in the areas and personal endorsement of the program, the women were able to increase the rates of participation by 115 percent and 50 percent, respectively, "when all conventional approaches to recruitment seemed to be exhausted" (Dorwaldt, Solomon, and Worden, 1988, p. 29). A model program that involved organization-based volunteers in locating and assisting the rural frail elderly yielded similar results. The program succeeded in identifying an additional 300 clientele, almost 20 percent of the target population, "in a locale where a sophisticated service delivery system had existed for 10 years" (Young, Goughler, and Larson, 1986, p. 344). The volunteer programs improved both the scope and the quality of public services.

In a number of ways, volunteers can enhance the responsiveness of government to citizens. First, through communication and contact with individuals and groups who donate their time to public agencies, officials have an opportunity to learn firsthand about community needs, expectations, and evaluations of services. Second, when volunteers assume some of the tasks of regular service workers, the latter can devote greater attention and expertise to areas or cases that in the absence of volunteer assistance would not receive sufficient consideration. Thus, collaboration between staff and volunteers can augment not only effectiveness but also responsiveness of services.

Finally, through volunteering, citizens transmit relatively specific information regarding their demands and preferences for public services that can assist officials in allocating resources more efficiently. Citizens can vote with their time: By contributing labor to the production of certain services rather than others, they signal domains where greater quantity and/or quality of activity are desired. Together, government officials and volunteers can then work to ameliorate these conditions. In sum, volunteers are not only different than employees, but also the difference can enhance the performance of government agencies.

From Intangible to Tangible Benefits. At some point, the intangibles of volunteer participation accumulate into concrete advantages for public organizations. Perhaps most important, citizen involvement builds public awareness of the operation of government agencies and the difficulties they encounter in delivering services. Such exposure can quickly erode negative political rhetoric indicting "the bureaucracy" to reveal the valuable work typically performed, often under trying conditions of budget cutbacks, escalating demands, and popular apathy, if not outright hostility. Through participation in these organizations, volunteers develop greater insight and appreciation for public agencies and their employees that can generate support in the larger community.

Volunteer familiarity with the public sector appears to breed respect, rather than contempt. Despite the oft-noted resistance of regular personnel to their involvement, volunteers are effective advocates of agency interests who help to further organizational missions, achieve increased appropriations, and thereby preserve government budgets and paid positions. Not only are they valuable to an agency in promoting community awareness and good public relations, but they can also engage in critical support activities with external constituencies. For example, partly as a result of the independence and credibility that the public attributes to them (see above), volunteers have earned the distinction of premier fund raisers.

They are just as adept at mobilizing popular support and lobbying centers of power. Unlike paid employees, volunteers are able to approach the public and funding authorities and not be seen as self-serving (Scott and Sontheimer, 1985, p. 23). Writes John Braithwaite (1974, p. 431), "as a missionary for better programs, one enthusiastic intelligent volunteer is worth several paid professionals." In California, library volunteers successfully pressed city councils and the state legislature to protect this institution from the depredations of Proposition 13 (Walter, 1987). On the national level, since its inception in 1964, the Service Corps of Retired Executives has been a staunch defender of the Small Business Administration. SCORE proved a very helpful ally in the battle to preserve the agency against President Reagan's bids to dismantle it during the mid-1980s. Further evidence of the potency of volunteers' political efforts appears in Vincent L. Marando's (1986, p. 22) study of recreation services in Maryland: "Volunteers encourage county expenditures while they contribute resources to recreation departments. . . . Volunteer requests and often their demands stimulate counties to provide more and higher quality recreation services. In Maryland, volunteers function as lobbyists to protect the recreation budget from expenditure cuts and in many instances exert pressure for increased expenditures. . . . Although recreation is not considered a vital service, it fared no worse than other services [in the annual state budget]. The role of volunteers at budget time appears to be important in the process of allocating public resources."

These examples do not appear to be isolated cases of volunteer involvement in the political process on behalf of sponsoring agencies. In a survey of localities with heavy volunteer participation covering five western states, 83 percent of a sample of volunteers and 89 percent of their supervisors agreed that "Volunteers support the program and budget of the department they work for." Somewhat fewer, but still over a majority of both volunteers (56 percent) and supervisors (76 percent), felt that "volunteers are more apt to support the city in tax and bond elections than the average citizen" (Duncombe, 1986).

The benefits of volunteers to public organizations extend to more immediate, internal functions as well. Although volunteering should not be treated as a credentialing process for paid employment with an agency, trained volunteers offer an attractive and convenient source of proven recruits. Some police departments view their reserve and other volunteer units as a reservoir of potential sworn officers (Sundeen and Siegel, 1986). In a similar manner, Small Business

Development Centers have hired accomplished volunteers away from SCORE. These situations arise as a natural outgrowth of the marketable skills that participants can acquire in volunteer programs.

Volunteers also add to the resource base necessary to innovation in public organizations. By applying the labor and talents of its volunteers, an agency can experiment with a policy option without having to obtain funding initially for a demonstration or pilot program. Though volunteer efforts are not free, they allow testing of promising changes and alternatives in organizational policies, procedures, and services without substantial cash outlays (Ellis, 1986, p. 49). Volunteers have led the way in pioneering novel programs in the social and human services that eventually became fully supported (Park, 1983; Schwartz, 1977; Becker, 1964). In a fiscal climate that imposes a hiring freeze, budget cutback, or mandate to implement new services (or improve existing ones) without adequate funding, the resource flexibility created by a successful volunteer program would be especially advantageous.

Summary and Implications

In three ways, volunteers can improve the quality and impact of government services: through their performance in the jobs assigned to them, facilitation of the work of paid staff, and introduction of unique attributes to public organizations. Contrary to stereotypes that conceive of volunteers as untrained "do-gooders" who wreak havoc rather than help, most public employees who have accepted voluntary assistance give positive appraisals to their accomplishments on the job. Though working with volunteers adds to supervisory duties of paid staff, here, too, evaluations are generally complimentary. The delegation of tasks to volunteers frees staff to devote greater time and attention to cases and problems that can profit from their qualifications and expertise. Far more than a paycheck distinguishes volunteers from employees. Volunteer motivations, perspectives and experiences, relationship to the organization, linkages to the community, and popular image are a source of intangible, as well as tangible, benefits to government agencies and clients.

Simply installing volunteers in public organizations cannot guarantee these advantages, however. Instead, government managers must take positive steps toward their attainment.

First, they must work to correct inaccurate images of volunteers that can keep employees from enlisting voluntary help. The information presented in this chapter, and in other research on volunteerism, may be useful for counteracting negative stereotypes. Perhaps more convincing to staff would be agency policies that treat volunteers and employees equally with respect to standards of conduct and performance on the job. In this manner, the volunteer program avoids the impression (erroneous or not) that service quality or amount might be sacrificed to accommodate the participation of lay citizens. Involving volunteers with employees in planning and operating the program is another method that can reduce stereotyping on both sides (see Chapter Six). Forums that bring the parties together, such as social activities, shared break periods, public meetings, awards presentations, and the like, can have the same salutary effect. Trained consultants in volunteer management also have experience in confronting and overcoming negative conceptions, so that organizations can return to a focus on missions and services.

Second, public agencies must provide means for realizing the "volunteer intangible," the host of nonmonetary benefits that citizens can bring to government services. As a start, volunteers should enjoy the opportunity to take on jobs where their special talents might be appreciated by clients, such as in direct service. Volunteers should also have the chance to express feedback and suggestions to the managers of departments in which they work. As an incentive to cooperation, employees and volunteers might be recognized jointly for any innovations or improvements stemming from volunteer involvement. To provide an additional outlet for feedback, the agency should establish the position of director of volunteer services. As Chapter Two showed, this office is essential to meeting the needs and aspirations of citizen participants and facilitating their varied contributions to the organization.

Finally, public managers must give careful attention to planning, design, and implementation of the volunteer program. Part Two of this book considers this subject in depth. Among the most crucial design issues, the agency must assess its needs for volunteers and identify their possible roles, obligate resources and institute procedures to recruit and screen citizens and ensure a fit to job openings, provide orientation and training for the government workplace, and link the volunteer program to operating departments. Token consideration of these factors can lead to serious deficiencies in volunteer morale, reliability, and retention that jeopardize the effectiveness not only of citizen participants but also of paid staff expected to collaborate with them. When such problems occur, officials normally show little hesitation in placing the blame on the volunteers. A more plausible explanation is that although public organizations have a vital interest in the gains in productivity that the approach can help them to achieve, they do not always recognize or take the steps necessary to develop and maintain a strong volunteer program.

4

Sharing Power and Authority with Volunteers: Issues of Volunteer Accountability

Public administration in both theory and practice has tended to assume that government officials are the ones actually providing public goods and services. . . . However, a large and growing share of government programs is now provided not by government but by a remarkable variety of proxies—third parties who are ultimately responsible for the quality and responsiveness of government goods and services. Donald F. Kettl, 1988b, pp. 9-10

The involvement of service volunteers in the public sector is part of a significant trend among jurisdictions in this country toward "government by proxy": the delivery of publicly funded goods and services by nongovernmental organizations and personnel. In the 1985 fiscal year, the federal government spent only about 14 percent of its budget on programs it administers itself, and half of this total went for operations, maintenance, and employment in the armed forces (Kettl, 1988a, p. 4). Some federal departments support as many as four indirect workers for every person on the payroll (Seidman and Gilmour, 1986, p. 120). This trend is not confined to the national level. An examination of total federal, state, and local spending in sixteen representative communities in 1982 shows that government delivered an average of only 39 percent of publicly financed services (Salamon, 1987, pp. 101–103). States use private providers for the management and operation of a growing number of functions, including hospitals and health centers, recreational facilities, water supply and wastewater treatment, public works and transportation, and prisons and juvenile corrections (Fixler and Poole, 1987). A similar pattern is evident at the local level, where cities and counties have turned to alternative service approaches, such as contracting, subsidies, and vouchers, to supplement the work of public employees (Valente and Manchester, 1984).

These changes have forced a redefinition of "street-level bureaucrats," a term coined by Michael Lipsky (1980) to denote public personnel, such as police officers, social workers, and teachers, who enjoy relatively great autonomy in providing government services. As Lester M. Salamon (1981, p. 261) observes, in the newer forms of government action, the service agents "are frequently not public employees at all, but bankers and businessmen, hospital administrators, and corporate tax accountants." Add to this list the great number of citizens who volunteer their time and skills to the public sector. For although contracts, grants, tax expenditures, loans and loan guarantees, insurance programs, and regulation are usually considered the chief instruments of government by proxy, the involvement of volunteers is yet another method through which governments fulfill significant service responsibilities.

Government by proxy is much more than the substitution of nongovernment personnel for public employees in the delivery of services. At root, it represents a sharing with third parties of the exercise of discretion in the use of public authority (Salamon, 1981). The crucial task facing government managers is to devise strategies to achieve effective performance and ensure accountability when the producers of services are not part of government and lie beyond its direct control. As Donald F. Kettl (1988a, 1988b) points out, public administration education must adjust to these new forms of government action. This chapter elucidates the challenges to public management arising from the introduction of volunteers as a proxy workforce in the delivery of services.

Volunteers and Government by Proxy

Like the recourse to the other proxies, government reliance on volunteers has become pervasive, especially at the local level. A 1982 survey undertaken by the International City Management Association (ICMA) estimated that more than one-half (56.5 percent) of a national sample of cities of over 4,500 population enlist volunteers to produce one or more services (Valente and Manchester, 1984). A more recent estimate from a survey by Sydney Duncombe (1985) placed the figure at over 70 percent (72.6 percent). Thus, a significant portion of the American citizenry donate time to the public sector. Based on a 1985 random sample survey of individuals by the Gallup Organization, Richard A. Sundeen (1989) reports that 9.5 percent of the adult population volunteers to at least one local government agency, 2.4 percent to a state government agency, and 1.3 percent to the federal government. In 1985, they supplied public organizations with a huge amount of productive labor, equivalent in total hours to 1.2 million full-time employees (Weisbrod, 1988, p. 202).

Although citizen volunteers may be best known as fire fighters and police auxiliaries, studies indicate that their activities on behalf of government are far more widespread. Volunteers are, indeed, common in the area of public safety, but they are also prevalent in the criminal justice system, health and human services, parks and recreation, culture and the arts, and education. Instances of volunteer involvement occur as well in government support functions, and in public works and transportation, albeit at lower rates. In all, Duncombe (1985) found that volunteers assisted cities in more than sixty types of work. A second ICMA survey, administered in 1988, reported volunteer participation in thirty-seven types of services, ranging from the arts to zoos (Morley, 1989).

Spurred on by fiscal stringency, the "social deficit" of unmet human needs, and the perception that the approach can achieve efficiencies, the participation of volunteers in the delivery of public services shows every sign of accelerating. In addition to these pragmatic forces, the linkage of volunteerism to values of patriotism and civic duty and obligation gives further impetus to this option. On just such grounds, for example, President Bush has appealed to "a thousand points of light," and legislative initiatives for national voluntary service from both political parties receive unprecedented attention not only in the media and in academic circles (Moskos, 1988; Danzig and Szanton, 1986), but also in the halls of Congress (Kuntz, 1989; Democratic Leadership Council, 1988).

It is not solely with respect to pervasiveness that government reliance on volunteers resembles the other proxy arrangements. While the traditional conception of volunteers envisions their role as ancillary to paid staff, the involvement of citizens has expanded well beyond subsidiary roles. Instead, like the street-level bureaucrats in these other forms, volunteers increasingly hold front-line positions that entail contact with clients and the exercise of discretion in the provision of publicly funded services. The range of jobs for which governments engage volunteers seems limited only by the ingenuity of public officials and the acceptance of paid staff. A partial listing includes: computer programming, economic development planning, business counseling, employee benefit and insurance planning, legal aid, ombudsperson services, job search assistance, park and natural resource protection and restoration, paramedical and emergency medical services, assistance in schools and libraries, building inspection and code enforcement, programs for the handicapped, energy conservation, building repair and renovation, and so on (see Farr, 1983, pp. 9-10).

Lack of Direct Supervision. A common motivation of public officials for incorporating volunteers is to reduce expenses, in Hill's (1980, p. 156) phrase, to provide services "on the cheap." The same motivation has meant that governments frequently operate volunteer programs with only minimal direct oversight or attention from paid personnel—in a manner sometimes replicated with the other proxy arrangements (see Kettl, 1988a).

In some cities, for example, volunteers are basically autonomous in running certain programs (see Martin, 1982), and in many, if not most public agencies, formal supervisory control seems modest, at best. In areas such as culture and the arts, recreation, natural resources, day care, and paramedical services, the number of volunteers can dwarf the number of paid personnel by several times. As a consequence, the ratio of government officials to the volunteers for whom they are nominally responsible can fall to levels far lower than would be countenanced in conventional supervisor-subordinate relationships in the public sector.

The Office of Business Development of the U.S. Small Business Administration offers a case in point. Business Development relies heavily on some 13,000 SCORE volunteers, dispersed around the country in more than 500 locations, to conduct prebusiness workshops, problem-solving clinics and business conferences, and on-site management counseling for SBA clients. In fiscal year 1988, SBA business development staff numbered 306 field positions. Perhaps half these officials, in addition to myriad other duties, have primary responsibility for the management and coordination of the volunteers. Of the twenty-seven central office positions that the SBA allocates to Business Development in Washington, D.C., just one is specifically directed to the volunteer program. Despite the scope and importance of this endeavor— the Small Business Administration (1989, p. 84) acknowledges that SCORE members "can be found in virtually every facet of business development effort"—the position has no support staff, but several additional major obligations.

In government and nonprofit organizations, this situation does not appear atypical. In his survey of local governments, Duncombe (1985, p. 363) discovered that only 21.9 percent of the sample of 534 cities with volunteer programs had an official designated as head. Even then, in many instances the municipality simply appended the func-

tion onto the existing job description of an administrative
assistant, personnel analyst, public services assistant, community services supervisor, or like position. Just 11.6 percent of the cities had made an evaluation study of the
volunteer program. Similarly, in a survey of 269 volunteer
managers in the northwest United States, their job titles
notwithstanding, only one-third of the sample devoted all
their work time to managing the volunteer program; nearly
four in ten (38 percent) spent less than half their time on
this obligation (Appel, Jimmerson, Macduff, and Long,
1988, p. 4). A lack of support for the position is a chronic
problem (see Scheier, 1988–89, 1988a, 1988b).

If these levels of formal attention and investment in
the management of volunteer programs by public and nonprofit organizations seem relatively meager, then the supervision of volunteers provided by line personnel can be
expected to be much worse. Employees often have little
stake in the volunteer program and may harbor indifference
or resentment toward it. Indeed, part of the rationale for
having a director of this operation is to encourage staff to
accept volunteers and to work actively with them. Attaining
this goal is a recognized problem in the best of circumstances, let alone without a demonstrated commitment
from the organization to its volunteer program (for example, Ellis, 1986; Wilson, 1976).

The era is long since past when government agencies
looked to service volunteers primarily for routine administrative, clerical, and manual chores. Volunteer activities have
spilled over into a very broad array of programs and jobs,
many of which allow for substantial discretion in attending
to the needs of clients and/or the institution itself. Public
organizations have demonstrated markedly less initiative in
matching this charge with a comparable investment in administration and oversight of the volunteer program. As a result,
volunteers have become a proxy workforce through which a
growing number of agencies deliver goods and services. What
are the challenges to public management raised by this form
of government by proxy?

Coping with Interdependence

The involvement of volunteers makes public organizations dependent on their citizen participants for the ultimate quality and responsiveness of government services. Government no longer maintains unilateral control. Instead, when volunteers meet with clients, advise and guide them, and otherwise assist in the delivery of goods and services, they share in the use of public authority. In this situation, the overriding concern for government managers, as it must be in dealing with any proxy, is to ensure that the exercise of discretion remains consistent with the goals and values of public endeavors.

In directly administered government programs enlisting only employees, conventional tools such as hierarchical chain of command and the organizational prerogative to order and sanction if necessary to gain member compliance are thought to keep this exercise in check. To the degree that the approach is effective, it is because paid personnel are dependent on the organization—for salaries, promotions and other perquisites, as well as the appraisals of performance by which these rewards are determined.

A comparable degree of dependence on the agency is lacking for volunteers, however. As Jone L. Pearce (1982) explains, leaving the organization costs them very little, and they can usually find many alternative uses for their free time, with equal opportunities for personal growth and community service. In contrast to employees, "volunteers may work according to their personal preferences because they have little to fear if they do not" (Pearce, 1982, p. 391). As a result, with these actors, public administrators cannot rely on the conventional administrative tools to influence and regulate behavior. Instead, they must devise strategies to cope with the interdependence between government and its citizen partners, a relationship in which the agency is usually at a disadvantage.

Differences in Values. Even so, the use of discretion by volunteers may remain within the bounds of the public interest, as represented by program goals. Accountability requires that volunteers are responsive to the policies enacted by public officials, and ultimately the citizenry. If volunteers understand and embrace these purposes and the values underlying them, and wield authority responsibly on behalf of government agencies, public administrators will have satisfied a critical exigency in the management of interdependence.

Yet proxies bring disparate values and aims to the delivery of government services (Kettl, 1988a, p. 15). Volunteers are no exception. While systematic data are not available to evaluate the relative frequency of their occurrence, clearly instances exist in which the outlook and actions of volunteers clash with the values and priorities of the public sector.

For example, in a volunteer health care program intended to help elderly residents in an inner-city neighborhood, some volunteers used their discretion to choose which inhabitants to assist and which not to among eligible clients (Wolf, 1985, p. 429). One volunteer refused "to visit the people at the other end of her block because they were 'bad' people and she wanted nothing to do with them." Despite the policy of a voluntary food distribution agency to provide longer term support to clients, many volunteers felt uncomfortable making the necessary inquiries and would not refer callers to a local welfare office (Pearce, 1982, p. 389). At a senior citizens center, two outreach volunteers began discussing their clients publicly, an obvious breach of confidentiality; though the director of volunteer services warned them and eventually took disciplinary action, the problem continued (Netting, 1987, pp. 250-251). In a local program designed to combat and prevent social ills such as poverty and illiteracy, volunteers expressed value disagreements not only with service recipients but also public agencies (Wineburg and Wineburg, 1987, pp. 11-12). Initially, volunteers tended "to be too judgmental about the lifestyles of their clients," and they became "frustrated because they do not understand why the welfare bureaucracy is like it is."

The SCORE Association provides a further example. One study, while careful to acknowledge that criticisms have been overwhelmingly balanced by favorable evaluations of

SCORE activities, reported prejudiced or condescending attitudes on the part of some volunteer business assistance counselors, particularly toward women and minority groups (Willing, 1982, p. 412). In a survey conducted by the author in 1986, only 14 percent of SBA business development officers questioned whether the volunteers did as well as employees in counseling the typical client seeking management assistance. By contrast, the number who had reservations about SCORE members' ability to counsel minority and women clients more than doubled to 30 percent. It should be noted that the latter assessment may reflect, in part, special SBA initiatives in place for minorities and women that complicate the provision of management assistance.

Sources for value disagreements between governments and service volunteers are plentiful. Public agencies endorse, and attempt to operate by, principles of fair and equal treatment of clients, universal selection and decision criteria, preservation of individual rights, and the provision of due process. Practices such as documentation, confidentiality, and compliance with rules and regulations enjoy an honored standing. Efficiency and effectiveness are pursued as well, but under bureaucratic pressures to serve huge constituencies, clients generally come to be seen as cases, and helping can become routine, often at the expense of genuine caring for individuals (for example, Wolf, 1985, pp. 425–426). Professional, but impersonal, attention is the norm.

For those without education or experience in public administration, these values may seem ponderous and formal at best and counterproductive and unfeeling at worst. To such an observer, the standards may appear to elevate process above results and the needs of the agency above those of service recipients. At some points during their involvement with an agency, volunteers are likely to find adherence to these values in conflict with their own motivation to help other people. In every major survey probing the motives for volunteering, the reason given most frequently is the desire to assist others— expressed by as many as 97 percent of a nationally representative sample in a 1987 study (VOLUNTEER-The National

Center, 1988). That volunteers may benefit as well from this activity should not obscure their interest in helping (for example, Van Til, 1988; Pearce, 1987).

One manifestation of the value conflict is the often-noted difficulty organizations encounter in inducing volunteers to complete necessary paperwork and to maintain accurate logs of hours donated and time spent on various tasks (see Chapter Two). On the one hand, record keeping is part of the lifeblood of bureaucracy. In service agencies, case counts and contact hours are typically the basis for allocations of funding and personnel, including resources for the volunteer program. On the other hand, many volunteers evidently do not understand or accept this perspective. For them, record keeping is dispensable and can even detract from more important objectives, such as assistance to clients.

Dependence and Influence. The exercise of public authority by volunteers is not confined to their decisions and actions in helping government to deliver services. Like other proxies, volunteers may also play a role in defining the goals of public programs. Sometimes the participation of volunteers in this capacity is overt and at the invitation of the agency. For instance, an organization may seek their participation in establishing a volunteer program and/or setting its objectives (for example, Ellis, 1986; Graff, 1984; Wilson, 1976). At other times, volunteer influence emerges not by design but as a consequence of the dependence of public organizations on them.

By introducing volunteers to meet burgeoning workloads, governments become reliant on these formerly excluded actors and, hence, potentially vulnerable to their preferences for agency missions, policies, and programs. As Salamon (1981, p. 260) elucidates, the third parties that public organizations enlist as partners in service delivery often find themselves in the "fortuitous position" of needing the government less than the government needs them. The result is an asymmetry in interdependence, in this case between volunteers and the agency, that stamps the respective social roles: The volunteer, writes Natalie J. Allen (1987, p. 258), is the "helper"; the agency, the "grateful recipient."

With mounting budget cutbacks and service obligations stimulating organizations in both the public and nonprofit sectors to recruit volunteers, not only are these participants very much in demand, but they also enjoy diverse options for contributing their time. As the comments of government officials confirm, the result is a growing dependency on volunteers. "The degree of our dependence on more than 5,000 volunteers cannot be overstated," attests the head of the Smithsonian Institution (Adams, 1988, p. 10); the Forest Service has "recognized dependency upon volunteers," states an official from that institution (Greer, 1985, p. 2). Spokespersons from a number of other government agencies acknowledge the inability to pursue organizational missions without the aid of volunteers (for example, Deitch and Thompson, 1985; Brown, 1983; Martin, 1982).

Dependence is a recognized source of power, although government officials are not likely to think of volunteers in this way. Instead, given the preoccupation with fiscal stress, public administrators tend to regard volunteers primarily (and some, no doubt, exclusively) in monetary terms to supplement agency resources and possibly cut costs. Yet volunteers are not merely caches of "free" labor to public bureaucracies but have their own ideas regarding program goals, content, and scope that they may seek to realize.

National surveys conducted by the Gallup Organization (1986, pp. 37–41) reveal that very few people (no more than 5 percent) volunteer simply as an economic response to help "keep taxes down." Based on sophisticated analysis of survey data, Jerald A. Schiff (1984, p. 210) suggests that individuals donate money largely to increase the outputs of an organization. In contrast, they "give time in order to gain influence over and/or information about the behavior of an organization." Similarly, Pearce (1982) found that members of agencies staffed predominantly by volunteers wielded substantially greater upward influence than did their counterparts in a matched set of organizations staffed entirely by employees.

Robert C. Dailey (1986, p. 29) speculates that the commitment of volunteers to an organization may rest on their perception that influence is possible.

Estimates are not feasible of the number of volunteers who wish to affect the policies and practices of the agencies to which they donate labor. In some government programs, however, the exercise of influence by volunteers is manifest. T. Zane Reeves's (1988, p. 2) analysis of the Peace Corps and VISTA, for example, illustrates how "ideology, as interpreted by political appointees, career employees, volunteers, and former volunteers, has played a major role in shaping agency goals, objectives, and project selection." Throughout the history of the organizations, volunteers and former volunteers have opposed the attempts of presidential appointees to leadership positions to redirect agency missions and activities according to different ideologies. Despite the persistent efforts of these officials to break down strong agency cultures, including a structural reorganization of the Peace Corps and VISTA (along with other federal volunteer programs) into a new ACTION agency in 1971, volunteers continued to express their dedication to an alternative set of values (Reeves, 1988, pp. 154–162).

While the Peace Corps and VISTA may be unique volunteer programs (participants receive a stipend, work on a full-time basis, live in the affected communities, and so on), volunteers strive to influence the goals and operations of government agencies with vastly different traditions. In many ways, the SCORE Association is the antithesis of the Peace Corps and VISTA. Most SCORE members are retired business executives, considerably older than these volunteers, and in all likelihood given their backgrounds, far more conservative. (Though SCORE was part of ACTION from 1971 through 1978, at the Congressional hearings over the inauguration of the agency, SCORE representatives objected to housing their association with such "radical" programs.) Nevertheless, SCORE volunteers have not hesitated to resist—and overturn—SBA policies, including several proposed transfers of the program, as well as initiatives to impose user fees for volunteer counseling and to charge the association for agency publications (the costs would then likely be passed on to clients). SCORE regularly protests its budget allotment from the SBA, which it argues is inadequate, and takes a stand on issues affecting members.

Conditions of Influence. To the degree that public organizations come to depend on volunteers, the latter gain opportunity for influence in agency affairs. In VISTA, the Peace Corps, SCORE, and other volunteer programs, dependence lies in the need government organizations have for contributed labor. These programs enlist huge numbers of volunteers relative to the size of the paid contingent. In addition, the organization of volunteers into associations within the agencies greatly facilitates communication, mobilization, and collective action. If the volunteers are members of an autonomous nonprofit organization that collaborates with government in the delivery of services, their influence might be further enhanced. (See Salamon, 1987, for a discussion of such public-private partnerships.)

The demand for labor is not the sole basis for government dependence on volunteers. Agencies may also rely on them for advocacy and for raising necessary funds, with analogous implications for influence. For example, volunteers may bear responsibility for obtaining some external funding for their program, perhaps as a cost-saving measure (see Chapter Two). Agency leaders should not be surprised if those who have acquired the funds also expect to be involved in determining how they are allocated.

A study of the Los Angeles Public Library system offers an illustration (Walter, 1987). Library officials counted on volunteers to solicit funds for the library, which management would then decide how to allocate. The citizens, in contrast, felt that the role of donor should carry with it the right to play decision maker as well. The struggle over control of the donated funds diminished confidence and trust between the volunteers and the library administration. While the volunteers correctly perceived that the library needs them, they in

turn rely on the competence and expertise of library professionals and the legitimacy of the public agency to improve
services. As a result of this interdependence, "the fund raiser
thus acquires a de facto organizational role as policy maker"
(Walter, 1987, p. 28).

As governments expand their reliance on volunteers for
labor, fund raising, or advocacy, and assist them in forming
associations, so too grow the prospects for volunteer influence. In addition to these forces, which sow dependence and,
hence, the foundation for power, volunteerism appears to be
taking a more political turn. Ilsley and Niemi (1981, pp. 1-2)
insist that all volunteer-based organizations include elements
of both service-oriented volunteering, such as assistance to
clients and staff, and advocacy activities, efforts to inform
agencies and the public of the need for change and to advance
that movement. One need look no further for a demonstration
than a volunteer program to restore and maintain New York
City's Central Park. Not only do volunteers contribute an
enormous amount of labor to this enterprise, but also "they
have the opportunity to . . . lobby their personal causes with
park and city officials directly. It is a tangible benefit of their
participation" (Hart, 1986, p. 38). Authorities in the field
have called for "empowerment"—for volunteer administrators
and citizen volunteers to realize the great quantity of time
they donate to recipient organizations, the value of the goods
and services they produce, the importance of the donations of
materials and money they stimulate, and the friendship and
goodwill they generate in the community and in the political
system (for example, Scheier, 1988-89, 1988a, 1988b; Wheeler,
1986-87; Schindler-Rainman, 1986-87; Naylor, 1985). These
are enduring bases for the recognition and use of power.

Summary and Implications

The involvement of service volunteers in the public sector is a
form of government by proxy. Increasingly, volunteers share
authority with government in the provision of public goods
and services, and exercise discretion and influence over this

process. By virtue of the growing dependence of government organizations on them, volunteers also have potential for influence in agency affairs. Like any proxy, volunteers bring disparate values and goals to the public arena, but governments seem more intent on delivering services economically than providing formal administration and oversight mechanisms for their citizen partners.

Government by proxy raises the essential challenge to public administrators of devising strategies to achieve effective performance and ensure meaningful accountability when the producers of services lie beyond direct managerial control. Formulation of administrative strategies equal to this challenge ought to be a high priority, but as yet the task has received little attention in the public administration community, other than in a handful of works (Kettl, 1988b, p. 10). The prevalence and importance of proxy arrangements notwithstanding, education programs in public administration continue to operate by the assumption that government employees are the chief agents for the delivery of services.

The participation of service volunteers in government organizations disputes this conception. Traditional approaches to public management will not suffice when those providing services and wielding discretion and authority on behalf of government are citizens, rather than employees. Part Two considers the design of public programs to realize effectiveness and accountability with volunteers.

Part Two

Building Effective Volunteer Programs

5

A Framework for Designing
and Organizing
Volunteer Programs

*Since the volunteer cannot be rewarded with
salary increments and formal professional
promotion, it is imperative that everything
possible be done to guarantee satisfaction from a
good work experience and meaningful adequate
recognition. Most of the universally recognized
principles of administration for employed
personnel are even more valid for volunteer
workers, who give their talents and time.*
Harriet H. Naylor, 1973, p. 173 (emphasis in
original)

*All too frequently when we fail to achieve
the results we want, we look for the causes
everywhere but the right place. Frequently it is
our inappropriate managerial methods. It is
much easier to blame others, such as . . . the
"unreliable volunteers."*   Marlene Wilson,
1976, p. 27

Designing a volunteer program to realize the full benefits of
the time and skills invested by citizen volunteers and government employees constitutes a profound challenge to public
managers. The stakes are high: Hastily or poorly conceived

programs can undermine the potential of volunteer involvement to expand and improve government services. In human terms, insufficient attention to program planning, organization, and implementation can result in volunteer "burnout" and disillusionment, staff resentment and frustration, and most distressing, the perpetuation of problems that gave impetus to voluntary action in the first place. Classic texts by Harriet Naylor (1973) and Marlene Wilson (1976) were among the first to bring this message home to practitioners, and in the process, they helped to launch the field of volunteer administration (see also Stenzel and Feeney, 1976). This chapter details the major components of an effective volunteer operation in the public sector.

Satisfying Internal Constituencies

The clientele reached by a government agency may be the chief beneficiary of a volunteer program, but the program must also serve two internal constituencies: the citizens who donate their time to the organization and the employees who are to work with them. Unless the needs of both groups are taken into account, the approach can be expected to founder. At the core of a successful program must be an appreciation for citizens' motivations for volunteering and employee perspectives on voluntary assistance.

Reasons for Volunteering. Surveys by the Gallup Organization have explored the reasons given by Americans for first volunteering and for continuing to volunteer. Since the initial survey in 1981, the motivations (as assessed by this methodology) have remained remarkably consistent. As in the earlier surveys, in the most recent, conducted in 1988 (Hodgkinson and Weitzman, 1988b), the response expressed most frequently—by over one-half the volunteers (56 percent)—was the desire to do something useful to help others. About one in five respondents (22 percent) had religious concerns. Motivations intrinsic to the work itself also ranked high. More than one-third (35 percent) said they enjoy doing the work; nearly as many (30 percent) had an interest in the activity; and close to one out of ten (9 percent) wished to learn and gain experience. (Because individuals may have several reasons for volunteering, the percentages do not sum to 100 percent.)

Survey methodology may not be the optimal technique for ascertaining motivations for volunteering (Smith, 1981). Studies using alternative approaches have demonstrated that recognition from peers and the organization, the opportunity for sociability, a need for affiliation with other people, avenues for personal growth, the desire to serve or support the goals of an organization, and a sense of contributing to larger purposes can also be salient motivations (for example, Van Til, 1988; Pearce, 1987; Moore, 1985; Sills, 1957).

Based on this research, volunteering should not be confused with self-sacrifice, contrary to popular stereotypes. Yet the decision to volunteer and to continue in this activity does seem to rest on a mixture of altruistic as well as instrumental motivations. Volunteers can—and most likely do—pursue both types of rewards simultaneously: One can certainly help others, derive strong interest and satisfaction in the work, learn and grow from the experience, and enjoy the company of friends and co-workers in the process. These rewards emanate from the quality and meaning of the volunteer work experience.

Government personnel systems do not typically accord high priority to such motivations. The rewards of public sector employment tend to be seniority-driven, and revolve around salary increases, promotion through the organizational ranks, job protections, and other tangible inducements. In order to incorporate volunteers into the workplace, government managers will have to adjust to the requirements of a group for whom, by definition, these incentives are not salient. Instead, the features and possible attractions of the work itself will have to receive greater emphasis. This focus does not mean that all volunteer positions must be created with an eye to job enhancement or enlargement, or the investment of significant task or other major obligations in them. In fact, the aversion of most volunteers to jobs that are "too big," and the difficulty of filling nonpaid positions that carry heavy administrative or leadership responsibilities, are well known. What it does mean is that public administrators will need to consider the activities that volunteers could usefully perform for the organization in light of the motives the tasks might engage.

Employee Perspectives. The greatest impediment to the successful introduction of volunteers into an organization is the often antagonistic reaction of paid staff (see Chapter Six). In general, volunteers are accused of uncertain reliability in fulfilling work commitments; lacking relevant training, skills, and experience for the tasks assigned; requiring excessive supervisory time, especially in relation to the assistance they might provide; and encroaching on employee prerogatives and perhaps job security. Given the liabilities commonly attributed to volunteers, employees are not inclined to welcome them.

A negative initial conception of volunteers may be characteristic, but it is not productive and must be overcome. Although resistance to the approach has commanded most attention, employees have good reasons for working with volunteers. As will be elaborated in Chapter Six, a well-designed volunteer program can yield significant benefits to government personnel. The involvement of volunteers can make paid jobs more satisfying and rewarding by allowing employees to delegate a portion of their defined duties, obtain assistance in areas where they feel inadequate, and concentrate on activities for which their formal education and/or training have prepared them. Volunteers offer perspectives and insights, as well as empathy and emotional support, otherwise not available to staff. By expanding employee jobs and fostering closer ties to the community, they also afford opportunities for professional development.

In confronting employee perspectives on volunteer involvement, public managers face two primary challenges. First, they must educate staff to the possible benefits of working with service volunteers. Employees will not work con-

structively with volunteers simply because they "have to" or
they are "supposed to"; alerting staff to the positive outcomes
of volunteerism is a much more persuasive technique. Second,
government managers must design and implement programs
that generate these advantages and ameliorate potential draw-
backs, so that the benefits to paid staff of including volunteers
outweigh the costs. As governments struggle to do more with
less, the kinds of assistance that volunteers can offer should
prove attractive to employees, especially if the help is rendered
on a timely basis, with requisite skills, and in a manner suited
to staff needs and job constraints. Few employees can reason-
ably object to shedding some of their duties and gaining additional resources and expertise.

   *Satisfying Internal Constituencies Through Program
Design.* Even the soundest plans to involve volunteers in a
government agency cannot guarantee acceptance by all staff
members, or a meaningful experience for all volunteers. Yet
a well-devised program can counteract potential resistance,
increase the degree as well as the quality of collaboration
between staff and volunteers, and thus improve services to an
agency's primary external constituency—clients. The foundation for an effective volunteer operation consists of five
general elements; the remainder of the chapter examines each
of them in turn.

1. *Organizing the volunteer program.* The program must be
    linked to the structure of the agency, and positions of
    leadership and management established to provide direc-
    tion and oversight for the volunteer operation.
2. *Matching volunteers and organizational needs.* The orga-
    nization must identify tasks that might be productively
    assigned to volunteers, prepare job descriptions for the
    positions to be staffed by citizens, and recruit and screen
    volunteers for the positions and place them accordingly.
3. *Educating citizens for volunteer service in the public sector.*
    Citizens should receive general orientation to the agency
    as well as specific training (as necessary) for the jobs
    assigned to them.

4. *Training employees in volunteer management and supervision.* In-service training should help employees appreciate workplace differences between paid staff and volunteers. Employees need to learn, and put into practice, successful techniques for working with volunteers.
5. *Evaluating and recognizing the volunteer effort.* Periodically, evaluation studies should assess the impacts of the volunteer program for clientele. Public organizations should also review the performance of individual volunteers and employees who work with them. Evaluation forms the basis for recognizing the contributions of all parties to agency goals.

Organizing the Volunteer Program

The volunteer program must be organized to respond to the motivations and requirements of volunteers and employees. With respect to volunteers, the program should have mechanisms for determining the types of work opportunities sought and meeting those preferences, and for engendering an organizational climate in which volunteers can pursue their goals with the acceptance, if not always the avid endorsement, of paid personnel. From the perspective of staff, the program must have the structures and procedures in place to assume the necessary burden of administration, and to generate a pool of capable volunteers matched to the tasks of participating offices and departments.

Management of a volunteer program constitutes a legitimate job in itself, which requires a significant investment of time and can benefit from specialized education and/or training. Should major program obligations, such as recruitment, orientation, screening, and training, be left instead to those employees who wish to include volunteers, the results would be predictable, though lamentable: Little volunteer involvement would occur, and staff might well question whether "volunteers are worth the effort." Consistent with the observation of Marlene Wilson (1976, p. 27) with which this chapter began, that scenario represents a failure not of volunteers, but of managerial methods. The volunteer program must be structured to ensure that its primary functions are carried out, and that the voluntary services made available are consonant with citizen motivations as well as staff needs.

Housing the Volunteer Program. Alternative structural arrangements are feasible for housing the volunteer program in a public agency (Valente and Manchester, 1984, pp. 56–57). In order of increasing comprehensiveness, they are ad hoc volunteer efforts, volunteer recruitment by an outside organization with government otherwise responsible for management, decentralization of the program to operating departments, and a centralized approach. Each option presents a distinctive menu of advantages and disadvantages.

Volunteer efforts may arise spontaneously in an ad hoc fashion to meet exigencies confronting public agencies, especially on a short-term basis. Normally, citizens motivated to share their background, training, skills, and interests with organizations that could profit from them are the catalyst. The fiscal stress experienced by the public sector in the late 1970s and throughout the 1980s may have quickened the helping impulse (see Chapter One). The SCORE Association started in this manner in the early 1960s, with retired business executives approaching the U.S. Small Business Administration to help the agency in attending to a huge constituency (Brudney, 1986). The responsiveness and alacrity with which an ad hoc effort can be launched and operating is inspiring: Within six months of its inception, SCORE supplied 2,000 volunteers to the SBA (crisis situations can provoke an even more dramatic reaction). Unfortunately, only selected parts or members of the organization may be aware of an ad hoc citizen effort and thus be able to avail themselves of it. As a senior SBA official interviewed by the author explained: "You see that broom closet down the hall? That was the SCORE office twenty years ago. That was all anyone knew about them. Heck, I was supposed to be in charge of SCORE, and I didn't know much more. What were those old guys doing around here, anyway? It took us a while to get organized."

Spontaneous help from citizens can infuse vitality into a public agency and alert officials to the possibilities of volunteerism. But because energy levels and zeal fade as emergencies are tamed, the ad hoc model is very vulnerable to the passage of time. A volunteer program requires not only a different type of ongoing, rather than sporadic, commitment from citizens, but also an organizational structure to sustain their contributions and make them accessible to employees. Unless the agency takes steps to institutionalize participation, it risks squandering the long-term benefits of the approach. Almost from the start, the SBA and the SCORE volunteers worked to develop an appropriate structure. In 1989, they celebrated the twenty-fifth anniversary of a partnership that has brought a continuous stream of volunteers to the agency and assistance to over 1 million small businesspersons.

A second option is to rely on the expertise and reputation of an established nonprofit organization, such as the United Way and its affiliates, for recruiting volunteers, but otherwise retain all managerial responsibilities within the agency. Some governments formalize this relationship through contract. Since recruitment is the most fundamental program function, and arguably the most problematic (see Chapter Seven for a full discussion), professional assistance can be highly desirable. This arrangement can be particularly helpful to an agency just beginning a volunteer program.

As in the delegation of any organizational function, however, quality control presents a necessary caution. Recruiters must be familiar with the government workplace, or the volunteers referred to the agency may not prove suitable. A recruiter may also have several organizations as clients, so that the priority attached to the requests of any one of them is unclear. More important, trusting recruitment to outsiders is a deterrent to developing this capacity internally, which is an essential aspect of a successful volunteer program. By all means, public organizations should nurture positive relationships with agencies in the community to attract volunteers and for other purposes. But they must avoid total dependence on external sources and strive to implement recruitment mechanisms of their own.

The volunteer program can also be decentralized in individual departments within a public agency or local government. The primary advantage offered by this approach is the flexibility to tailor programs to the needs of specific organizational units and to introduce volunteers where support for them is greatest. Yet duplication of effort across several departments, difficulties in locating sufficient expertise in volunteer management to afford multiple programs, and problems in coordination—particularly restrictions in the ability to shift volunteers to more suitable positions or to offer them opportunities for job enrichment—are significant liabilities. In addition, the selective approach can unwittingly generate disincentives for public managers to include volunteers (Brudney, 1989a, p. 117): Top officials may mistakenly equate non-paid work with unimportant activities to the detriment of a department's standing in the organization, or they may seize on the willingness to enlist volunteers as an excuse to deny a unit essential increases in budget and paid personnel. Such misunderstandings must be ameliorated prior to the introduction of volunteers.

Despite the limitations, the decentralized approach may serve an agency quite well in starting a pilot or experimental program, the results of which might guide the organization in moving toward more extensive volunteer involvement. Alternatively, a lack of tasks appropriate for volunteers in some parts of the agency, or perhaps strong opposition from various quarters, may confine voluntary assistance to selected departments.

Although volunteer participation in government is not a new phenomenon, the final structural arrangement, a centralized program serving an entire public agency or jurisdiction, is a rather recent initiative (Valente and Manchester, 1984; Hatry, 1983). With this approach, a single office is responsible for management and coordination of the program, while volunteers are actually deployed and supervised in line departments of the organization. The office provides guidelines, technical assistance, screening, training, and all other administration for volunteer activity throughout the agency. The advantages of centralization for averting dupli- cation of effort, assigning volunteers so as to meet their needs as well as those of the organization, and producing efficient and effective voluntary services are considerable. However, the program demands broad support across the organization, especially at the top, to overcome issues that may be raised by departmental staff and any limitation in resources. Because such backing is not often forthcoming, most volunteer activ- ity in local governments remains specific to individual city departments (Hatry, 1983, p. 47).

Director of Volunteer Services. Regardless of the struc- tural arrangement chosen to house the volunteer effort, the program should have a position bearing overall responsibility for management and representation of the volunteers, here called the "director of volunteer services" (DVS). The position serves both symbolic and practical purposes.

The manner in which the office is staffed sends a force- ful message to employees regarding the significance attached to the volunteer program by organizational leadership. Al- though governments have tried an assortment of staffing options, including volunteers, personnel with existing duties, and employee committees, a paid DVS position demonstrates a sense of commitment and priorities not evident through the other means. For the same reason, in the formal structure of the organization, the office should be located as close to the apex of the hierarchy as feasible.

These attributes of the office carry important practical advantages as well. For example, the DVS should enjoy pre- rogatives and obligations commensurate with positions at the same level in the organization, including participation in relevant decision making and policy making and access to superiors. In this manner, the incumbent can represent the volunteers before the relevant department(s) or the organiza- tion as a whole, promote their interests, and help to ensure that officials appreciate their contributions. A part- or full- time (as necessary) paid position lodges accountability for the program squarely with the DVS, presents a focal point for contact with the volunteer operation for those inside as well as outside the organization, implements a core structure for program administration, and rewards the office holder in relation to the success of the volunteers.

In addition to these roles, the DVS has important duties that further substantiate the need for a dedicated position (Ellis, 1986, pp. 45–49). The DVS is responsible for volunteer recruitment and publicity, a critical function requiring active outreach in the community and highly flexible working hours. The incumbent must communicate with department and organizational officials to ascertain workloads and requirements for voluntary assistance. In this regard, the DVS interviews and screens all applicants for volunteer positions, maintains appropriate records, places volunteers in job assignments, provides liaison supervision, and monitors performance. The office must coordinate the bewildering variety of schedules and backgrounds brought by volunteers to the agency. The DVS also bears responsibility for orientation and training, as well as evaluation and recognition, of volunteers. Since employees are usually unfamiliar with the approach, they, too, may require education; the DVS is the in-house source of expertise on all facets of volunteer involvement and management. Finally, as the chief advocate of the program, the DVS endeavors not only to express the volunteer perspective, but also to allay the apprehensions of paid staff and facilitate collaboration.

As programs increase in size, the DVS may have to share these obligations with volunteers and/or staff, but the duties must be performed. Given the scope of the job tasks, Ellis (1986, p. 54) recommends that secretarial support for the position is imperative.

Matching Volunteers and Organizational Needs

An effective volunteer program matches two basic components: the desires, skills, and interests of citizens for volunteer opportunities, and the requirements of government organizations for voluntary assistance. Successful matching is a result of (1) identifying organizational tasks that might best be performed by volunteers, (2) preparing descriptions for volunteer jobs that elaborate the essential responsibilities, and (3) recruiting and screening applicants for volunteer positions and placing them accordingly.

Assessing Organizational Needs for Volunteers. A volunteer program should not begin with recruitment. Public officials must first determine objectives for the program and the specific organizational tasks and responsibilities that can be productively assigned to volunteers. Although most of the attention surrounding the involvement of volunteers in the public sector centers on efficiency considerations, programs may also be designed to improve responsiveness, increase capability, facilitate innovation, and so on. In order to build organizational acceptance and commitment, employees should participate in the goal-setting process (see Chapter Six).

Their participation is integral as well to ascertaining organizational needs for volunteers. A survey of employees, or at a minimum of department heads and key officials, can yield important information on activities most amenable to volunteer involvement and attitudes toward the approach. Because most government personnel have not had experience with involving volunteers in their workplace, they may bear negative opinions and be reluctant to enlist voluntary help. Staff members may also lack knowledge regarding how volunteers might assist them, or how they might collaborate effectively with nontraditional workers. To overcome such obstacles, the director of volunteer services should arrange for orientation and/or training in volunteer management aimed at overcoming stereotypes and demonstrating the possibilities and advantages of working with volunteers (see below).

In the end, an employee survey should yield data on activities most appropriate for volunteer participation as well as organizational departments and officials most and least receptive to volunteers. This information is, of course, crucial to planning and implementing the program. Yet assessing agency needs for volunteers, enlarging areas for their involvement, and educating staff to the approach should be seen not as a one-time exercise, but as an ongoing responsibility of the DVS.

Job Descriptions for Volunteer Positions. Naylor's (1973) insight into the parallels between the administration of employed personnel and volunteer workers noted at the outset of this chapter is especially pertinent with respect to job specifications, placement, recognition, and evaluation. Studies undertaken by the International City Management Association on volunteer programs in local governments indicate that "volunteer job descriptions are really no different than job descriptions for paid personnel. A volunteer will need the same information a paid employee would need to determine whether the position is of interest" (Manchester and Bogart, 1988, p. 59). Specifications for volunteer positions should include title, required skills, time requirement, proposed starting date (and ending date, if applicable), responsibilities, authority, reporting relationships, and so on. The DVS should have background or training in task analysis and job design to develop positions that appeal to the interests and aspirations of citizen applicants.

Job descriptions are very helpful to prospective volunteers in appraising whether the opportunities afforded by a government agency are likely to meet their needs and competencies. They are equally useful to the organization. First, the preparation of job descriptions necessitates organizational deliberation concerning the objectives for volunteer involvement, a worthwhile undertaking in its own right and one that sets the general criteria for ultimate evaluation of the program. Second, the creation of formal volunteer positions helps to alleviate idle, frequently dubious, employee speculation concerning the rationale for introducing volunteers, which can frustrate a viable partnership. Third, job descriptions publicize volunteer activities, so that more staff become aware of these contributions and are able to request assistance. Fourth, by specifying the parameters of volunteer jobs, the agency simultaneously preserves the integrity, prerogatives, and authority of paid positions; they are two sides of the same coin. Clear definitions governing both types of positions can defuse potential tensions and antagonisms that might otherwise undermine employee-volunteer relationships. Moreover, the acceptance of personal responsibility for important organizational tasks by volunteers enhances the reliability of their work performance (Pearce, 1978). In sum, job descriptions for volunteer positions facilitate the matching of agency requirements with citizen talents and interests crucial to a productive volunteer program.

Recruiting, Screening, and Placing Volunteers. Job descriptions for volunteer positions are also at the core of successful recruitment. Recruiting volunteers should not be an undifferentiated search for person-power irrespective of qualifications, but a selective mission to locate and entice citizens with appropriate backgrounds and aspirations to fill designated agency needs that intrigue them. Although some generalized public relations is necessary to give visibility to this effort, targeted recruitment, rather than broad appeals for "help," is a more effective strategy. (Methods for attracting and retaining capable volunteers are discussed further in Chapter Seven.) The careful matching of citizens with positions improves not only volunteer motivation but also organizational performance (Wilson, 1976, pp. 101-103).

Just as for paid positions, the personal interview is the method of choice to assess the basic fit of prospective volunteers to organizational opportunities. Although some may object to a screening interview, conducted by the DVS or other program official, as contrary to the volunteer spirit, it actually serves the best interests of all involved. The first responsibility of a public agency is to its clients, who can hardly be expected to benefit from misplaced or deficient volunteer assistance. For this reason, the program should be under no obligation to accept all interested volunteers. An agency can say "no" to applicants, provided that the screening process is sensitive enough to uncover unique as well as prosaic skills, unusual as well as common backgrounds and potentialities. In such situations, every effort must be made to refer the applicant to more suitable volunteer openings elsewhere in the community.

Prospective volunteers deserve an interview to elucidate their motivations and desires for government service, and to have the organization take them seriously. The interview should clarify the expectations not only of the volunteer but also the sponsoring agency. Inadequate screening can result in misassignments to positions that underutilize applicants' talents and energies or, conversely, that demand too much of particular incumbents. In either case, volunteer burnout and attrition are the likely outcomes. Screening volunteers to achieve suitable job placements also contributes to organizational productivity—a factor that improves the morale of staff internally and the reputation of the agency externally.

To encourage assignment of volunteers throughout the organization, the procedures for employees to seek their assistance should be made as easy as possible. While a staff member's request for volunteer help must be specific, the experience of some programs demonstrates that it can be reduced to a simple, one-page form (Goetter, 1987). In deference to paid personnel, the official to whom the volunteer will report enjoys the right to interview applicants to evaluate their commitment to the organization, appropriateness for certain positions, and compatibility with co-workers. In addition, like other agency staff, the volunteer should serve a probationary period. After assignment is effected, the volunteer becomes the joint responsibility of the line supervisor and the director of volunteer services. The DVS or designated program official should be available to support staff in all aspects of volunteer management and to monitor and enhance the work experience of volunteers.

Educating Citizens for Volunteer Service in the Public Sector

If an agency is to realize the full benefits of volunteer participation in the delivery of government services, both citizens and employees must gain knowledge about the approach.

This section discusses orientation and training for volunteers. The following section turns to education for public administrators.

Most volunteers to public organizations will not possess background or credentials in government employment. Orientation sessions can familiarize them with the philosophy, norms, traditions, and basic rules and procedures of the sponsoring organization. In addition, orientation should expose participants to the distinctiveness of the work environment in which they have chosen to donate their time and talents. That is, preservice education should elaborate the charge of public authority underlying the missions of government agencies, the relatively close scrutiny under which these institutions operate and attendant requirements for documentation of activity, and the importance of care and deliberation in the use of discretion and the application of public funds. Even at this early stage of volunteer involvement, the organization can begin to inculcate a sense of accountability for performance so crucial to effective management of government by proxy (see Chapter Four).

The agency should also provide for the in-service training of volunteers. For many positions, volunteers will possess the relevant competencies, or can acquire or refine them quite easily on the job (for example, city hall receptionist, museum tour guide, library reader for children, and so forth). Depending on the work history of volunteers, job assignments in other government domains—for example, drug and alcohol rehabilitation, economic development planning, or law enforcement—will likely call for more formalized training. Should volunteer staff hold positions of responsibility for major elements of the program, such as orientation, budgeting, overall management, or evaluation, advanced leadership training may prove necessary.

Since public agencies may be held liable for the actions of volunteers, they have a vital interest in providing requisite training (see Chapter Eight for a discussion of liability issues concerning volunteers). Sound procedures for orientation and training offer one of the best assurances that organizations have that volunteers will be competent for the jobs assigned and cognizant of relevant policies and procedures. In addition, developing a corps of such "job-ready" volunteers is, arguably, the most compelling step that program officials can take to satisfy paid staff that volunteers are worth the effort and to gain acceptance for the approach (see above).

Training should impress upon volunteers the importance of their work to the goals of the organization, and instill a strong sense of personal responsibility for the tasks assigned (Pearce, 1978, pp. 280–282). The director of volunteer services, as well as department managers, should reinforce this message by their treatment of volunteers as crucial, rather than peripheral, human resources. Organizations that socialize volunteers to understand that their labor has a direct bearing on the functioning of the agency, and whose employees act accordingly, are most likely to be rewarded with reliable and productive volunteer service.

Some texts counsel public officials to keep orientation and training sessions brief, so as not to dissuade potential volunteers (for example, Farr, 1983). While in-service education should not be tedious for volunteer (or employed) personnel, it must be of sufficient depth to present a fair and accurate description of the agency, its work requirements, and nonpaid positions. This function, too, is integral to ensuring a proper fit between the motives, talents, and interests of applicants and the conditions and openings for volunteer service within the agency. Yet an organization should not stress correct process, form, and procedure to the point that training threatens to create detachment toward clients and rather mechanical provision of services (Clary, 1987). Instead, government officials will want to preserve and foster the "volunteer intangible," especially the enthusiasm, perspective, caring, and emotional support that citizens can contribute to a public agency and service recipients (see Chapter Three).

For most volunteers, opportunities for continuing education and growth are positive inducements, valued either in themselves and/or instrumentally for obtaining marketable job skills. If the positions that governments make available to volunteers have been designed to appeal to these needs, the time devoted to orientation and training should be of little consequence.

Training Employees in Volunteer Management and Supervision

Volunteer programs ask public managers to integrate novel human resources into their work activities, though "there is little in their professional education, their bureaucratic experience, or their professional literature to guide them" (Walter, 1987, p. 23). Training for employees in working with volunteers can help to compensate for this lack of background knowledge and motivation.

Training should center around issues of managerial control. Volunteers are much less dependent on the organization than are paid staff members, who must earn their livelihood from it. Most volunteers can leave the organization and find comparable opportunities for their time with far less effort and inconvenience than can employees. As a result, supervisors do not have as much control over volunteers (Pearce, 1982, 1978). Volunteers can afford to be more selective in their acceptance of work assignments. They may not be as faithful in observance of agency rules and regulations, particularly those considered burdensome or "red tape." Since nearly all who volunteer do so on a part-time basis, they will generally have less information about organizational policy and procedures. Social interaction is part of the fun and spark of volunteering, and participants may insist on this aspect of the job more so than employees.

Given the relative autonomy of volunteers, a heavy-handed approach to supervision can be expected to elicit antagonism and attrition, rather than compliance. Traditional organizational inducements—the "three p's" of pay, promotion, and perquisites—are not operative for volunteers. Conventional organizational sanctions, too, are likely to prove abortive; appeals to hierarchical authority are far less apt to sway volunteers than employees. Instead, government managers must apply a different set of incentives to motivate and direct volunteer behavior toward agency goals. Persuasion, negotiation, coaching, and teamwork are much more effectual strategies for this purpose. For example, in a study of volunteers in a major public library system, administrators who embraced this style of "management-by-partnership" enjoyed greater success in dealing with volunteers and meeting objectives than did those intent on control (Walter, 1987, p. 31).

Training for employees should do more than advance changes in managerial style. It should also alert organizational leadership and program staff to measures that they can implement to facilitate the task of volunteer supervision. Based on a comparative study of organizations staffed predominately by volunteers and those staffed entirely by employees, Jone L. Pearce (1982, 1978) determined that the "psychological contract" between members and the organization, or the set of mutual expectations, both implicit and explicit, governing their relationship, is more ambiguous and broad for volunteers than for employees. To channel volunteer talents and energies productively, she advises agencies to elucidate the behaviors expected from nonpaid staff.

How can public organizations do so? The procedures discussed earlier in this chapter offer a viable approach to elaborate the psychological contract between volunteers and the agency and to promote mutual understanding of this relationship. Creating formal positions for volunteers and preparing the associated job descriptions, interviewing applicants and giving them mutually satisfactory work assignments, and presenting orientation and training are potent means to define what volunteer service means to the agency and to citizens, and to coordinate the needs and motives of both sides. Probably no factor aids more in supervising volunteers (and paid staff) than placing them in positions where they can put their strongest motivations and best skills to work.

A complementary approach for solidifying the member-organization contract is to enact and circulate policies delineating professional conduct for all participants. By setting standards as high for volunteers as for paid staff, a public agency builds trust and credibility, increased respect and requests for volunteers, a healthy work environment, and quality services (Goetter, 1987; Deitch and Thompson, 1985; Wilson, 1984). Organizational policy should encompass absenteeism, tardiness, appropriate dress, confidentiality, deportment while representing the agency, treatment of clients, limits of authority, and so forth. Policy should also elaborate the rights and responsibilities of all organization members, to protect volunteers from arbitrary treatment or exploitation, and to relieve employees from apprehension concerning loss of authority or job security. A handbook distributed to both citizen participants and paid staff summarizing these provisions, as well as other signal aspects of the volunteer program, is well worth the investment of public funds. The handbook offers a common frame of reference for understanding volunteer service to the agency.

One issue that policy must address is possible termination of volunteers. An old adage holds that "volunteers cannot be fired." Certainly, separation from the agency should be a last resort only after other remedies, such as reassignment, have been exhausted. However, this maxim must give way should volunteers continually fail to meet basic standards of professionalism promulgated by the agency and judged essential to performance. "If a teacher plans a lesson that requires a volunteer's help and the volunteer doesn't show up, that teacher probably will decide the volunteer program is more work than it's worth" (Goetter, 1987, p. 34). If such behavior occurs repeatedly, public goals—and the volunteer program itself—are put at risk, so the director of volunteer services must take decisive action. Policy should stipulate that before reaching this juncture, the DVS would have ascertained the nature of the problem from the volunteer and any affected employees and worked with them to find possible solutions.

As recommended in Chapter Six, to build ownership and commitment, public officials should include volunteers and employees in planning the volunteer program. The policies and precepts that emerge from their deliberations assist the organization in specifying desired standards of professional conduct and in attaining them. In her sample of volunteer organizations, Pearce (1978, pp. 276-277) found that the ones most successful in clarifying the volunteer-agency relationship suffered the lowest rates of turnover. These organizations had notebooks with all written policies, formal job descriptions, training manuals, and so forth. "In fact, in each case their socialization procedures were more elaborate than the procedures of their employing counterparts." In contrast, the volunteer organization with the highest turnover in her sample had none of these things.

In sum, employee training in volunteer administration should consider not only questions of managerial technique but also means to firm up the psychological contract between the organization and its volunteers. Volunteers are less dependent than paid staff on the agency, and for this reason, managerial styles must adjust to accommodate a more autonomous workforce. Without organizational initiatives to impart a shared conception of volunteer service for employees and citizens, however, managerial adaptations in themselves are likely to prove insufficient.

Managing the SCORE Program. The results of a survey undertaken by the author of SBA business development officers (BDOs) reveals some of the workplace differences between volunteers and employees and suggests implications for public management. The BDOs, who act as agency coordinators for the SCORE program, were asked to compare the proficiency of the volunteers with that of "regular SBA employees" in nine areas. Respondents could rate volunteer performance as "much worse," "somewhat worse," "about the same," "somewhat better," and "much better." Table 5.1 presents the results (response categories have been collapsed for ease of interpretation).

As might have been anticipated, the domains in which the SCORE volunteers fare least well are completion of necessary paperwork and knowledge of relevant SBA rules and

Table 5.1. How Do SCORE Volunteers Compare to Regular SBA
Employees in Nine Activity Areas?

Activity*	Worse (%)	Same (%)	Better (%)
Ability to counsel SBA clients	14.1	36.4	49.5
Dependability in work commitments	22.2	59.6	18.2
Quality of work performed	27.2	52.6	20.2
On-time performance of work	30.3	51.5	18.2
Willingness to do any job task	34.4	35.4	30.2
Making efficient use of your time	35.7	43.9	20.4
Willingness to take direction	37.4	35.4	27.2
Completion of necessary paperwork	66.7	28.3	5.0
Knowledge of SBA rules and procedures	75.8	21.2	3.0

*$N = 99$ for all items except "Making efficient use of your time" ($N = 98$).

procedures. Nearly twice as many BDOs rated the volunteers worse than employees on paperwork (66.7 percent) and rules and regulations (75.8 percent) than on any of the other items. Although sizable minorities took a different view, over one-third of the BDOs judged the volunteers behind SBA personnel on willingness to do any job task (34.4 percent), making efficient use of the official's time (35.7 percent), and willingness to take direction (37.4 percent).

Nevertheless, an arresting finding of Table 5.1 is that two of the three volunteer activities evaluated most positively by the BDOs are the ability to counsel SBA clients and the quality of work performed. Half the BDOs (49.5 percent) rated volunteer management counseling above that of employees, and 72.8 percent appraised the quality of work as at least comparable. Their assessments of volunteer dependability in fulfilling work commitments (77.8 percent "same" or "better") and on-time performance of work (69.7 percent) also rank high. Additionally, excessive socializing on the job is not a problem: In an item not shown in the table, 79.2 percent of the BDOs rejected the statement that "SCORE more closely resembles a social club than an organization to help small business."

These responses demonstrate that despite reduced control over volunteers, a well-managed program need not sacrifice organizational effectiveness. Supervisory practices at the Small Business Administration are instrumental to this result. First, numerous SBA handbooks and other publications, as well as solid procedures for volunteer recruitment, screening, orientation, training, and placement, help to create mutual expectations that facilitate supervision. Second, the SCORE volunteers have great latitude in accepting or rejecting work assignments, although persistent inactivity is not tolerated and can jeopardize membership status. Third, the tasks performed by the volunteers provide intrinsic motivation: In a survey of chairpersons of SCORE chapters around the country, 89.7 percent felt that the volunteer program offers "stimulating work," and 81.7 percent considered the cases assigned for management counseling "challenging and interesting." Fourth, the volunteers are responsible for major facets of the program, including recruitment, training, and reporting. Finally, while the volunteers enjoy substantial autonomy, the SBA and the SCORE Association hold them to high standards of professional conduct and service to small business.

Evaluating and Recognizing the Volunteer Effort

According to researchers, evaluation is carried out less often and less well than the other central elements of a volunteer program (for example, Allen, 1987; Utterback and Heyman, 1984). In a study of 534 cities over 4,500 population that had volunteers, Sydney Duncombe (1985, p. 363) found that just 62 (11.6 percent) had made an evaluation study. Government officials are reluctant to appear to question the value of well-intentioned helping efforts. In addition, they may worry about the effects of an evaluation policy on volunteer recruitment and retention, and on public relations. Nevertheless, for individual volunteers and the paid staff who work with them, and for the volunteer operation as a whole, evaluation and recognition activities are essential program functions.

Evaluation of Volunteers and Employees. The fears of organizational leadership notwithstanding, volunteers should view assessment favorably. A powerful motivation for volunteering is to achieve worthwhile and visible results; evaluation of performance can guide volunteers toward improvement on this dimension. No citizen contributes his or her time to have the labor wasted in misdirected activity, or to repeat easily remedied mistakes and misjudgments. That an organization might take one's work so lightly as to allow such inappropriate behavior to persist is an insult to the volunteer and an affront to standards of professionalism crucial to job effectiveness and employee acceptance (see above).

Susan J. Ellis (1986, pp. 81–82) points out that evaluation is actually a form of compliment: Performance appraisal indicates that the work merits review, and that the individual has the capability and will to do a better job. For many volunteers, moreover, volunteering is a way to acquire desirable job skills. To deny feedback to those who give their time for organizational purposes, and who could benefit from this knowledge, is a disservice to the volunteer.

The employee to whom a volunteer reports should prepare the appraisal, in conjunction with the director of volunteer services. But an agency-initiated appraisal is not the only method. Volunteers might also evaluate their own performance and personal experience in a public agency (Manchester and Bogart, 1988; McHenry, 1988). The assessment should tap volunteer satisfaction with important facets of the work assignment, including job duties, schedule, support, training, opportunities for personal growth, and so on. The self-assessment is also a valuable tool to obtain feedback on agency management and supervision of volunteers: Employees should learn from the process as well. Regardless of the type of evaluation, the goal ought to be to ascertain the degree to which the needs and expectations of the volunteer and the organization are met, so that job assignments can be continued, amended, or refined as necessary.

Agency officials might recognize and show their appreciation to volunteers through a great variety of activities: award or social events (luncheons, banquets, ceremonies), media attention (newsletters, newspapers), certificates (for tenure or special achievement), expansion of opportunities (for learning, training, management), and, especially, personal expressions of gratitude from employees or clients. A heartfelt "thank you" can be all the acknowledgment many volunteers want or need. Others require more formal recognition. The director of volunteer services should make letters of recommendation available to all volunteers who request them.

A volunteer services approach requires the participation of not only volunteers but also public employees. If government officials are committed to having paid staff and volunteers work as partners, program functions of evaluation and recognition should apply to both members of the team. Thus, employees expected to work with volunteers should have pertinent responsibilities written into job descriptions. Equally important, performance appraisal for the designated positions must assess requisite skills in volunteer management. Just as demonstrated talent in this domain should be encouraged and rewarded, an employee's aversion to volunteers, or poor record with them, should not go overlooked and, implicitly, condoned. As elaborated above, organizational training should develop competencies in volunteer supervision. (Chapter Six provides an extended discussion of techniques to motivate and recognize staff collaboration with volunteers.)

Recognition activities for volunteer programs normally focus on citizen participants. But employees value recognition as well, especially when awards ceremonies, social events, media coverage, agency publications, and the like bring their efforts and accomplishments with volunteers to the attention of organizational leadership. Similarly, feedback on employee achievement from volunteers and the director of volunteer services belongs in agency personnel files. By taking seriously the evaluation and recognition of paid staff in working with volunteers, public officials provide incentives for an effective partnership.

Evaluation of the Volunteer Program. While volunteer programs must satisfy constituencies internal to the organization, their overriding rationale is to improve external conditions or the prospects of clients. Agencies that mobilize volunteers for public purposes should be held accountable for the use of government funds, facilities, labor, and authority, and for the investment of citizen time and talents. Too often, however, what passes for "evaluation" of this effort is a compilation of number of volunteers, hours donated, and client contacts or visits. Some researchers complain that associated costs have been neglected (Utterback and Heyman, 1984, p. 229). Impressive and significant though these data may be, they tap the inputs or resources to a volunteer program, rather than its results or accomplishments.

Much as they would be expected to do for any other unit of the organization, public officials should periodically assess the outcomes of a volunteer program against its goals or mission. Volunteer activity is other-directed; it should do more than gratify donors and accommodate employees. Evaluators need to review the aggregate performance of the volunteers in assisting clients, ameliorating community problems, expediting agency operations, and meeting additional objectives. Not only does the assessment yield information that can improve program functioning, but it also reinforces for all concerned—citizen participants, paid staff, and agency clients—the importance of the volunteer component to the organization.

A second, recommended type of evaluation pertains to the processes of a volunteer program. Officials should determine that procedures to meet essential functions discussed in this chapter (volunteer recruitment, training, placement, and so forth) are in place, and that they are operating effectively. Additionally, the evaluation should assess the satisfaction of volunteers and staff members with the program. Continuing struggles with recruiting suitable volunteers, arresting high rates of volunteer burnout and turnover, relieving staff antagonisms, reaching mutually agreeable placements, and the like, point to flaws in program design that must be addressed. By diagnosing such problems, a process evaluation can enhance the achievement of external objectives.

Summary and Implications

Underlying the success of a government volunteer program are five general elements: program organization, a system to match volunteer and agency needs, education for citizens in volunteer service, employee training in volunteer management and supervision, and a commitment to evaluation and recognition of performance. If volunteer efforts stagnate or go awry, officials should seek causes and remedies in these elements, rather than in putative failings of volunteers, such as unreliability, or lack of relevant job knowledge (Wilson, 1976). Surely, these liabilities must be overcome, but they are reflections on the program, rather than on its citizen participants.

An effective volunteer program can usefully draw on principles of administration for employed personnel (Naylor, 1973). But the learning should flow in both directions: If a government organization devoted the same level of energy and care as recommended for the management of volunteers to designing paid jobs and recruiting for these needs, interviewing and placing applicants, discerning motivations and responding to them, and evaluating and recognizing accomplishment, the benefits realized by employees and the agency would be more than worth the effort.

6

Planning and Managing
Volunteer Programs to
Overcome Staff Resistance

Volunteer program problems come and go. Only one has persevered near the top of the problem parade for ten years: paid staff and agency non-support of volunteers. Ivan H. Scheier, 1977, p. 32

In the operation of volunteer programs, no impediment looms as large or as obstinate as the often indifferent or antagonistic reception of paid staff. Ivan Scheier's assessment of volunteer-staff relations is one of the most striking, but he is hardly alone. The issue has a timeless quality. In 1977, according to Scheier (1977, p. 32), this relationship could already be considered an "Old Failure." His conclusion seems just as apt some ten or fifteen years later. "It is one of those things everyone talks about—but very few really have done much to change the situation," writes Marlene Wilson (1981, p. 21). "It was . . . the number one problem in volunteerism nationally and in Canada in the '70s. And it will escalate to become a critical, survival issue in the '80s for volunteer programs in agencies and organizations." Adds Linda Graff (1984, p. 20): "The issues are going to be around for a while and the potential for tensions to increase exists."

The consequences of these tensions are serious: The quality of volunteer-staff relations affects the viability of vol-

119

unteer programs in several ways (Allen, 1987, p. 259). Because volunteers must frequently rely on staff members for assistance and advice, employee attitudes are readily transmitted to them. A lack of support for volunteers can undermine the enthusiasm as well as the caring and concern citizen participants would otherwise invest in government programs. If staff do not understand, accept, and appreciate the role of volunteers, they can reduce the jobs assigned to them to errands, thus, robbing the tasks of their motivating aspects. Such attitudes toward volunteers, moreover, can spill over to clients. Should employees betray negative opinions to service recipients through their words or actions, either consciously or unconsciously, clients may come to accept this outlook as well. An organizational climate dominated by hostility and suspicion is hardly conducive to volunteer effectiveness or retention. Thus, it should not be surprising that the satisfaction of volunteers with the respect, appreciation, support, and assistance accorded them by staff influences their decision to remain with an agency or to seek other, more constructive outlets for their time (Scheier, 1981; Pierucci and Noel, 1980).

A problem that has endured for as long as this one is not likely to yield to a single, easy solution, and yet the success of the volunteer program demands that it be addressed. This chapter presents a unified strategy to better volunteer-staff relations. Though some rough spots in their interaction might be expected, conflict between the two parties is wasteful of human resources—and spirit—and detracts from the capability to pursue organizational missions. The strategy consists of five major components:

1. Determine the goals underlying the participation of volunteers.
2. Examine, and amend as necessary, agency policy and legislation pertinent to volunteers.
3. Ensure the commitment and support of top agency management for a volunteer program.
4. Involve management, staff members, and volunteers in

planning the program and in crucial decisions regarding sharing the workplace.

5. Educate staff to the advantages of working with volunteers and reward them for effective collaboration.

Why Volunteers?

The first step in planning a volunteer program must be to determine the purposes for introducing the new personnel into the organization. For what reasons are volunteers sought? In a period in which demands for more and better government services are confronted by scarcity in budget and personnel, the question may seem hardly worth asking. The need for donated labor should be manifest.

If the sole rationale that officials can muster for a volunteer component is to save public dollars, however, they court major disappointment. As discussed in Chapter Two, volunteer programs will not reduce budgetary obligations, unless, of course, they are intended as a method to displace paid staff—a move sure to exacerbate the very tensions that have defeated many volunteer programs. Instead, from the perspective of efficiency, what volunteers offer government agencies is the capacity to make more productive application of existing funds and person-power. With a relatively small investment of resources, volunteers have the potential to increase the level and quality of services that an agency can deliver to the public. While costs are not spared in this situation, to the degree that volunteers improve the return on public expenditures, they extend resources yet available to government to meet pressing needs for assistance and services.

To many government officials, these reasons may be the decisive "bottom line" for incorporating volunteers. "The point is that they are an available resource in a time of diminishing resources," states one authority (Strickler, 1987, p. 28). Additional or different purposes may drive a volunteer program, however. Agency leadership may decide to enlist volunteers to interject a more vibrant dimension of commitment and caring into organizational relationships with clients. Or, the goal may be to learn more about the community, nurture closer ties to the citizenry, and strengthen awareness and support among the populace. Volunteers may be sought to reach clients inaccessible through normal bureaucratic channels, or to provide special skills, such as fund raising or computer programming, not readily available to an agency. The purpose may be to staff an experimental program otherwise doomed to fiscal austerity. Enhancing responsiveness to client groups may be still another rationale. And so on.

That the list of possible motivations for establishing a volunteer program is lengthy attests to the vitality of the approach. Before seeking volunteers, public managers should settle on the ends for their agency. An explicit statement of goals advances several important facets of program design and functioning. First, it begins to define the types of volunteer positions that will be needed, and the number of individuals required to fill these roles. Such information is at the core of eventual recruitment and training of volunteers. Second, it aids in delineating concrete objectives against which the program might be evaluated, once in operation. Evaluation results are instrumental to improving the program and obtaining the funding necessary to support volunteers.

Finally, a statement of the specific ends underlying volunteer involvement can help to alleviate the apprehensions of paid staff that volunteers may intrude on their professional prerogatives or threaten their job security. Without a rationale for the program, employees are left to invent their own, and during a period of budgetary restraint and staff cutbacks, it should be little wonder that suspicions are easily aroused. Clarifying the goals for voluntary assistance can dampen such speculation and offer some security for employees, especially if they are included in planning for the volunteer program (see below).

Legislation, Organizational Policy, and Volunteers

In designing the volunteer effort, public managers need to examine the legislative environment. Statute law and/or policy governing an organization can inhibit or even prohibit volunteer involvement. The most noteworthy example is a federal regulation that proscribes national agencies from enlisting the services of volunteers, except in emergency situations affecting the safety of human life or the protection of property, unless a law has been passed specifically exempting the agency (Title 31, Section 1342 of the United States Code). Although Congress has overridden the provision in a number of instances—including the Small Business Act of 1953, the Volunteers in the Parks Act of 1969, and the Volunteers in the National Forests Act of 1972—it constitutes an obvious impediment to volunteerism in the public sector and a consolation to reluctant or antagonistic staff. President Reagan's Task Force on Private Sector Initiatives recommended lifting the prohibition, and a resolution to this effect was introduced in the U.S. House of Representatives in 1983, but the law remains intact (Manser, 1987, p. 847).

Similar restrictions on voluntary services can exist in state and local governments. For example, most larger American cities prohibit volunteer fire fighters, as do several smaller towns (McChesney, 1986, p. 69). Public managers interested in establishing a volunteer program in their agency must research pertinent legislation and, if necessary, work to overturn contrary statutes. In some instances, appropriate legislation may already be in place. Passed in 1977, the Virginia State Government Volunteers Act established a Division of Volunteerism to provide assistance to local and state agencies and encourages volunteer participation in government (Hatry, 1983, p. 48).

Organizational policies can exert nearly comparable effects on an ongoing volunteer program, either negatively or positively. On the one hand, Jim Utterback and Steven R. Heyman (1984, p. 232) found that the enactment of a policy requiring clinical staff at a community mental health center to devote 50 percent of their time to direct service disrupted "a thriving volunteer program." Cooperation between volunteers and clinicians gave way to competition for clients, with the result that approximately one-third of the volunteers reported feeling resented by staff. On the other hand, organizational policy can facilitate volunteer participation. In their landmark study *Social Workers and Volunteers,* Anthea Holme and Joan Maizels (1978, p. 69) discovered a much higher rate and intensity of volunteer involvement by probation officers than social workers in Great Britain. In trying to account for these differences, they judged "of considerable importance, undoubtedly, the influence of central policy in the probation service since 1965, which has actively encouraged the use of volunteers."

The predilections of employees need not be the sole factor in individual decisions to work with volunteers. Legislation and organizational policy can also act as a potent force to stimulate—or constrain—reliance on nonpaid personnel.

Top-Level Support for Volunteers

Assessing the legislative and policy environment of an agency for impediments to voluntary services is one thing; taking action to surmount them is quite another. Winning amendment or repeal of obstructive statutes, and developing and implementing new policies to foster volunteerism, require intervention from top agency leadership. No matter how fervently volunteer proponents and managers may press for these changes, organizational leaders are ultimately responsible for setting a policy, tone, and example to accomplish them. Without their complete support, a volunteer program is almost certain to founder (for example, Ellis, 1986; Valente, 1985; Farr, 1983; Scheier, 1981).

Open to top agency officials are a number of concrete measures to demonstrate commitment to the volunteer program. When they work with volunteers themselves, assist in publicity and recruitment for the program, include the director of volunteer services (or similarly titled individual) in staff meetings, attend recognition ceremonies, and incorporate skills in volunteer management into employee performance appraisals, they send an unmistakable message regarding the significance of volunteers to the agency. Again, these are decisions that top administrators, rather than the director of volunteer services, must take and implement.

Management involvement should begin at the earliest stages of program planning. Administration representatives are a reliable source of information on organizational policies and procedures. In addition, they can obligate agency personnel, such as clerical assistance, to the planning process; authorize release time for staff and urge them to participate; and ratify and expedite rules and procedures to facilitate volunteer participation, such as new record keeping and reporting systems. They can also ameliorate employees' anxiety and promote the innovations called for by a volunteer program: "There is no substitute for participation in task force [planning] meetings by a representative of the administration. Such participation provides support to those who are attempting to change established patterns of behavior. In fact, the presence of administration at all major meetings often allayed the underlying tensions that emerged when staff felt their authority was being challenged by the volunteers and the new volunteer program" (Silverman, Hepner, Ricci, and Wick, 1984, p. 28).

While support from the apex of an organization cannot alone guarantee the success of a volunteer undertaking, it is a highly desirable, if not necessary, condition for program well-being. High-level backing from the U.S. Small Business Administration, including the participation of the head of the agency, was pivotal to the founding and growth of the Service Corps of Retired Executives (Brudney, 1986); by no means is the SBA an isolated instance (for example, Wilson, 1976; Valente, 1985). Conversely, unless top officials are willing to pledge the authority and resources of an agency to a volunteer program, the project must be seriously reevaluated.

Staff Involvement in Planning the Volunteer Program

A precept in the field of organizational development is to include groups to be affected by a new policy or program in its design and implementation. Involvement adds to the knowledge base for crafting policy and builds a sense of ownership and commitment that can prove very beneficial in gaining acceptance for innovation. Because the incorporation of volunteers into an agency can impose changes widely perceived by employees as not only significant but also detrimental to the quality of work life, staff participation is especially important. The planning process should include the three principal actors in the volunteer effort: agency management, who as described above must be on board for the program to proceed; staff, or their bargaining agent, such as a public employee union; and volunteers themselves, or their delegates (Graff, 1984, p. 17). The sharing of needs, perspectives, and information that ensues can help to reconcile staff apprehensions and volunteer interests with the service demands and constraints facing a government agency.

Recognition of Staff Views. One major purpose served by involving employees is to address specifically and concretely possible misgivings regarding the introduction of volunteers. Volunteer administrators, and the pertinent literature as well, are sometimes guilty of portraying volunteer-staff relations as a struggle between generous citizens who "just want to help," and "selfish" staff, who seem to care only about their own situation (see Wilson, 1981; Scheier, 1977). The stereotypes are erroneous and detract from the central issues of volunteer services. Volunteers present an organization with a highly variable mix of talents, skills, energy, and work habits and attitudes: The major challenge of program design is to meld these diverse pieces into an organizational whole both satisfying to volunteers and productive for the agency.

Quite apart from any defensiveness about the organizational status quo, responsible government administrators have legitimate reasons to question the participation of volunteers. Public service professionals are genuinely concerned about possible declines in service quality, the protection of client confidentiality and other rights, the training and preparation of the newcomers to handle complex problems, and the potential for withdrawal of government funding. Understandably, the introduction of nonpaid personnel to handle similar or related work responsibilities is not always a comforting thought to government employees, who like other workers value job security. Even when they have received appropriate pledges that "volunteers supplement, not supplant, paid staff," this principle of volunteerism has not been honored universally (see Chapter Two).

At the same time, some staff may harbor less charitable presumptions about volunteers. They may regard as inappropriate the involvement of those without specialized training in service delivery, fear that volunteers will monitor their own job performance, belittle volunteer capabilities, and denigrate volunteer commitment and reliability. Until such beliefs are voiced and addressed, the prospects for acceptance of volunteers are dim.

No doubt, in the planning process, administration, staff, and volunteers will learn about the concerns and intentions of one another. In addition, to ensure that all parties may benefit from the accumulated knowledge in the field, agency officials should strongly consider the use of more formal means of instruction. Spokespersons from successful volunteer programs, as well as trainers, consultants, and other specialists in volunteer administration can ease the introduction of the new participants. Depending on the backgrounds of employees and the types of jobs to be assigned to volunteers, general orientation and/or specialized training sessions may need to be scheduled. The dissemination of pertinent literature is also of obvious value. Much of it is nontechnical and readily accessible to a fresh audience. (The quarterly journals *Voluntary Action Leadership* and the *Journal of Volunteer Administration* would be especially helpful.) Easily digested synopses of the literature (perhaps drafted through contractual arrangement) present another option.

The participation of government personnel, or their representatives, in planning the volunteer program offers an important forum to subject the "conventional wisdom" surrounding the approach to critical scrutiny. Volunteerism is rarely a topic in the formal education of public managers; very few have had the opportunity to accumulate background in this emerging area of study and practice (Young, 1987). Since staff members are expected to work in partnership with volunteers, they deserve an airing of their views and a realistic assessment of the task before them. Education and training are much more fruitful ways to deal with any misconceptions than is scorn or stereotype.

Taking Volunteers Seriously. If volunteers or volunteer delegates can be identified, they, too, should be included in the planning process. A primary goal is to create an organizational climate in which their input is welcomed and respected, and volunteers constitute a valued member of the work team, rather than a cumbersome obligation or decorative frill. A receptive organizational climate is essential to the health of a volunteer program (for example, Salmon, 1985; Brown, 1981; Ilsley and Niemi, 1981; Wilson, 1976). As with paid employees, organizational commitment increases when volunteers participate in decision making (Knoke, 1981). Participation is no less meaningful to many volunteers, to instill a sense of self-confidence and personal worth—attributes that enhance job satisfaction, self-confidence, and ultimately retention by the agency.

From the organizational perspective, involving volunteers in program planning and decision making is yet another way that top administrators can affirm their support for the program. It is also a highly practical means to assimilate into the agency the "volunteer intangible"—the special knowledge, insight, and caring that citizens can lend to government services (see Chapter Three). Additionally, the inclusion of staff and volunteers in planning helps to align expectations regarding the relative work responsibilities of each party. In sum, volunteer involvement provides the foundation for an organizational climate in which volunteers are accepted as partners in service delivery, and their contributions are recognized and appreciated.

Sharing the Workplace

Probably the largest stumbling block in designing the volunteer program is determining how work responsibilities should be allotted between paid staff and volunteers. What jobs are employees to perform, and what jobs volunteers? Overall policies, such as "volunteers do not do the work of paid staff," or "volunteers ought to support the work of employees," have their place as important statements of guiding philosophy that give reasonable assurances to staff members. On a practical level, however, general guidelines can become easily blurred (Graff, 1984, p. 17; Park, 1983, pp. 137–138).

While volunteers typically do not perform the work of paid staff, and most of the time act in supportive roles, job definitions are quite dynamic within an agency, and the status of a given position (paid/nonpaid) varies widely across agencies. As an organization grows and matures, jobs formerly held by volunteers can migrate to paid staff. It is easy to see, for example, that volunteers might initially handle clerical duties, but the need for these chores becomes so great and ongoing over time that an agency hires a secretary. The same trend applies to the provision of direct services. Historical analyses confirm that service professionals have gradually assumed tasks once performed on a volunteer basis (for example, Park, 1983; Ellis and Noyes, 1978; Schwartz, 1977; Becker, 1964). Change in job status can also occur in the opposite direction: Over a twenty-year period, SBA business development officers steadily relinquished the client counseling function to SCORE volunteers. (In 1987, the SBA ceased crediting business development staff for this activity.)

In a like manner, little commonality exists in the classification of positions across organizations. In one public library, cataloging acquisitions may be the province of paid employees, while in another, volunteers are responsible. Legal services may be donated in one agency, compensated monetarily in a second one. Some federal and state agencies have public personnel assisting owners of small businesses, while other institutions rely on experienced volunteers.

Without an intrinsic basis to designate a task as "volunteer" or "staff," the *process* by which work responsibilities are allocated assumes paramount importance. Actions taken by any one party are not likely to further the best interests of the volunteer program. Unilateral decisions by agency management regarding the scope of volunteer jobs can quicken resentment and resistance from paid staff that will plague the program from its inception. The well-intentioned aspirations of volunteers may intrude on functions judged crucial by employees. And staff may take too limited a view of the competence and potential of volunteers.

Discovering Common Interests. A more effective method to reach these determinations is to involve all three parties in decisions to add volunteer positions within an agency or to alter paid job descriptions (Graff, 1984, p. 18). When staff, volunteers, and administration participate jointly, employees should find that they have an unexpected ally in volunteers.

Staff members fear job "displacement"—that is, that public agencies may recruit volunteers to do the same work as employees, thus jeopardizing job security. The literature leaves no question, however, that volunteer scholars and managers endorse labor's stance that the substitution of nonpaid workers for paid is unethical. No evidence exists that volunteers feel any differently (see Chapter Two). Hence, if agency administration intend to use volunteers to reallocate funds away from designated positions, they can anticipate resistance not only from employees but also from volunteers. Should officials persist in this course despite opposition, the strategy will ultimately prove self-defeating, for it will severely damage the trust and collaboration fundamental to the success of a volunteer program.

More difficult to address, but probably more typical, is possible "replacement" of staff, a situation in which cutbacks in public funding render the loss of paid positions inevitable, and an agency seeks volunteers to compensate for the shortfall (Graff, 1984, p. 18). Chapter One showed that this scenario is an increasingly common one in the public sector and is responsible, at least in part, for the growth of volunteer services during the 1980s. Here, the ethical issues are less clear: As opposed to displacement, factors other than the incorporation of volunteers are the cause of the lost jobs, and volunteer involvement allows the agency to maintain a measure of service to deserving clients. Yet, because services continue to be provided at some level, replacement can temper protest from client groups, agency management, and the general public to restore funding.

Involving staff, volunteers, and management in program planning cannot avoid the pain of job loss, but it can help to assess the options open to an agency and to clarify the rationale for the introduction of volunteers. Top officials are ultimately responsible for mobilizing whatever resources are necessary to achieve organizational goals on behalf of clients: They should have every opportunity to elaborate the circumstances motivating the call for volunteers. If reductions in agency budget are the catalyst, they might also outline alternative responses to the problem, such as contracting with the private sector. In fact, a serious evaluation of the options can be a powerful incentive for employees to realize the merits of citizen volunteers and to accept them as partners in the delivery of public services (Brudney, 1989b).

Staff as well as volunteer delegates to the planning process deserve such explication. At the same time, they should exercise a critical review function over the rationale and design of the volunteer program. Again, staff should discover that they have more in common than in conflict with volunteers. Like employees, volunteers can be expected to resist plans that sacrifice jobs arbitrarily. Volunteers do not believe any more than do staff members that paid positions are expendable, nor are they indifferent to the prospect of displacing public personnel. On the contrary, the great bulk of volunteers who care enough to donate their time to an agency are troubled by the effects of cutbacks on client welfare. Yet, if cuts cannot be avoided, volunteers—and the agency—must make the best of a decline situation (Park, 1983, p. 136). Some volunteers will choose to contribute their time to direct service activities. But others will reject this mode of volunteering in favor of policy development and advocacy, with the goals of focusing public attention on the problem and reacquiring lost funding. Jane Mallory Park (1983, p. 136) is optimistic that "over the long haul, they will probably help create as many positions as have been lost."

The most enduring basis for cooperative relationships is for representatives of management, employees, and volunteers to work out in advance of program implementation explicit understandings regarding the rationale for the involvement of volunteers, the nature of the jobs they are to perform, and the boundaries of their work (Ellis, 1986; Graff, 1984; Brown, 1981; Wilson, 1976). Conditions of fiscal stringency reinforce the need for this procedure: Clear agreements are more pressing in times of austerity than in more flush periods, in order to alleviate the heightened tensions arising from sharing the workplace. One thing seems certain. If employees and volunteers are left to come to their own understandings in the absence of firm guidance from the agency, the results will rarely be satisfactory for either party, or for the organization as a whole.

Allocating Tasks.   The agreement should designate (or provide the foundation for distinguishing) the jobs assigned to volunteers and those held by paid staff. The respective tasks should be codified in formal job descriptions not only for paid but also nonpaid workers, with the stipulation that neither group will occupy the positions reserved for the other. Dividing the work to be done does not mean that all volunteer positions must be in supportive roles to employee endeavors (Ellis, 1986, p. 88). For example, in some Maryland counties, paid staff facilitate and support the activities of volunteers in delivering recreation services, rather than the reverse (Marando, 1986). Many organizations rely on donated labor for highly technical, professional tasks—such as accounting, economic development, and computer applications—not provided by employees and which they otherwise could not obtain. More important is that the delegation of tasks take into account the unique capabilities that staff and volunteers might bring toward meeting organizational needs and goals.

If the rationale for volunteer involvement is to add a new dimension to an agency—for instance, a pilot program, or more intensive contact with clients, or greater community support—the designation of tasks should not be so controversial. By design, the innovations lie beyond existing staff capacity; moreover, organizations have traditionally recognized the merits of volunteers for these purposes. Careful analysis of the new projects can identify the specific positions to be staffed by volunteers. Aside from a minimal number of liaison personnel, most employees might be affected little, if at all. Unless public agencies were to receive significantly increased funding, and leaders were convinced that it should be put toward these rather than competing ends, potential (paid) jobs are not sacrificed. Indeed, volunteer programs have often spawned new positions (for example, Wineburg and Wineburg, 1987; Marando, 1986; Hart, 1986; Scott and Sontheimer, 1985). Under these circumstances, staff opposition to the introduction of volunteers seems reflexive and unwarranted. Full explication of the program and its goals should help to ameliorate any problems.

If, instead, volunteers are sought as a means to adapt to reductions in budget or to ease the burden on a staff stretched thin by increasing client demands, sharing the workplace can be more trying. Here, volunteers are more fully integrated into the diverse operations of an agency, rather than assigned to distinct volunteer units relatively separate from employee domains. What is more, given the rationale for involving volunteers, the principal aim is to maintain or perhaps augment services by having the new personnel relieve staff of some duties. To allocate work responsibilities in this situation, Ellis (1986, pp. 89-90) recommends that an agency reassess the job descriptions of the entire staff. Prime candidates for delegation to volunteers are tasks with the following characteristics:

- Those performed periodically, such as once a week, rather than on a daily or inflexible basis
- Those that do not require the specialized training or expertise of paid personnel
- Those that might be done more effectively by someone with special training in that skill
- Those for which the position occupant feels uncomfortable or unprepared

The culmination of the task analysis should be a new set of job descriptions for employees and a second set for volunteers that are sensitive to prevailing organizational conditions. Staff "are primarily now assigned to the most important, daily functions," while volunteers "handle work that can be done on a once-a-week basis or that makes use of special talents for which the volunteers have been recruited" (Ellis, 1986, p. 90). The intent is to achieve the most effective deployment of both paid and nonpaid personnel. The cost is a reallocation of job responsibilities. As discussed above, joint consultation among top management, staff or their bargaining agent, and volunteers or their delegates in the planning process greatly enhances the prospect that appropriate changes can be identified, accepted, and implemented successfully.

Benefits to Staff from the Participation of Volunteers

Involving staff in the design of the volunteer program can help to ensure that their interests will be considered. But consideration alone cannot guarantee a positive motivation to work with volunteers. Employees may come to tolerate volunteers as a legitimate organizational response to adverse conditions, yet not accept them as able partners in the delivery of services. If volunteers remain in this state on the periphery of the organization rather than in its mainstream, some of their value will be dissipated. In contrast, to the degree that employees perceive immediate advantages from working with volunteers, they will be more likely to include them in important job activities. Agency leadership can advance this goal in two ways. First, they should make staff aware of the benefits of volunteers. Second, they should incorporate skills in volunteer management into the job description and performance apprais-al of employees expected to interact with these personnel.

Emphasizing the Positive. Too often, those responsi-ble for the volunteer program are inclined to "apologize" for this mode of services, as if it were an unfortunate accommo-dation to unpleasant realities. Involvement of volunteers by staff members should not be cast in this light as a favor to the program, or as a way of mollifying insistent leaders. The advantages of volunteers are usually presented at the agency level; for example, volunteers facilitate organizational effi-ciency and community relations. To individual employees, these goals may not be persuasive reasons for working with volunteers. A well-designed volunteer operation, however, also yields tangible benefits to paid personnel. And top agency officials and the director of volunteer services should not hes-itate to educate them.

The greatest immediate payoff of volunteers for em-ployees is the potential to make their jobs more satisfying and rewarding. The introduction of volunteers extends staff members a rare chance to delegate unwanted tasks that sap professional time, patience, and enthusiasm. Volunteers do many of the little things that should be done, but which the press of organization demands makes difficult or tedious for staff to accomplish. Volunteer jobs are not exclusively in sup-port roles. Careful job descriptions can net recruits with spe-cialized skills, training, and experience in areas in which staff members feel inadequate. As a result, employees gain access to needed expertise, which the organization could not ordi-narily afford, that can help them to perform better on the job. Conversely, the presence of volunteers frees staff to concentrate on duties for which their background and formal education particularly qualify them. These tasks are usually the ones that rank high in intrinsic challenge and stimulation for pub-lic personnel.

A second area in which volunteer participation carries immediate benefits for public administrators is professional development. In many cases, the presence of volunteers affords employees in nonmanagerial positions an unanticipated opportunity to exercise and develop skills in supervision for the first time. Continuing interaction with individual volunteers and volunteer groups and associations builds a solid foundation for dealing with community interests. Increasingly, government organizations are willing to support education in volunteer management for those willing to take on the responsibility. In short, working with volunteers opens a viable avenue for staff to accumulate desirable talents and to demonstrate the acquired competencies to superordinate officials.

Finally, in volunteers, staff will find individuals capable of shouldering not only the physical but also the mental strains of the workplace. Volunteers who work closely with employees share an interest in a given policy domain and understand its gains and setbacks, its aspirations and stumbling blocks. They are both a sounding board for staff ideas and frustrations and a novel source of insight and inspiration. Public administrators are charged with attending to the most complex and intransigent of societal problems, in an environment often suspicious of their activities and skeptical of government interventions. The empathy and emotional support offered by volunteers can be a helpful factor in combating "burnout" in a demanding profession. Of course, this relationship flows in both directions: By fully integrating citizens who wish to donate their time into public agencies, staff remove the crucial impediment to a gratifying volunteer experience.

Kathleen M. Brown (1981, p. 23) advises that if staff members do not seem to recognize the value of volunteers, directors of volunteer services need to remind them "of all the things that wouldn't get done and all the services the organization could no longer provide if volunteers weren't involved." They should point out as well the direct benefits employees can realize through incorporating volunteers: more rewarding positions, options for professional development, and support on the job. Staff are likely to find the latter set of reasons more compelling.

Closing the Loop: Rewarding Employees. Public administrators face a variety of demands that compete for their attention on the job. Devoting time and energy to establishing good working relations with volunteers may not rank high among them. Yet organization leaders possess powerful tools to alter the precedence assigned to this endeavor.

Officials can confirm for employees the importance of attending to volunteer management when they (1) write these skills into job descriptions as appropriate, and (2) follow through by evaluating personnel on this dimension. These acts elevate the status of volunteer management from a "desirable" quality (one that is therefore dispensable in the crush of contending priorities) to an essential talent. Moreover, they provide the incentive for employees to undergo training to acquire this expertise, an investment that government agencies will find it in their best interest to underwrite. If public officials are sincere about incorporating volunteers into the organization, they must not only make staff aware of the associated benefits but also credit them for the time and effort expended on this activity.

A failure to follow through on this commitment yields a predictable, if lamentable, outcome. Although the U.S. Forest Service asks all managers to develop volunteer resources, many have not done so. One Forest Service official explains that "most managers have seen neither reward nor recognition for developing good programs. As a result, managers who are hard pressed may opt for other ways to get the job done" (Greer, 1985, p. 2).

Job descriptions and performance appraisals are primary tools that management can apply to spur employee behavior consistent with the goals of the volunteer program. In addition, Scheier (1981) recommends other techniques to foster constructive alliances between volunteers and staff. Since teamwork is the objective, both members of the team ought to be recognized for outstanding joint performance in agency newsletters and publications, presentations to the public, and award ceremonies and banquets. Normally, these forums are oriented to agency volunteers, with scant attention paid to staff members who have collaborated so well with them. The employees merit organizational appreciation as well. Personnel files should include receipt not only of such honors but also letters of commendation from the director of volunteer services and individual volunteers and groups. As with other evidence of extra time and effort devoted to volunteers, these items, too, should be considered in the performance evaluation of employees who have earned them.

Summary and Implications

Productive working relationships between volunteers and staff do not emerge by accident. Instead, the tone and substance of volunteer involvement is set in the earliest stages of planning for the volunteer program. Organizational leaders have at their disposal a series of concrete procedures to deal with possible staff resistance and to facilitate introduction of volunteer personnel.

First, top officials need to make manifest the purposes underlying the volunteer program. Not only does clarity assist in alleviating staff apprehensions, but it also guides job descriptions for volunteers, standards for program evaluation, and recruitment of citizens. Second, officials should review the legislative and policy environment of the agency for obstacles to the implementation of volunteer services. Statutes must be amended as necessary, and new ones encouraging volunteer involvement deserve a hearing. Third, agency leaders should seek and support the participation of staff members or their representatives (public employee unions) and volunteers or their delegates in program planning and design. No better method exists to gain the input and earn the dedication of those on whom the success of the program ultimately rests. Fourth, joint involvement in the planning process is vital to work out the legitimate problems and concerns occasioned by sharing the workplace. In such sensitive deliberations, process is just as important as results: Affected parties should feel that they have been taken seriously, and that their views have been received and respected. Finally, agency leadership as well as administrators responsible for the volunteer program should seize every opportunity to communicate the advantages of volunteer involvement not only for the agency but also for individual staff members. To demonstrate the depth of their resolve, top officials should include in employee job descriptions skills in volunteer management as appropriate, and evaluate this dimension in the assessment of performance.

Most of the burden for the implementation and ultimate success of a volunteer program must fall on top organizational officials. To the degree that they are willing to commit the authority and resources of an agency to this undertaking, and they are sincere about integrating participants into program planning and design, public organizations and volunteers should benefit.

Government employees should benefit, too. Before they can do so, however, they must overcome antagonistic attitudes that have given rise to unflattering stereotypes and undermined volunteer programs. Learning must occur: Volunteers are not responsible for fiscal conditions that have precipitated cutbacks in funding and staff in the public sector. Volunteers are no more pleased by these developments than are public personnel or affected constituencies. Volunteers do not seek to take jobs away from, or displace, government employees. Even when the loss of regular positions cannot be avoided, many volunteers are reluctant to step into the breach, and do so only as a last resort to maintain some level of service to clients. Volunteers do not differ from staff in decrying the fiscal climate that has made such choices necessary. Undoubtedly, they would prefer simply to augment existing organizational capacity. In short, volunteers are not the "enemy."

These lessons are not the only ones for public administrators. Volunteers offer immediate advantages to staff members, in addition to those reaped by their organizations. Volunteers can make the time spent on the job more productive and gratifying, open doors for professional development, and provide empathy and emotional support. In an era in which initiatives to "privatize" government have captured the fancy and approbation of political leaders and the populace, public employees should realize the strong allies they have in volunteers.

7

Attracting and Retaining
Able Volunteers

*The volunteer spirit is still alive and well in
America.* President Ronald Reagan, 1982

*Even the most avid fan of statistics inevitably
collides with a number that seems totally
unbelievable. . . . [I]n 1985, 48 percent of
Americans over the age of 14 reported they did
volunteer work. That caused my calculator to self-
destruct. . . . [D]oes every other person do
volunteer work? It's not me and not (I think)
nearly half my friends. Are all the nonvolunteers
on the East Coast offset by the fact that everyone
in Illinois, Iowa, and Idaho volunteers?*
Robert J. Samuelson, 1987, p. 49

Any effort by government to reap the advantages of volunteer
involvement discussed throughout this text is critically dependent on the availability and willingness of citizens to donate
their time to public organizations. The views of Ronald Reagan and Robert J. Samuelson, a regular columnist for *Newsweek* magazine, reflect the extremes of opinion encountered
on this issue. To the president and many others who extol the
virtues of volunteering—but are not involved in managing
these programs—availability is not problematic. For them,

141

volunteering is a part of "the American personality," an activity longed for "out of the goodness of our hearts and a sense of community pride and neighborliness" (see Bendick and Levinson, 1984, pp. 455–462; Adams, 1987).

While that characterization may have some validity, Samuelson takes a much more skeptical view regarding the magnitude and eagerness of the volunteer population. He is joined by many, if not most, directors of volunteer programs, who find that recruitment is one of the most demanding aspects of the job. Jane Mallory Park (1983, pp. 138–139) refers to a "recruitment illusion," the presumed existence of a nearly boundless reservoir of volunteers that could compensate for gaps in organizational funding and staffing, were program officials just imaginative and enterprising enough to tap into it. Without discouraging public administrators from adopting innovative approaches and an optimistic outlook essential to successful recruiting, the reality is that the volunteer pool is limited, and competition among agencies for its services is keen. Few of even the most assiduous organizations can boast of a waiting list of volunteers.

This chapter elaborates strategies to assist public agencies in recruiting and retaining able volunteers. Using data collected in national surveys, the chapter first provides reliable estimates of the number of volunteers potentially available to government organizations. It then assesses trends that will likely affect the size of this population and the ability of governments to attract citizens from it. The final sections of the chapter are devoted to recruitment and retention of high-quality volunteers.

The Availability of Volunteers to Public Agencies

Attempts to measure the dimensions of volunteer activity upon which government organizations might draw must rest fundamentally on the definition of the key term. Unfortunately, little consensus exists on its parameters. According to the Gallup Organization (1981, p. ii), responsible for a series of national surveys on volunteerism, "not only can researchers

in the area not agree upon a clear definition of what constitutes volunteer activity, but it is likely that the public has
varying perceptions as well." Within public administration
and political science, volunteering has been variously understood as involvement in community and neighborhood associations, participation on citizen panels or review boards,
membership in civic groups or clubs, advocacy on social
issues, campaign work for political candidates, as well as
donations of time to public agencies to aid in the delivery of
services. Each of these definitions might produce a different
estimate of the size of the volunteer population. Here the
emphasis is on direct service volunteers to offices of government (see Chapter One).

Defining Government Volunteers. This book focuses
on volunteer programs operating within public agencies
or departments. The volunteer activity must be accepted,
requested, sponsored, or directed by a governmental institution. Partnership agreements, in which publicly financed services are provided through nonprofit organizations or in
cooperation with them, do not constitute government volunteer programs (unless, of course, the public agencies involved
employ volunteers). As will be seen below, the growth of the
nonprofit sector, which relies heavily on volunteer labor,
may render availability increasingly problematic for other
organizations.

Volunteers do not receive direct monetary compensation
for their donations of time and energy. Nevertheless, agencies
may choose to reimburse them for the out-of-pocket costs
incurred and, less frequently, to provide a modest stipend well
below prevailing wage rates, a convention sanctioned by the
Peace Corps and some fire departments and state parks (for
example, Marando, 1986; Farr, 1983; Pattakos, 1982; Smith,
1972). While volunteering should not be confused with self-
sacrifice (benefits include sociability, career exploration and
development, and various forms of personal enhancement),
this activity is oriented toward helping others. Just as volunteering is not aimed at material gain, it cannot be mandated

or coerced; compulsion significantly alters the character of the endeavor (Van Til, 1988, pp. 5–9). Thus, defendants in court-ordered restitution programs that mandate community service are not considered "volunteers" in the present inquiry.

As opposed to "informal" volunteering, which is practiced alone by individuals outside of an organizational context, agencies require a regular commitment of time from volunteers. While virtually any donation of labor may seem welcome, particularly in a period of fiscal stringency, sporadic or one-time-only instances of volunteering are difficult to integrate into established organizational work routines and may even prove counterproductive when the costs of recruitment, training, and supervision are taken into account. For this reason, a growing number of organizations ask interested citizens to dedicate a set amount of hours on a weekly or monthly basis to volunteering, a procedure recommended by Paul J. Ilsley and John A. Niemi (1981, p. 64) as part of a volunteer work agreement with the agency.

The use of work agreements highlights the fact that the positions staffed by volunteers help governments to meet extant needs and fill pressing gaps in services and programs (Farr, 1983, p. 8). Volunteer activities do not comprise "make-work" tasks but, instead, have a market counterpart (Wolozin, 1975, p. 23). Thus, with the exception of natural emergencies or disasters—which call for a sporadic, yet intense response— just as for paid employees, a regular investment of time by volunteers is necessary for effective job performance.

In sum, volunteers to government contribute time in an organizational setting, in programs sponsored by public agencies. Although they are not compensated monetarily, the tasks they carry out have a market value and can be "very valuable services" to the organization and its clients (Smith, 1981, p. 23). Volunteers surely derive psychic, social, and other rewards, but the primary beneficiaries are those assisted through their activities. A minimum level time commitment from volunteers is essential to the functioning of the organization and the production of public goods and services. Based on this definition, the following section assesses the magnitude of the volunteer population potentially accessible to governmental institutions.

Estimating the Size of the Volunteer Pool. Because no comprehensive study has been undertaken of citizens willing to donate time to government agencies, estimates of availability must remain tentative. Nevertheless, survey research on the volunteer behavior of Americans yields insight into the size of this pool.

The Gallup Organization has conducted three major surveys probing citizen volunteerism, the first for 1981 (Gallup Organization, 1981), the second for 1985 (Gallup Organization, 1986), and the most recent for 1987 (Hodgkinson and Weitzman, 1988b); future plans call for biennial replication of the survey. The Independent Sector, a nonprofit coalition of corporate, foundation, and voluntary organizations that commissioned the surveys, chose to define volunteering very broadly as "working in some way to help others for no monetary pay." While this definition encompassed traditional forms of volunteering—such as donating time to a hospital, school, or civic organization—it also produced responses that Gallup (1981, p. iii) acknowledged "might normally not have been classified as volunteer activity." Examples include singing in a church choir, taking care of a neighbor's pet, and helping a friend move.

Even with such an expansive definition, the rate of volunteering has declined over the period encompassed by the surveys, from 52 percent of the American public in 1981, to 48 percent in 1985, to 45 percent in 1987. Other studies corroborate a decline. Using a virtually identical definition of volunteering ("helping others in some way for no monetary payment"), a second national survey conducted in 1985 estimated that 47 percent of Americans had volunteered during that year (Hodgkinson and Weitzman, 1986).

These data suggest that while the incidence of volunteering has fallen, the absolute level remains quite high, at least as delineated by the Independent Sector. For purposes of government agencies that wish to enlist volunteers, however, the percentages are inflated: They encompass any act of volunteering over a twelve-month period, whether one-time-only or ongoing, alone or in an organizational setting. The Gallup surveys ascertained further information that can be used to refine the estimates in accordance with the definition of government volunteers elaborated above.

To begin, citizens who report volunteering over shorter time intervals than one year—for example, in the past month or week—are more likely to be regularly involved in volunteer work than are those who participated no more frequently than per annum. In the 1985 survey, 36 percent said that they had volunteered in the past month (compared to 35 percent in 1987), and one-quarter (24 percent) had been active in the past week (Hodgkinson and Weitzman, 1988b, p. 9; Gallup Organization, 1986, pp. 2–4).

Data on the number of hours donated by volunteers allow further refinement. The Independent Sector advises that "if an individual has done no volunteer work or has spent less than one hour per week on volunteer work during the last week we may speculate that the individual is in volunteer work on a sporadic basis or for a one-time cause" (Gallup Organization, 1986, p. 3). In 1985, while most of those volunteering in the past week had contributed a minimum of two hours, application of this criterion reduces the quantity of "regular volunteers" to 20 percent of the population (Gallup Organization, 1986, pp. 3–4). As intimated by the decrease in the annual rates of volunteer activity examined above, the size of this group also appears to have declined since 1981, when the initial Gallup survey found that 31 percent of Americans had donated two or more hours per week (Gallup Organization, 1981, pp. iv–v).

These figures provide a more accurate reading of the pool of volunteers prized by government (and other) agencies, but they continue to overstate their availability in two ways. First, many volunteers prefer to donate their time informally, outside of the auspices of an organization. For example, while Gallup estimated that just over half the population had volunteered in some manner in 1981, the results of a second

Gallup (1982, p. 176) survey undertaken less than a year later revealed that significantly fewer people were formally involved in charity or social service activities (32 percent), or were members of voluntary organizations (34 percent).

Based on such comparisons, Murray S. Weitzman (1983, p. 271) concludes that "it is apparent that volunteer work performed in informal settings is substantial," perhaps as great in the aggregate as that contributed to organizations. In 1985, informal volunteers may have comprised as many as one-third of the citizens donating time on a weekly or monthly basis. (Because multiple responses were permitted to determine the types of activities engaged in by volunteers, precise estimates of the percent involved solely in informal work are not feasible; see Gallup Organization, 1986, pp. 28–31.) If this correction were applied to the 20 percent of Americans identified as regular volunteers in the analysis above, it would attenuate the group to between 13 and 14 percent of the population. Figure 7.1 briefly reviews the process for arriving at the final estimate. Weitzman (1983, p. 271) concurs that probably less than 15 percent of the population accounts for some 80 percent of the time that is contributed to recipient organizations.

A second element affecting the availability of this group to government is the predominance of religious organizations in securing the participation of volunteers, in some surveys

Figure 7.1 Estimation Process for the Number of Volunteers Potentially Available to Government Agencies

48 percent—> of the American public volunteered during 1985, on a regular or sporadic basis, formally or informally	36 percent—> volunteered in the past month	24 percent—> volunteered in the past week	20 percent—> volunteered in the past week and contributed at least two hours ("regular volunteers")	13 to 14 percent of these, at a minimum, volunteered in a "formal" or organizational setting

Source: Based on data from Gallup Organization (1986, pp. 2-4, 28-31).

as much as 50 percent of all voluntary activity (for example, Hodgkinson and Weitzman, 1988b; Gallup Organization, 1981; ACTION, 1974; U.S. Department of Labor, 1969). The 1985 Gallup survey confirms this finding. More than 40 percent of those who had volunteered in the past week or in the past month donated time to religious institutions (Gallup Organization, 1986, pp. 28-31). The percentage involved in religious work exclusively cannot be determined (again due to a multiple response format), but religious organizations attracted at least twice the number of volunteers as did any other endeavor. Whether many of these volunteers should be considered accessible to government is questionable.

According to its broad definition of the term, Independent Sector (1986, p. 4) is correct that "volunteer activity remains a pervasive activity for nearly half of the American population." Should public administrators base their recruitment efforts on that expectation, however, they will be in for major disappointment. Volunteering to an agency, governmental or otherwise, is very different than volunteering spontaneously and informally. Survey research does not allow precise estimates of the number of citizens who donate their time on a regular basis, in an organizational setting, to nonreligious institutions, but the percentage is a fraction of the entire volunteer pool. While this group may yet seem large, governments are not the only—or even the most desirable—employers of volunteers. Moreover, other factors point to a continuing diminution in supply.

Trends Affecting the Availability of Volunteers

The Availability Problem.   As the analysis above would suggest, finding sufficient volunteers has become a primary concern to managers of government volunteer programs. In the mid-1980s, Sydney Duncombe (1985, 1986) surveyed local officials in a 20 percent sample of cities with a population of at least 4,500 regarding the participation of service volunteers. By a margin of nearly 20 percent, the problem cited most frequently in cities that had volunteer programs was "getting enough people to volunteer," identified by more than half the officials (56.2 percent). By contrast, the more prosaic obstacles to successful programs, such as volunteer supervision (37.8 percent), liability coverage (21.3 percent), support from managers (16.3 percent), and absenteeism (16.3 percent), lagged far behind (Duncombe, 1985, p. 362).

In a follow-up to the 1985 survey, Duncombe examined volunteer programs in forty cities in five western states that apply this service option extensively (California, Idaho, Nevada, Oregon, and Washington). Again, the most serious difficulty reported was, "I do not have enough volunteers." More than 40 percent of the sample of volunteer supervisors considered this factor "a disadvantage" (31 percent) or "a major disadvantage" (10 percent)—far more than rated any of seven other putative liabilities of the approach this consequential (Duncombe, 1986, p. 298).

A study of emergency medical squads in New Jersey, a state in which 92 percent of these units are staffed by volunteers, offers an illustration (Gora and Nemerowicz, 1985, pp. 65–67). One-third of the twenty-one squads examined had experienced no problems in recruitment. At the other extreme, one-third had suffered severe recruitment problems, with the result that squad size had fallen to 63 percent or less than the level judged optimal by the squad leader. In four units, lack of volunteers affected the ability to provide 24-hour emergency coverage; one of the squads could not cover the day shift, and a second had to pay paramedics during the day. A *New York Times* article chronicled the search for "Vanishing Volunteers" in one New Jersey town (Hanley, 1988, p. B-1): "Volunteerism today, such as it is, is represented by a trickle of new residents willing to join town boards. In 1987, 13 people offered to serve out of about 15,000 residents. . . . No newcomers, though, are joining the fire department . . . or the rescue squad. Volunteers are their lifeblood, but as in suburbs everywhere, their membership is stagnant. Demands for their services mount steadily as population grows, but the new residents who rely on them for health and safety do not appear to have the time or enthusiasm to help."

Similarly, Kettering, an Ohio city of 62,000, once boasted a waiting list of volunteers to its fire department. In 1986, however, the city hired a manager of volunteer services to "go to the people, because the people are no longer coming to it" (Rastikis, 1986, p. 27). Although projecting to the future is inherently risky, indications are that the recruitment pinch will intensify over the next decade.

Competition for Volunteers. Several developments exacerbate the availability of volunteers to the public sector. First, as a result of cutbacks in government support to nonprofit organizations amounting to 20 percent since 1980, and a decline in direct federal spending for human services estimated at more than $113 billion over this period, the demand for volunteers is rising (see Allen, 1987, pp. 257–258; Agranoff and Pattakos, 1984, pp. 79–81; Valente and Manchester, 1984, p. 71; Watts and Edwards, 1983, pp. 9–10). For example, the Minnesota Office of Volunteer Services (1987, p. vi) has established a goal to expand the number of volunteers in the state by 25 percent and the average number of hours they donate by the same percentage by 1990. In response to an aggregate decrease in funding of 17 percent between 1980 and 1985, U.S. state parks have sought more volunteers. In a survey of all state park directors conducted in May, 1985, thirty of the fifty (60 percent) reported that they were making significantly more use of nonprofit groups and volunteers to provide visitor services. Many park systems experienced difficulties in attracting volunteers (Myers and Reid, 1986, pp. 51, 81).

Nonprofit agencies have also stepped up their efforts to recruit volunteers. A 1982 survey disclosed that the strategy adopted most frequently by nonprofit organizations to cope with the cutbacks in federal support was to place greater reliance on volunteers. Nearly one-third of the nonprofit agencies surveyed indicated they had increased their use of volunteers over the preceding year (Weisbrod, 1988, p. 130). Acknowledging that the objectives will not be easy to attain, a task force constituted by Independent Sector (1987, p. 21) has resolved to boost volunteering by 50 percent and double charitable giving by 1992.

As fiscal stringency has threatened the capacity of national, state, and local governments, as well as the non-profit sector, to maintain service levels, volunteers—especially those prepared to make an ongoing contribution to an organization—have become an increasingly valuable resource. The director of a school library volunteer program assures her peers that volunteers are "everywhere!" (Farynowski, 1987, p. 11), but so too are the agencies that seek their help. Nearly two decades ago, Harriet S. Naylor (1973, p. 19) foresaw that the growth of government-based volunteer programs for economic and social purposes could lead to competition for volunteers. Ivan H. Scheier concurs that the number of organizations competing for the services of volunteers has outpaced the supply. He cautions that "organizations which want to keep their volunteers will have to work harder to make the volunteer experience personally more empowering and visibly impactful on problems" (in Rydberg and Peterson, 1980, p. 14).

This domain may not favor the public sector. On the contrary, nonprofit agencies often possess attributes salient to volunteers that yield an advantage over governments in recruitment and retention. These characteristics include a tradition of working with volunteers; increased flexibility and less fragmentation in approach; closeness to the field and smaller scale of operations; greater capacity to focus on the full range of client needs and tailor services to them, rather than concentrate on isolated problems; and significant diversity in both the content of services and in the institutional framework within which they are provided (Salamon, 1987; Salamon, Musselwhite, and Abramson, 1984). Given this listing, without partnership agreements with nonprofit organizations, governments may well encounter stiff competition for desirable volunteers (see below).

Despite these manifest advantages, evidence suggests that the nonprofit sector has not been immune to problems of volunteer availability. Less than one-quarter of a sample of administrators of Virginia human service agencies polled in 1980 believed that recruiting volunteers was as easy then as it had been five years before (Watts and Edwards, 1983, p. 20).

The League of Women Voters experienced a decrease in membership of about 8 percent between 1978 and 1980, and between 1969 and 1979, the American Red Cross reportedly suffered a loss of one-third of its more than two million volunteers (Clotfelter, 1985, p. 143). Attenuation in the rate of volunteering among key demographic groups is at least partially responsible. According to the Gallup surveys discussed above, between 1981 and 1985 the rate of volunteering (broadly defined) fell by 19 percent among single people, 11 percent among people aged 18 to 24, and 5 percent among women. Citing a need to arrest these declines, Independent Sector has announced a major program to increase the knowledge and practice of volunteerism in nonprofit and government agencies (O'Connell, 1987, p. 104). Similarly, Vernon M. Goetcheus (1984, p. 44) has urged public and other organizations "to find new ways to help the growing numbers of women in the work force plan to continue to be volunteers."

A pair of important stipulations enacted by the Tax Reform Act of 1986 may further diminish the supply of volunteers: the reduction in personal income tax rates and the more restrictive treatment of the deductibility of charitable contributions. Since a drop in tax rates makes paid work more valuable to individuals, and thus increases their "cost" of volunteering, economists Jerald A. Schiff and Burton A. Weisbrod anticipate that the amount of donated labor should fall. They estimate that "a one dollar increase in the after-tax wage, for the typical individual, will reduce annual volunteering by 4.8 hours, or approximately 20 percent of mean hours volunteered" (Schiff and Weisbrod, 1986, p. 627). As leaders of nonprofit organizations fear, the reduction in the tax deductibility of charitable contributions will lessen monetary gifts. Receiving less attention, however, is the fact that because giving money is related to donating time (for example, Hodgkinson and Weitzman, 1986; Clotfelter, 1985; Gallup Organization, 1986, 1981), this change can be expected to indirectly decrease the amount of time volunteered—and the impact could be much greater than the tax-rate effect (Schiff and Weisbrod, 1986, p. 628). With respect to volunteerism, perhaps the only potentially positive influence of the 1986 tax-code changes would be to augment income. If tax reform does so, it may increase hours volunteered, for higher-income people can be expected to volunteer more; but this effect is unlikely to offset the negative incentives of the cut in tax rates (Weisbrod, 1988, p. 139; Schiff and Weisbrod, 1986, p. 628).

Recruiting High-Quality Volunteers

This chapter has shown that from the standpoint of organizations that regularly depend on volunteers for service production, the size of the available pool is much more modest than conventional estimates might intimate, and that trends, although speculative, portend further reductions in supply. Agencies have already begun to feel these effects. At least three articles published during the 1980s question by their titles whether volunteers have become an "endangered species" (Parker, 1988; Ellis, 1985a; Rehm, 1980). Like those discussions, the purpose of the present inquiry is not to bemoan the decline in numbers but to alert government, as well as nonprofit, organizations and administrators that "they must sell their programs to volunteers" (Rehm, 1980, p. 24). This section elaborates strategies for attracting capable volunteers; the following section turns to retention of volunteers.

Organizational Culture. Fortunately, not all government volunteer programs should encounter serious problems in recruitment and retention. T. Zane Reeves's (1988, pp. 3-7) study of the Peace Corps and VISTA shows that the fostering of a "commitment culture" within public organizations—a shared set of simply stated values, a clear sense of agency mission, an action orientation, and frequent interaction with clients—can prove a great boon in attracting and keeping volunteers. Throughout six presidential administrations, the success of the Peace Corps and VISTA in this domain has been directly related to the vitality of their organizational cultures. For example, Reeves (1988, p. 110) found that in the late 1970s, the Peace Corps "had reached a new low in both management and morale. Indeed, it no longer had a coherent organizational culture." Correspondingly, the U.S. General Accounting Office (1979, pp. 26-39) issued a report in 1979 that chastised the Peace Corps and ACTION for severe lapses in the volunteer programs. Otherwise known for their special appeal to volunteers, these agencies had witnessed a costly, threefold escalation in the rate of early termination by recruits, from 11 percent in 1961 to 38 percent in 1975.

The significance of organizational culture for volunteer programs is not limited to the Peace Corps and ACTION but applies more generally. Ilsley and Niemi (1981, pp. 11-15) stress that clear and succinct articulation of an organizational mission, incorporating explicit recognition of the importance of both volunteers and paid staff toward its attainment, is fundamental to program effectiveness. Naylor (1973, p. 22) adds that organizations must forward ideals dedicated to service to others. Staff and volunteer leadership must strive to find ways to translate these ideals into meaningful action. Agency objectives and goals must be clearly expressed for people who care, so they can see the organization as a place to make an important contribution to society through volunteering.

Since smaller size may promote a more easily identifiable sense of purpose, city and county governments may have an advantage in building and sustaining a commitment culture. Although no precise comparative statistics exist, volunteer programs in the public sector do appear to be most common at the local level (see Chapter One). Nevertheless, Reeves's (1988) analysis demonstrates that a culture with strong allure to volunteers is attainable in larger bureaucracies as well. Certainly, where established, a commitment culture is an asset to volunteer programs and to the overall goals of an agency. But for agencies lacking this attribute, changing organizational culture is both a slow and unpredictable process. Should time frame, attitudes, or other characteristics prevent such change, potent options remain open to bolster volunteer recruitment.

Job Design for Volunteer Positions. Chief among them is the careful design of nonpaid positions to appeal to the needs and aspirations of potential volunteers. As Jon Van Til (1988) argues, the fact that volunteering benefits others does not preclude participants from selecting work that also satisfies more personal objectives. Benjamin Gidron (1980, p. 361) agrees that "volunteer workers are not totally altruistic; they want to do a worthwhile, rewarding job and they will try to make sure that the job they have chosen fulfills some of their needs." Martha A. Shulman (1982, p. 6) concludes, "in general, volunteers are likely to participate in activities they enjoy and those that give them a feeling of accomplishment and personal growth." Yet another authority states: "Job satisfaction is 'pay' for volunteers. Instead of salary administration, we must touch the interests and objectives of each worker, each in appropriate ways" (Naylor, 1985, p. 27). According to this scholarship, the most effective volunteer recruitment strategy for government (and other) organizations is the creation of jobs that offer opportunities for enjoyment or challenge, interesting or meaningful work, personal growth, and/or social interaction.

In general, social service organizations find that volunteers are able to meet these needs especially well in jobs that entail direct contact with clients. Indeed, the popular conception of volunteering embraces the notion of direct service (see Chapter One). The immediate sense of feedback, vitality, and usefulness attainable in such positions can offer meaning and motivation to the volunteer. The cover story of the July 10, 1989, issue of *Newsweek* magazine, entitled "The New Volunteers: America's Unsung Heroes," provides an illustration. Many of the volunteers featured in the issue attributed their involvement to the satisfactions gained from seeing firsthand the results of their helping behavior for other people. Similarly, an empirical study of service volunteers in Israel concluded that job satisfaction rests on the assignment to tasks that allow volunteers opportunity for self-expression and the chance to see their achievements (Gidron, 1983, p. 32).

In some government agencies, volunteers' preferences to be close to clients or the "action" can lead to a strong complementarity of interests between them and paid staff. Among business development officers at the U.S. Small Business Administration, for instance, staffing the "help desk," at which they respond to client walk-in and telephone requests for assistance with managerial problems, is a task acceded to only as a last resort. In unguarded moments, some employees will even allow that a stint on the help desk "interferes" with their normal job duties. In contrast, most SCORE volunteers enjoy this assignment and are able to assist the business development staff (and SBA clients) at the same time.

Recruiters for government volunteer programs should not assume that direct service positions are the only ones that might attract citizens. Based on a review of research on the motivations of volunteers, Van Til (1988, pp. 24–32) concludes that people have multiple reasons for volunteering, both other- and self-oriented, and that "different organizational tasks appeal to different motivational forces." Even repetitive tasks usually regarded as menial (the traditional chore of stuffing envelopes, for example) might prove suitable to individuals who would like to help out, but want no more from volunteering than relief from the pressures of paid employment.

By no means, however, should such chores be the only ones reserved for volunteers, or a prerequisite for more ambitious assignments. Administrative positions and those supporting the work of paid staff can also lure volunteers. According to the 1988 Gallup survey on volunteering (Hodgkinson and Weitzman, 1988b, p. 8), the second largest group of respondents who had done volunteer work in the past month described their job as an aide/assistant to a paid employee (assisting the elderly or handicapped formed the largest category). To still other people, volunteer opportunities that encompass wide latitude for leadership, management, and creativity are highly desirable.

In sum, the key to recruitment of volunteers in the public sector is not the design of positions that are singularly demanding, but a choice of jobs to appeal to a range of aspirations. As Chapter Six explains, the most constructive method to achieve this objective is to involve employees, management, and citizens in assessing organizational needs for volunteers and developing appropriate job descriptions for nonpaid staff.

Adapting Public Organizations to Volunteers. Beyond job design, government agencies can take very practical steps to facilitate and accommodate volunteer participation. To remedy shortfalls in recruitment, organizations should consider flexible schedules for volunteering outside of the traditional work week. Evening and weekend hours can open this activity to new audiences (Langton, 1988a; Borkman, 1986) and benefit clients as well. Susan J. Ellis (1985a) maintains that volunteer organizations have not begun to tap the large numbers of potential members who do not work "normal" hours. These include occupants of jobs that require shift work, evening hours, weekend days, and variable schedules.

Volunteer jobs that can be performed outside the agency, for example, in the home or at the place of paid employment, can gain citizens who want to make a contribution but need or prefer to work off-site. Another condition that may be particularly salient to this group are positions stipulated for a fixed term, preferably in a contract (Dorwaldt, Solomon, and Worden, 1988). In a national survey, eight out of ten nonvolunteers (79 percent) said that a short-term assignment would be an important incentive in getting them to volunteer (VOLUNTEER-The National Center, 1988).

Public organizations can also attract more volunteers by bringing involvement within the means of all income groups. While volunteers expect to give their time for free, they do not anticipate having to "pay" for the privilege. Agency policies that provide for reimbursement for expenses incurred—for instance, for transportation, parking, meals, and uniforms—would lessen the cost of volunteering. According to survey research, organizational assistance in supplying or locating affordable child care would be especially welcome

(VOLUNTEER-The National Center, 1988). The New York State Senate has considered legislation in this area to help persuade volunteers (Agranoff and Pattakos, 1984, p. 81).

Similarly, while volunteers are not compensated monetarily for their labor, government agencies can tender other inducements that augment the value to individuals of donating time. Most public organizations have at their disposal an assortment of low-cost incentives that can stimulate volunteerism. Many participants, for example, appreciate the self-development aspects of volunteering. Public agencies should give orientation and training to nonpaid workers and seek cooperative agreements with educational institutions to grant academic credit for volunteer activities. Organizations can encourage career exploration by offering citizens opportunities for advancement, promotion, and supervision in volunteer positions. Placement functions can be equally alluring: Agencies should document the work experience of volunteers, provide them with job and academic references, and assist them in securing paid positions if sought, either internally or with other employers. Governments can also spur volunteerism by soliciting on employment application forms a listing and description of nonpaid work experience and considering this background in assessing candidates for job openings. In 1988, the U.S. Congress passed a concurrent resolution encouraging both public and private organizations to do so (see Chapter Eight).

Every Volunteer a Potential Recruiter. The national Gallup surveys (Hodgkinson and Weitzman, 1988b, pp. 27-28; Gallup Organization, 1986, pp. 35-36) underscore the significance of such measures for volunteer recruitment. Advertisements for volunteers, whether appearing on television, radio, or in print, seem largely ineffectual as recruitment devices. Just 5.3 percent of the volunteers in the most recent survey (1987) learned about the activities to which they donate time through the media. Yet, because the surveys include among the "volunteer" group those engaged in informal activities, such as helping friends and neighbors, they underestimate the effectiveness of the media in attracting volunteers to organizations (Watts and Edwards, 1983, p. 19). Media advertisements crafted to meet specific agency needs and carefully marketed to the correct audiences certainly merit the attention of government recruiters; quite often, public service announcements are a viable option. Newspaper and magazine coverage can also prove helpful. The SCORE Association, for example, credits a *Reader's Digest* article published early in its history with a significant jump in membership.

Nevertheless, the best sources for recruitment are volunteers who share positive experiences with others. Based on the Gallup surveys (Hodgkinson and Weitzman, 1988b, pp. 27-28; Gallup Organization, 1986, pp. 35-36), most individuals learn about opportunities for volunteering through personal contacts with participants—for example, from someone who asks them to serve (40.4 percent) or from a family member or friend involved in the activity (27.6 percent). Fewer than one in five (19.2 percent) seek out the activity on their own. (These data are from the 1987 survey. Because of multiple responses, the percentages do not sum to 100 percent). If each volunteer can, thus, be conceived as a potential recruiter, the message seems manifest: Organizations will succeed in attracting and retaining new members to the degree that government volunteer service gives participants a sense of meaning or fulfillment that they wish to relate to other people.

The SCORE Association has used the personal touch in recruiting to great advantage. In a survey administered to chairpersons of the SCORE chapters by the author, nearly 70 percent agreed (52.6 percent) or agreed strongly (16.5 percent) that "members often bring in their friends to the chapter to join SCORE." According to one chairperson: "Recruitment isn't a problem for us. People want to belong to the chapter. We place ads in the yellow pages or on a billboard or two if we can get them for free. But those are really to attract clients, not to get members. Members bring in members; it's that simple."

Recruiting at the Workplace. Personal contact is not the sole technique for recruitment for SCORE or other government-based volunteer programs. In the 1987 Gallup survey, 39.3 percent of the volunteers learned about their chosen activity as a result of participation in an organization (Hodgkinson and Weitzman, 1988b, pp. 27–28). Very frequently, this discovery occurs at the workplace: In a national survey, one out of five employed respondents (21 percent) said that their employers had urged them to become involved in volunteer activities. Of this group, 60 percent actually did become involved, compared to just 39 percent of the employed respondents who had received no prompting from their employer (VOLUNTEER–The National Center, 1988).

Public agencies should forge closer ties to private organizations that promote and/or sponsor employee volunteerism, and they should encourage firms without such programs to reevaluate their community service policies. In addition, officials might undertake outreach to meet job holders at the workplace, demonstrate the importance of volunteerism, and apprise them of relevant nonpaid openings. This avenue may net the further advantage of yielding volunteers who can assist governments in areas requiring high levels of technical expertise. Since those who hold paid employment are more likely to volunteer than those who do not, "organizations and agencies . . . must look to the workplace as the most natural and potentially most successful way to reach and recruit those people into active service" (Vizza, Allen, and Keller, 1986, p. 20).

Also not to be overlooked for recruitment (and other) purposes are partnership agreements with voluntary action centers and voluntary and nonprofit organizations, which can apprise members, clients, and citizens of the range of volunteer opportunities afforded by the community. Pooled or cooperative arrangements for recruitment among public and nonprofit agencies would limit the competition for high-quality volunteers that might otherwise disadvantage government bureaucracies. In 1988, the SCORE Association concluded an agreement with the American Association of Retired Persons that allows chapters to draw on the huge AARP talent bank for volunteer counselors and clerical assistants. In addition, some SCORE chapters obtain volunteer clerical help through private, nonprofit, and public organizations.

Nontraditional Volunteers.   Other tactics to invigorate recruitment include greater attention to nontraditional sources of volunteers. Although women continue to participate at a higher rate than men, and most participants are white and married, the conventional image of the volunteer cannot be sustained empirically. In 1987, the rate of volunteering by males (43.8 percent) lagged only slightly behind the rate for females (46.7 percent); 39.7 percent of single people and over one-quarter of blacks (27.7 percent) and Hispanics (26.8 percent) engaged in volunteer activity (Hodgkinson and Weitzman, 1988b, pp. 13–20).

As the profile of the "typical" volunteer fades, recruitment opportunities open to public organizations. For example, the fastest growing segment of the U.S. population is the group over sixty-five years of age, and retirement often introduces lifestyle changes conducive to volunteering. An equally promising source of volunteers that has only begun to be tapped consists of students at the college or even the high school level. About 25 percent of American colleges and dozens of high schools have recently instituted volunteer work in the curriculum. Since 1987, the California State University system has encouraged (but not required) students to perform thirty hours of community service annually. School officials state that about a quarter of the system's 400,000 students participate in the program (Kantrowitz, 1989, p. 37). In 1989, the Illinois state legislature passed similar legislation to create a volunteer program on each state college and university campus. Not only would the nontraditional sources augment the supply of volunteers, but also they would bring a diversity of useful perspectives and insights to government agencies.

Retaining Volunteers

As vital a function as recruitment may be, it is not the endpoint of working with volunteers; it is the beginning. Public administrators must be just as committed to nurturing and retaining volunteers as productive members of the organization. Researchers have given somewhat less attention to the retention function, perhaps because the methods for enticing volunteers to continue with an agency appear to be quite consistent with the strategies discussed above for attracting them. Moreover, retention begins with effective recruitment: Government organizations that make a sincere effort to develop a climate receptive to volunteering, match volunteer competencies and preferences to nonpaid positions, adapt the workplace to citizens, and implement outreach policies are more apt to make mutually satisfying volunteer placements that will endure over time.

Ann DeWitt Watts and Patricia Klobus Edwards (1983, p. 18) examined recruitment and retention strategies employed by human service agencies in five Virginia cities. They concluded that the approaches to retaining volunteers, such as reimbursement, training, promotion to paid employment, flexible scheduling, and increased responsibility, "are not wholly unlike those of recruitment." Correspondingly, the Gallup surveys indicate that "the reasons most frequently mentioned for continuing to volunteer are the same reasons most frequently mentioned for first becoming involved in a volunteer activity" (Gallup Organization, 1986, p. 40; compare Hodgkinson and Weitzman, 1988b, p. 27). Over the three surveys (for the years 1981, 1985, and 1987), close to a majority and usually more express a desire to do something useful, followed by enjoyment of the work, an interest in the activity, a family member or friend who might benefit, and religious concerns.

These results notwithstanding, some significant differences separate the processes of volunteer recruitment from retention. As might be expected, once citizens become members of an agency, the immediate rewards of the work experience, such as the social aspects of volunteering and the job itself, tend to rise in importance. Based on research on volunteer visitors, firefighters, and school volunteers, Jone L. Pearce (1983b) found that these subjects stated that they joined the

organization for predominantly service reasons, but friend-
ships and social interaction were more influential in their
decision to remain with it. While the long-range rewards of
helping others, supporting organizational goals, and making
a contribution decreased in importance to them (albeit the
scores remained at high levels), the rewards of meeting people and enjoying the company of friends and co-workers
increased. Similarly, in a study of volunteers to local government, the importance attached by participants to doing something useful or benefiting a family member or friend dropped
over time, but interest in or enjoyment of the work grew as a
motivation (Sundeen, 1989; compare Chambré, 1989). An analysis of volunteers in a probation setting determined that volunteers who had stayed with the program for a longer period
reported spending less time on administrative tasks such as
filling out forms and reports and attending meetings (Pierucci
and Noel, 1980).

Pearce (1983b, p. 148) argues that "the rewards individuals expected from volunteering are often not the rewards
most salient to them once they have become volunteers. Further, this shift in the rewards of volunteering, if not anticipated and managed, can result in the rapid departure of many
new volunteers." To counteract this possibility, public administrators have several options. To reinforce volunteers' initial
emphasis on service motivations, they might be placed in
positions where they can contribute directly to organizational
goals, for example, through contact with clients or participation in policy activities. Additionally, agencies should offer
entry-level counseling and careful placement to assist volunteers in reaching their personal goals, and attempt to foster a
work environment conducive to their efforts. Training programs and orientation sessions should present an accurate
picture of the rewards of volunteering, so that citizens—and
the organizations they serve—do not fall victim to unrealistic
expectations of the experience (Pearce, 1983b, p. 154).

Government agencies will also need to do a better job
of responding to their volunteers. While an organization may
have a standard set of activities designed to bring in new

recruits, retention is a dynamic process of reviewing performance, growth, and aspirations with the volunteer and modifying work assignments accordingly. In addition to the methods discussed above, to motivate the continued involvement of volunteers, organizations may offer a variety of inducements, depending on individual circumstances. These include a series of steps toward greater responsibilities, participation in problem solving and decision making, opportunities for training, supportive feedback and evaluation, and documentation of work performed. Agencies have also discovered that formal recognition of the contributions of a volunteer, especially in a public forum such as an awards dinner or newspaper article, "is almost universally welcomed" (Scott and Sontheimer, 1985, p. 28). In sum, factors over which program managers enjoy control are instrumental to retention of volunteers (compare Pierucci and Noel, 1980).

Even so, public administrators must recognize that despite their most diligent efforts, some turnover among volunteers is inevitable, just as it is for paid staff. Volunteering to an organization demands a degree of self-discipline and dedication, as well as a willingness to adjust individual priorities. Not all volunteers are willing to make the commitment. After they join an agency, some will discover that the rewards of volunteering do not merit the adjustments in lifestyle; alternatively, changes in personal circumstances (for example, ill health) may force an end to contributing one's time. Turnover cannot be eliminated, but by exercising responsiveness to the needs of volunteers, program officials should be able to keep it within reasonable bounds.

From the perspective of the clients and goals of public organizations, moreover, turnover is not always detrimental. While attempts at reconciliation should be the first, preferred solution, separation is sometimes the only answer to dissipating conflict that saps the vitality and resources of volunteers and agencies from the objectives at hand. Dissatisfied volunteers can seek involvement in organizations closer to their policy preferences and concerns, which can in turn benefit from the infusion of energy and support. Volunteerism will be most effective as a response to societal problems if citizens have a variety of outlets for making a contribution.

Summary and Implications

Government-based volunteer programs call for individuals to make a regular investment of their time and talents in an organizational setting. In so doing, volunteers assist public agencies in meeting extant job needs as well as the demands of the populace for services. While participants reap a variety of rewards from their involvement, they are not compensated directly for the value of their labor. Instead, volunteering is primarily helping behavior, and the major beneficiaries are agency clients.

Crucial to the success of these programs is the availability of citizens willing to donate their time to government bureaucracies. Estimates from national surveys reveal that nearly half the population engages in volunteer behavior of one sort or another. When more restrictive definitions are applied, however, such as the one specified above, the percentage of Americans who can be considered potentially accessible for volunteer service in the public sector drops appreciably. Emerging trends intimate both a continuing diminution in the supply of volunteers and a rise in organizational demands for their assistance.

Given these trends, public administrators should expect volunteer recruitment and retention to become increasingly challenging. Fortunately, their institutions can offer a range of options to attract and sustain the contributions of high-quality volunteers. Some agencies benefit from a commitment culture that is especially salient to volunteers. Short of this attribute, much lies within the reach of government officials: careful job design of nonpaid positions, facilitation and support of volunteer service, nonmaterial inducements extended to the volunteer, closer ties to the workplace and to other organizations, and outreach to nontraditional sources of volunteers. While all of these strategies have demonstrated success, the most effective is to ensure that the volunteer experience is one worth communicating. Satisfied volunteers make the most persuasive recruiters of other volunteers.

Part Three

Promoting Voluntary
Efforts

8

Encouraging
Volunteer Involvement
in the Public Sector

*In general, there has been a shift from emphasis
on the 'good cause' to emphasis on accountability
and results. The greatest and most important
change has been with respect to the volunteers—
their role, their treatment, their numbers.*
Peter F. Drucker, 1988, p. 30

*Without discounting the common-sense wisdom
of making volunteering pleasurable and
companionable, it is much more useful to view it
as work than as play. For one thing this implies a
different kind of social purpose which should
encourage both the volunteer and the users of
volunteer services to take the activities more
seriously.*   Jane Mallory Park, 1983, pp. 79–80

Writing in the Sept. 8, 1988, issue of the *Wall Street Journal*,
renowned business expert Peter Drucker attempted to account
for the tremendous gains in productivity achieved by many
nonprofit organizations over the past two decades. According
to Drucker, the Third Sector has embraced principles of "management" not only for its paid staff, but also for the huge
cohort of volunteers continually attracted to its missions. Not
content with altruistic yet haphazard volunteer initiatives,

168

the successful agencies carefully screened, trained, supervised, and evaluated their nonpaid personnel. Both the organization and the volunteer prospered as a result.

In a book aptly titled *Meaning Well Is Not Enough*, Jane Mallory Park reaches a similar conclusion. Good intentions and a noble cause may bring volunteers to an agency, but passion and commitment alone do not produce desirable results. To be effective, volunteer activities must be organized and managed. Accountability means making the best use of all organization resources to confront the problems at hand. Those resources include volunteers. The problems will take no less.

The preceding chapters have made the same case with respect to the participation of service volunteers in the public sector. For government organizations, volunteer activities are neither a windfall of "free" labor that can resolve all predicaments, nor a burden of frivolous "do-gooding" that they have no choice but to accept. Instead, the participation of volunteers is a legitimate service option, which like other methods can be managed, shaped, and adapted. Taking these activities "more seriously," in Park's phrase, requires officials to involve volunteers in ways that further the goals of public agencies, respond to the motivations and aspirations of volunteers, and recognize and compliment the jobs of employees.

The 1980s witnessed substantial growth in service volunteers in government. The factors most responsible for this rise—an uncertain fiscal climate, inexorable popular demands on government, the interdependence of the public and nonprofit sectors, political preferences for alternatives to the standard model of delivering services—show no signs of abating. By all reports, public organizations will rely on volunteers even more into the foreseeable future. But as earlier chapters have shown, having volunteers is no guarantee that these valuable human resources will be incorporated wisely or well. Students and practitioners of public administration with an enduring commitment to the approach should guide its implementation. This chapter examines steps that government officials can take to encourage responsible volunteer programs in the public sector, and areas of research that academicians might pursue to advance this development.

Encouraging a Volunteer Approach: Practice

Several avenues lie open to government officials and public administrators to promote effective volunteer programs. They should consider strategies in four broad areas: legislation and organizational policy; insurance coverage; demonstration projects; and education, training, and knowledge dissemination.

Legislation and Organizational Policy. President Bush, like recent predecessors in the office, has shown great interest in volunteerism. To maintain this high profile and to facilitate broader acceptance and application of the approach, public officials should work to enact pertinent legislation.

National public service has attracted most attention. In June 1989, more than twenty bills pending before the 101st Congress called for some form of national service, including the "Citizenship and National Service Act," "American Conservation and Youth Service Corps," and the "National Community Service Act of 1989" (Kuntz, 1989, pp. 1555–1556). President Bush has proposed his own plan, a "Points of Light Initiative Foundation," that would urge volunteerism by all Americans. (This proposal expands the focus of an earlier "YES to America" initiative, for "Youth Entering Service.") National public service has spurred lively debate in the popular media as well as in scholarly books and journals (for example, Moskos, 1988; Danzig and Szanton, 1986).

Elaborate national programs are not the sole means for encouraging volunteerism. Closer to "home" in their departments and organizations, public officials can take more immediate steps. High on the list of priorities should be action to amend or repeal Title 31, Section 1342 of the United States Code, which requires Congress to pass legislation specifically authorizing a federal agency to enlist the services of volunteers (see Chapter Six). While public agencies must respect the rights of employees and entrust to volunteers only those activities for which they possess necessary qualifications, the regulation is detrimental to agency improvement and renewal, and inimical to the spirit and purposes of volunteerism. State and local governments can have similar laws that would need to be revised or overturned to allow volunteers. For instance, many American cities and towns prohibit volunteer personnel in fire departments (McChesney, 1986, p. 69).

No comprehensive study has assessed the impacts of organizational policies on the willingness of public employees to work with volunteers. Nevertheless, evidence from case studies suggests that these effects can be dramatic, ranging from impeding a volunteer program (Utterback and Heyman, 1984) to increasing staff demand for voluntary assistance (Holme and Maizels, 1978). Public officials can facilitate the adoption of volunteer programs by ensuring that appropriate legislation and policy are in place in their agencies.

Enactment of these measures would make volunteers more welcome in government, but service volunteering is a two-way street. Public officials should also press for legislation and policy that lend dignity to this activity, and that recognize volunteers for the valuable work performed. A good example is a position statement adopted by the National Governors' Association on August 1, 1989, pledging support for national service. The governors resolved to "encourage creativity and diversity among programs so that citizens of all ages have an opportunity to serve, providing assistance to individuals and programs to help them achieve their goals."

Another example is House of Representatives Concurrent Resolution 61, "Volunteers and the Importance of Volunteerism," passed by both Houses of Congress in August 1988. The Resolution declares: "That it is the sense of the Congress that experience in volunteer work should be taken into account by the Federal Government, State, and local governments, charitable and service organizations and private employers in the consideration of applicants for employment, and that provisions should be made for a listing and description of volunteer work on employment application forms." As of this writing, the federal government, over thirty-five states, and a number of local governments accept volunteer experience on applications for employment, as do about 100 major companies in their hiring practices.

A third illustration of how legislation can acknowledge the value of volunteer service is by increasing the amount that citizens can deduct on their federal income tax returns for use of private automobiles to carry out volunteer activities. As part of the Deficit Reduction Act of 1984 (effective Jan. 1, 1985), Congress raised the deduction from 9 to 12 cents per mile. Although progress remains to be made to equalize the volunteer mileage deduction with the business rate of 20 cents per mile, the change reflects growing societal appreciation for volunteerism. Further ways that Congress might recognize and extend volunteer service include authorizing deduction on income tax returns of child-care expenses incurred while volunteering, and allowing volunteers all benefits of the tax code whether or not they itemize deductions.

Policies encouraging agencies to expand volunteer opportunities, as well as legislation urging employers to accept volunteer experience in job applications, and changing the federal income tax code to accommodate the work aspects of volunteering, are part of taking the approach seriously. Such initiatives deserve the support of public administrators.

Insurance Coverage.   Another issue that should command the attention of government officials is insurance coverage for volunteers. Volunteers who deliver services for public and nonprofit agencies are subject to the same events that affect paid staff and that could create conditions normally requiring protection through insurance. Thus, insurance coverage ought to be as natural for volunteers to an agency as it is for employees. This step is, again, a matter of treating volunteer involvement seriously. Depending on the nature of volunteer jobs and the program, coverage might include accident insurance, automobile insurance, personal liability, professional liability, and directors and officers liability (VOLUNTEER–The National Center, 1989).

Public and nonprofit organizations have not been

immune to "America's growing liability crisis [that] threatens volunteering" (Langton, 1986, p. 30). For example, the *New York Times* (Sept. 13, 1987, p. 70) reports that the city of Quincy, Massachusetts, lost its volunteer police auxiliary because city officials feared lawsuits. In a national survey conducted in 1987, 11 percent of the sample who said they did not volunteer gave as a reason concern about volunteer legal liability (VOLUNTEER-The National Center, 1988).

Spiraling insurance premiums (up to 300 percent and over) have forced hard choices on nonprofit organizations between purchasing liability protection and providing the services that are their raison d'être. "The cost of liability insurance has become so high that many nonprofit organizations cannot afford to provide this protection for their volunteers" (Haberek, 1987, p. 15). In certain instances, coverage is simply not available. Widespread fears of exposure to personal liability have deterred individuals from joining voluntary boards of directors and volunteering in a direct service capacity, as well as precipitated withdrawal from these activities. Nonprofit organizations report greater caution and reluctance among potential board members, and decreased willingness among service volunteers to act as drivers, have events in their homes, and chaperon trips (Langton, 1986). The anxiety over personal lawsuit strikes at the heart of volunteering.

Although many local governments have been successful in securing affordable insurance coverage for volunteers (Farr, 1983, p. 21), experts concur on the gravity of the liability situation. Findings from a 1986 survey of 2,532 chief executive officers, board members, executives, and professionals from business, government, education, and nonprofit organizations are instructive (Peat, Marwick, and Mitchell, 1987, pp. 4-9). Six in ten survey respondents indicated that liability insurance coverage for boards of directors and organizational officers posed a problem that may grow into a crisis, and about one-third said that the problem had already reached emergency proportions. Of the public officials surveyed, 78 percent felt that liability questions were having at least some negative effect on organizational governance, and 9 percent said that either a considerable amount or a great deal of damage had already been done. (Percentages were nearly identical for the entire sample.) Close to 90 percent of all respondents favored legislation by the states that would specifically address the liability concerns of trustees and directors of nonprofit organizations.

As of 1989, a federal bill that endorses this remedy, the "Volunteer Protection Act" (H.R. 911), awaited consideration by the Congress. First introduced in 1987, the bill encourages states to pass laws exempting volunteers who work on behalf of governments and nonprofit organizations from personal financial liability in the event of lawsuit brought against the organization. The Act is intended to protect the volunteer from exposure; the organization remains legally liable to any injured party (Haberek, 1987). As an incentive for action by the states, the bill would increase by one percent the Social Service Block Grant funds of those that comply. State laws vary widely on the legal liability of volunteers (McCurley, 1987).

Legislation does not relieve government and nonprofit organizations from the obligation to obtain insurance coverage for volunteers. In the first place, the laws only address the area of volunteer liability. In the second, the objective seems to be to reduce premiums by limiting exposure to liability, so that insurance protection falls within the means of more organizations. Short of legislation, however, much can still be done to alleviate the problem.

Although an agency cannot eliminate the threat of lawsuits, responsible operation of a volunteer program can minimize the opportunity for their occurrence. Chapter Five presented the central elements: Recruit and screen volunteers carefully; orient them to the public sector work environment; provide training and continuing education to do the job; manage and oversee activity; evaluate and recognize performance. Even if Congress were to pass the Volunteer Protection Act, it would shield volunteers from personal liability only when they acted within the scope of their duties, in good faith, and in a manner that could not be judged willful or wanton misconduct. Effective program design offers the surest path to this outcome.

Demonstration Projects. Volunteer demonstration projects have had a checkered past in this country, although these ventures have been directed primarily to integrating volunteers into communities, rather than into government agencies (Reeves, 1988). The government of the Province of Manitoba, Canada, however, has developed a project model specifically tailored to public organizations that has considerable promise for application to the United States. Entitled the "Volunteers in Public Service Program" (VIPS), the program attempts to combine goals of promotion of volunteerism in the public sector with the creation of alternative means for people to obtain valid work experience and training (Old, 1986–87).

As originally formulated, VIPS created and funded volunteer program manager trainee positions in government agencies that had been selected to participate in the program. A training period lasting from three to twenty-four months allowed trainees to learn necessary skills, and the organizations to build the foundation for successful volunteer involvement. At the conclusion of the training period, the agency was expected to provide funds from its own budget to continue the volunteer program. Each volunteer demonstration project team consisted of four members: In addition to the VIPS program manager, the designated agency, and the volunteer program manager trainee for the agency, a private volunteer center supplied technical assistance to the project (Old, 1986–87, p. 43).

Through a series of steps, the demonstration projects sought to implement structured volunteer programs in the public sector. First, VIPS publicized the program within government and received and reviewed applications from interested agencies and departments. With the assistance of the volunteer center, VIPS staff selected the agencies, based on their potential for volunteer jobs, resources available to support the program, and commitment to continuing the endeavor. Next, team members interviewed applicants for the volunteer program manager trainee position. The final decision was left to the agency, with the advice of VIPS. The volunteer center provided orientation and training to the individual selected, as well as to staff of the participating organization. The remainder of the training period under VIPS funding was devoted to program development, implementation, monitoring, and evaluation. As the volunteer program took hold in the agency, VIPS gradually withdrew, ceding control to the volunteer program manager trainee, whose role correspondingly increased. Similarly, the participation of the volunteer center receded after the early stages of program development.

In the seven-year history of the demonstration projects (1978 to 1985), fifty-one government agencies initiated volunteer programs with VIPS support, and thirty-one continued to operate them on their own (61 percent). While the lack of baseline data on attrition rates for volunteer programs makes this record difficult to evaluate, a VIPS official credits the projects with "a significant impact on the growth of volunteer involvement in the provincial government" (Old, 1986–87, p. 46). VIPS generated approximately 500 volunteers per year, contributing an average of almost 20,000 hours to the public sector. Other program benefits included: positive public relations for government; a pool of trained volunteer program managers who gained employment inside and outside government; training and work experience for volunteers, many of whom later found paid jobs; and transfer of VIPS models, resources, and expertise to nongovernment agencies developing volunteer programs.

As a consequence of a redefinition of its mission in 1985–86, VIPS has embraced a broader conception of its role in the coordination and promotion of volunteerism in Canadian government, and no longer sponsors demonstration projects (Old, 1986–87, p. 47). However, the VIPS project model bears emulation in the United States. At the national level, ACTION, the "Federal Domestic Volunteer Agency," would seem the logical choice to house such a program.

Although ACTION funds volunteer demonstration projects, they lack the focus and comprehensiveness of the VIPS model. At the state level, the State Offices of Volunteerism (see Chapter One) might oversee demonstration projects; larger municipalities might also have sufficient departments and potential for volunteer involvement to make them worthwhile.

Regardless of the appropriate organizational auspices, demonstration projects based on the VIPS framework would offer a useful method for establishing sound volunteer programs in American governments. In designing a model project, public officials would do well to consider the following attributes:

- An application and review process to ensure the interest of the agency in a volunteer program
- The provision of seed money to begin and develop the program
- The availability of technical assistance to support the effort
- The participation of the agency in the selection of the volunteer program manager to incorporate organizational perspectives
- The ability to adapt the volunteer program to fit the context of each agency
- The gradual assumption of program "ownership" by the volunteer manager and the organization to build acceptance and commitment

Education, Training, and Knowledge Dissemination. Academic treatment of the broad domain of volunteerism and philanthropy, much less the narrower topic of volunteer program development and management, is rarely a component of public administration graduate education. A primary reason is that the area has only recently begun to emerge as a distinctive field of scholarly inquiry. In 1977, John G. Simon, who founded the first academic program dedicated to study of the voluntary, nonprofit sector in that year, compared our knowledge to "the dark side of the moon" (in Hodgkinson,

1988, p. 1). In 1988, the Independent Sector organization could identify twenty such academic centers and institutional programs; sixteen had come into existence within the past five years, a majority were less than three years old, and only two had operated for a decade (Hodgkinson, 1988, p. 5).

Despite this great surge of activity, research and teaching on volunteerism and philanthropy have had relatively little impact on graduate education in public administration (Young, 1987). A report prepared by an Ad Hoc Committee for Nonprofit Management of the National Association of Schools of Public Affairs and Administration (NASPAA) recommended that accredited schools include knowledge of the nonprofit sector in their curricula for all students of public administration, whether or not they intend to manage nonprofit organizations. It also urged NASPAA to work cooperatively with other professional and scholarly associations to develop the field of nonprofit management studies (Young, 1987, pp. 31-32). Working with volunteers is endemic to this field (for example, Connors, 1988).

As formulated, the recommendations would make knowledge regarding volunteer administration more accessible to students of public administration. But as scholars of "government by proxy" (for example, Salamon, 1989, 1987, 1981; Kettl, 1988a, 1988b; Seidman and Gilmour, 1986) correctly observe, the discipline still tends to view the job of the administrator as producing government services, rather than managing activities of the variety of resources who increasingly deliver them—including nonprofit organizations and volunteers (see Chapter Four for a complete exposition). Certainly by the late 1980s, "contracting out" had pierced this assumption: Application of this method to government services has become so pervasive that no student enrolled in a reputable master of public administration (M.P.A.) or doctor of public administration (D.P.A. or Ph.D.) program could (or should) hope to avoid it.

By objective criteria such as the numbers of citizen participants, services affected, and sponsoring organizations, the involvement of volunteers in the production of government services is also prominent. But the scope and importance of the approach have not penetrated the field to nearly the degree that has contracting. Coverage of volunteerism and volunteer programs is not a standard feature of public administration curricula at any level.

This book has advocated education and training for public administrators as probably the best strategy for encouraging responsible and effective participation of volunteers in delivering government services. In three ways, public officials can play a vital role in furthering knowledge of volunteer program development and management: (1) requiring skills in this area for appropriate positions in government, (2) supporting continuing education for employees, and (3) participating in the dissemination of relevant information.

Too often, public and nonprofit organizations initiate volunteer programs without due consideration for leadership. According to one survey, only about one in five local government volunteer programs had an official designated as head, and in many cases the chief qualification appeared to be the individual's willingness to take on additional job responsibilities (Duncombe, 1985, p. 363). Organizations tend to assume that this person will absorb the new duties while continuing present assignments, and with no adjustment to salary. Writes one authority, "It is frequently difficult to ascertain if this assignment should be regarded as a promotion or demotion" (Wilson, 1976, p. 16). Should we be surprised when programs created in this manner fail to meet expectations, or to survive?

If volunteers and volunteer programs are to be taken seriously, public administrators must recognize the special training and competencies necessary for positions of leadership. By writing these qualifications into job descriptions, government officials present a catalyst not only to applicants to acquire the requisite background, but also to schools of public affairs and administration (as well as those in other disciplines) to provide it through their curricula. Further, the requirements should not be confined to job descriptions but carry over to evaluation of performance once in the position. Were these changes to be enacted on a large scale, they would lend force to the NASPAA recommendations regarding nonprofit management education. The demands of the marketplace for employment in government are unlikely to go overlooked for long among accredited degree programs in public administration.

Similarly, government agencies that have volunteers should be prepared to underwrite in-service education for public administrators who work with them, as well as for employees who could potentially benefit from voluntary assistance. Training might take place in the agency or, alternatively, be conducted off-site. In the latter case, the organization should bear the financial obligation and grant the associated release time. The same policy should apply for government personnel with a more sustained interest or demonstrated aptitude in volunteer program development and management. Provided that the individual agrees to return to the agency for a prescribed term of service, the organization should fund (in whole or in part) more thorough education in the field, for example, a degree or certificate awarded by one of the academic centers specializing in the study of volunteerism and philanthropy. Such arrangements are not uncommon in other areas of public administration.

Finally, public officials and managers with responsibility for volunteers need to become more active in interchange with practitioners inside and outside of government. Findings from a survey of government agencies and nonprofit organizations in eastern Massachusetts that have volunteers suggest that public administrators do not always have an outward orientation (Langton, 1988b, p. 27). For example, just 44 percent of the government agencies in the sample, compared to 71 percent of the nonprofit organizations, accepted an invitation from the study sponsors to attend a workshop on strengthening volunteer service. Only 48 percent of the government officials indicated that they would like volunteers referred to them, versus 78 percent of the nonprofit organizations. And less than half of the public agencies (44 percent) agreed to serve as a potential resource contact on volunteerism, compared to 74 percent of the nonprofit sample.

Other developments are more encouraging. Most of the State Offices of Volunteerism hold an annual meeting for volunteers and managers to review ideas, techniques, and challenges. The publication of a *Manual* by the ACTION agency elaborating start-up and operational procedures for these offices (Schwartz, 1989) spreads the necessary information to all states, whether they have an office or not. In addition, beginning in 1988, the directors of the State Offices have agreed to convene yearly at one of the major conferences of volunteer administrators to discuss common issues and problems.

Managers of volunteer programs in the public sector can take advantage of several means to exchange knowledge and experience with other professionals in the field. Participation in networks of volunteer administrators such as DOVIA (Directors of Volunteers in Agencies) is one avenue. Another is through the relevant journals; several are oriented toward practitioners (for example, *Voluntary Action Leadership* and the *Journal of Volunteer Administration*). Public officials can benefit not only from the treatment of important topics, but also the opportunity to publish their own ideas and to review those of others. Annual conferences of practitioners, leaders, and scholars in the field of volunteerism, such as those sponsored by VOLUNTEER–The National Center, the Association for Volunteer Administration, and the Association of Voluntary Action Scholars, offer the ideal setting for productive interchange. Public administrators could learn at these meetings, but they also have much to share.

Encouraging a Volunteer Approach: Research

Public administration scholars have only recently begun to devote the sustained attention to the involvement of service volunteers in government agencies that the scope and significance of this practice would seem to warrant. As they strive to build on this foundation, research in several areas could inform present application of the method, as well as future attempts to extend volunteer efforts in the public sector.

Assessing the Magnitude and Nature of Volunteer Involvement. Researchers have amassed relatively little empirically based information on the extent and characteristics of volunteer participation in the production of government goods and services. Aside from surveys of city and county governments sponsored by the International City Management Association in 1982 and 1988 (Morley, 1989; Valente and Manchester, 1984), and studies conducted by Sydney Duncombe (1985, 1986) in the mid-1980s, systematic knowledge of the dimensions of volunteer involvement in the public sector is quite limited. Even the reliability of the ICMA data is imperiled by generally low municipal response rates. Some State Offices of Volunteerism (umbrella organizations set up in most states to promote and coordinate volunteer programs within government and to support federal and private voluntary efforts) attempt to conduct an annual census of volunteer participation in government departments and nonprofit organizations in their state. However, the information is not widely available, and in any case, it is collected in only a minority of states. At the federal level, no comparable survey exists.

The Independent Sector, a nonprofit coalition of some 650 corporate, foundation, and voluntary organizations, has announced plans to underwrite biennial national surveys of the volunteer behavior of the American populace. The Independent Sector previously commissioned surveys on this subject by the Gallup Organization in 1981, 1985, and 1987, which were discussed extensively in previous chapters. This series constitutes a valuable resource for the study of volunteerism.

Yet, for purposes of research on service volunteering in government, the series is less useful. According to estimates from the 1985 survey, a comparatively modest percentage of the population donates time to government bureaucracies as opposed to nonprofit organizations (13.2 percent versus 46.1 percent) (Sundeen, 1989, p. 558). In addition, the Gallup survey items have not been altogether successful in determining the auspices (public or private) of the agencies to which citizens volunteer. Given these circumstances, much of the service volunteering in the public sector likely goes undetected in random sample surveys. In order to assess the magnitude and nature of this activity, research should be undertaken to identify government offices that recruit volunteers and the types of volunteer programs that they sponsor.

In sum, with the exception of local government, the extent of volunteer involvement in the public sector is a matter of informed speculation. Perhaps more important, across jurisdictions, the types of activities performed by volunteers, the organizational arrangements to support them, the results of their efforts, the reactions of paid personnel, and the like remain elusive questions. Systematic research concerning the breadth of volunteer participation, the service areas affected, the types of jobs held, and the broader implications of the approach for government agencies could inform present and future practice.

Overcoming Employee Resistance to Volunteers. Experts concur that one of the most common as well as enduring impediments to the introduction of volunteers, whether in government or private organizations, is opposition from paid staff. Yet government reliance on volunteer personnel increased over the past decade. How have public organizations confronted, and to some degree apparently surmounted, the traditional inclination of administrators to keep the participation of citizens in agency operations at arm's length (Levine, 1984, p. 185)?

One explanation, widely accepted in the literature, points to fiscal stress as the catalyst, but empirical evidence is inconclusive. James M. Ferris (1988, p. 18) showed that local governments with heavier tax burdens are more likely to have voluntary arrangements for the delivery of one or more services. By contrast, cities that must operate under legal limits on their ability to tax residents actually rely less on volunteers than do communities without the restrictions—despite the "common wisdom that such constraints encourage the use of alternative service delivery arrangements such as coproduction." Based on analysis of a different data set, Richard A. Sundeen (1989) came to the opposite conclusion. The relationship between fiscal pressures and the involvement of service volunteers in government awaits further inquiry.

Additional explanations for the increase in public sector volunteerism have received less systematic scrutiny. Consistent with literature in the field (for example, Ellis, 1986), Brudney (1986) found that the support of top agency leadership was instrumental to the establishment of a volunteer program at the U.S. Small Business Administration. His examination also identified as contributing factors sharp growth in the workload of the agency, far outpacing increases in its paid contingent, and the ready availability of a large pool of volunteers with the requisite skills to compensate. Thus, acceptance of volunteers may hinge on the perceived benefits to be realized by employees.

At least two other sets of variables merit consideration. First, as discussed above, statute law and/or policies specifying the personnel practices of government agencies would seem to exert a powerful influence on the adoption (or the rejection) of volunteer assistance. By altering employee calculations of incentives and sanctions, such formal actions might well affect the implementation of new procedures on the job. Second, Chapter Six elaborated and recommended an approach for involving paid staff in the design and operation of volunteer programs. Application of these techniques should be associated with greater approval of volunteers, but research has not tested this hypothesis empirically. Studies that explicated strategies available to public managers to overcome possible staff antagonism toward volunteers, and that examined the relative efficacy of the various methods, would be a welcome contribution to the literature.

Reaching Agreements on Work Roles. Closely associated with the reaction of employees to the introduction of service volunteers into government organizations is the challenge of sharing the workplace with a formerly excluded group. Two issues are involved: (1) How do public administrators and volunteers reach mutual understandings regarding the work roles to be assumed by each party? (2) Which job responsibilities might most profitably be delegated to volunteers, and which retained by paid staff?

Little is known about the first of these questions. As Virginia Walter (1987, p. 23; emphasis in original) states, "what is missing from the literature at this point is evidence about *how* coproduction is in fact implemented, how bureaucrats and volunteers negotiate the murky boundaries between politics and administration to collaborate in the provision of public services." Similarly, Stuart Langton (1988a, p. 6) notes that although great potential exists for more volunteering, "the question that has not been studied is how can agencies and organizations cope with a big increase in citizen participation." On the one hand, some scholars argue that fluid, open-systems arrangements are crucial to integrating the activities of citizens and bureaucrats for public purposes (for example, Clary, 1985). On the other, classic treatments of organizational volunteerism hold that clarity of authority structures, job definitions, and reporting relationships, for both volunteers and paid staff, are essential to the success of these programs (for example, Ilsley and Niemi, 1981; Wilson, 1976; Naylor, 1973). Given the importance of employee-volunteer agreements to the health of public sector volunteerism, the process by which they are attained deserves further study.

The second issue, concerning the proper allocation of duties between volunteers and staff to further organizational goals, has been the subject of lively speculation. Several recommendations center on volunteers' part-time status: Thus, they should be assigned tasks that can be performed periodically, rather than daily or according to an inflexible schedule; or ones that might impose too great emotional stress if conducted by an employee on a full-time basis (for example, hospice care); or those that require only intermittent attention to the work (see Pearce, 1978). Other recommendations focus on the background, training, and work preferences of staff and volunteers: Volunteers should handle the jobs that do not demand the specialized expertise of paid personnel. Alternatively, they might assume duties for which the position occupant feels uncomfortable or unprepared, or for which the volunteer possesses special training, skill, or expertise.

The degree to which public agencies attend to such provisos in delegating work responsibilities, and the relative efficacy of the resulting patterns for enhancing organizational productivity (as well as other key outcomes), have not been determined. As governments have solicited service volunteers, and they, in turn, have sought meaningful involvement, glib phrases that might have once guided the allocation of tasks—for example, "volunteers supplement, not supplant, the work of paid staff"—have lost their meaning. As shown in the preceding chapters, volunteers perform a very broad range of jobs in the public sector, from the highly professional to the highly routine. Even across organizations of the same type, volunteer assignments can differ markedly. Research is needed on how employees and volunteers come to share the public workplace, and the effects on government agencies of various methods and criteria for the allocation of tasks.

Evaluating the Volunteer Program. To foster accountability, improvement, and responsiveness (to both external and internal constituencies) by a volunteer program, this book has endorsed the concept of evaluation. When officials treat the evaluation function responsibly, the methodology most commonly applied is a variant of cost-effectiveness analysis developed by G. Neil Karn (1983, 1982–83).

Karn proposes that the monetary "worth" of volunteer services be set at the fair market value or purchase price for equivalent paid work, normally based on the job classification pay schedule of the sponsoring agency. If the schedule lacks a commensurate category, several proxies are viable, based on comparable positions in other governmental or nonprofit organizations, or in the private sector. To determine the economic value of the volunteer program, the analyst calculates the equivalent monetary price of all donated labor and weighs it against the direct and indirect costs of the program to the agency. Chapter Two elaborated the technique and applied it to the U.S. Small Business Administration and SCORE (Figure 2.1 presents a summary).

As great an advancement as this methodology offers over alternative evaluation procedures (for example, imputing to volunteer labor a dollar value equal to the minimum wage or an arbitrary amount), research should be directed to refining the technique and expanding the assessment. First, as discussed throughout, the impact of volunteers on the organization extends beyond their own labor; in well-designed programs, participants contribute to the productivity of paid staff. Too often, evaluations omit this element from the accounting. Second, the economic approaches are insensitive to the quality and effectiveness of the work performed. For some tasks, volunteers are reputed to hold advantages over staff, while for others the opposite would hold true. Yet these differences are not reflected in the "value" of the labor to the organization.

Third and perhaps most important, if the characteristic that imbues volunteering with its unique status is the act of giving without remuneration, then to assess its value primarily in monetary terms is not only ironic, but also a subtle form of "disempowerment" (Scheier, 1988b, 1988a). While the dollar equivalent returned by a volunteer program for the public funds invested is a powerful statistic that should be ascertained, the program should be held accountable in its own right for progress toward prescribed objectives. The present inquiry has emphasized goals of service to clients and to the organization as the proper basis for evaluation.

As suggested in Chapter Five, the impacts of a volunteer program for citizen participants and public employees deserve attention as well. Few studies systematically assess tangible gains registered by volunteers, such as skills and competencies acquired, let alone more tenuous effects, for example, a boost in self-confidence, or an increase in neighboring or citizenship behavior that would be extremely difficult to duplicate through other means. With respect to employees, whether agency leaders appreciate and reward skills in volunteer management, or, instead, seem to be interested in the method only insofar as it can reduce paid staff and budget, should not evade assessment. The impacts for public personnel might range from approbation and organizational advancement to demeaning stereotypes regarding the functions of a department in which volunteer labor can suffice. An appraisal of the scope and complexity outlined here would not be an easy undertaking, of course, but the field could benefit from broader evaluation perspectives.

Examining Other Forms of Volunteering in the Public Sector. This book has concentrated on formal volunteer programs operating under the auspices of government. Typically, these programs are designed to incorporate citizens' contributions of time and talents into existing hierarchical structures to assist public agencies in delivering goods and services, and in pursuing other policy goals. An endeavor that attracts over 23 million Americans yearly, and that ranks second only to contracting as an alternative service delivery approach among cities and counties, must be considered significant. Yet official programs sponsored by government organizations constitute only one of many diverse forums for volunteering.

Louis E. Weschler and Alvin H. Mushkatel (1987) offer a framework that might guide future research on this issue. They distinguish three types of volunteer activity in the public sector. The first of these, "coproduction," refers to the participation of citizens in the actual creation of public goods and services or in associated overhead functions. As discussed in Chapter One, the government volunteer programs elaborated in this study are examples of coproduction, as are citizen self-help groups and neighborhood associations, which frequently operate with only indirect, nonhierarchical linkages to public institutions. "Coprovision" entails the involvement of citizens in decision making and policy making regarding the goods and services to be provided in a community, the amount and quality, the recipients, and so forth. This mode has an explicitly political connotation; it includes service on advisory and review boards and policy committees, as well as so-called "advocacy volunteering," or attempts to bring about changes in governmental policies and procedures. Finally, "cofinancing" pertains to citizen participation in the aggregation of sufficient resources to produce the goods or services authorized in (co)provision decisions. Volunteer efforts in organizational fund raising are the most noteworthy example.

Thus, volunteer activity in the public sector spans involvement in service production, decision making, and the acquisition of funding, inside or outside a government bureaucracy. Volunteers can assist a public school system in a variety of ways, or lend their hands in an autonomous child-care center for disadvantaged households. They can sit on a local government planning commission or zoning board, or mobilize a protest group to oppose their decisions. Citizens can solicit donations just as readily for a municipal police or fire department as they can for a private, voluntary organization. Although no firm figures exist, citizen participation in the vast number of self-help and mutual aid groups, voluntary associations, and nonprofit organizations with ramifications for the public sector likely far exceeds the volume of government-sponsored volunteer programs. Scholars should continue to explore these modes of involvement, with special emphasis on their implications for expanding volunteer opportunities, increasing access to public officials and decisions, and enhancing the level and quality of community services.

Summary and Implications

A disparity exists between popular conceptions of the free spirit, creative spontaneity, and genuine caring of volunteers, and the image of government bureaucracies as highly structured, rule-bound, and impersonal. Can the two be reconciled?

To some, no doubt, "management" of volunteers, particularly by an institution of government, is not a felicitous prospect. Nevertheless, this chapter—and this book—have elaborated methods for scholars and practitioners to improve the administration of volunteers in the public sector. Refusal or failure to acquire and apply requisite skills for this purpose do not portend a return to "freedom" for volunteers, but an invitation for frustration. A pioneer in the field of volunteer administration, Harriet H. Naylor (1985, p. 29) illustrated the dilemma well: "Remember that people don't seek volunteering to be 'managed!' But they have a right to expect an orderly and appropriate placement, orientation and training, supervision in the sense of a knowledgeable person to turn to, and recognition for their uniqueness, abilities, accomplishments, growth, and changing objectives."

Government agencies do not seek volunteers to stamp out the qualities that make them unique and valuable participants. But they have a right to establish and manage programs intended to marshal and sustain the best efforts that people can contribute to the public sector.

9

Guidelines for
Successful Public Sector
Volunteer Programs

*Often in the past the volunteer program has been
seen as a rather low-status part of the total
agency organization. . . . However, this is
changing rapidly, with volunteer programs and
departments taking on new and added
importance as their value as a part of human
service organizations is being proved.*
Eva Schindler-Rainman, 1988, p. 20.6

Noted volunteerism educator Eva Schindler-Rainman's observation parallels the analysis of earlier chapters in this book.
Increasingly, government organizations are turning to volunteers to assist in the delivery of public goods and services.
Officials have begun to recognize explicitly the scope and
significance of the time and skills donated to public agencies
and to encourage volunteer contributions. The key to mar-
shaling and sustaining these efforts is the volunteer program. This concluding chapter offers recommendations to
strengthen existing volunteer programs and to guide the development of new ones in the public sector. The recommendations focus on the challenge first raised in Chapter Four (and
addressed throughout Part Two) of enhancing the effectiveness and accountability of volunteer services.

Recommendations

Provide Adequate Funding for the Volunteer Program. Successful organization and management of a volunteer operation begins with a realistic assessment of the monetary support requisite to this undertaking. Too often in the public sector, the recourse to volunteers is an ill-conceived attempt to produce services "on the cheap" (Hill, 1980, p. 156). Volunteer programs are not costless, and they are not self-managing. Despite popular belief to the contrary, these programs necessitate expenditures for recruitment, screening, orientation, training, materials, facilities, publicity, recognition, evaluation—and supervision by agency staff. Simply introducing volunteers into an organization does not solve the problems that any service-delivery arrangement will create in terms of administration and coordination, nor satisfy the need for oversight and monitoring. Instead, agency leadership must invest in the design of a robust volunteer program (Chapter Five presents a discussion of design issues).

Unless public officials are willing to give their backing to the volunteer program and commit the funds required to underwrite essential functions, all parties will suffer. Volunteers will consume inordinate amounts of employee time; citizen participants will become frustrated and tend to leave the program; and clients will see no improvement in the assistance they receive. Without adequate financial and supervisory support for volunteers, government agencies will have neither high performance nor accountability.

Share Power with Volunteers. Volunteers are not public employees, yet in the delivery of many services, they wield discretion and authority on behalf of government agencies. Public officials need to broaden their understanding of volunteer participation to include this facet and to establish mechanisms to increase accountability.

One very promising approach is to involve volunteers with agency staff in planning and decision making regarding the volunteer program, including issues of overall mission and the boundaries of responsibility for each party (see Chapter Six). Some public organizations have moved to formalize power-sharing by placing volunteers in positions of management, leadership, and training for the program (for example, Caldwell, 1988; Snider, 1985). For example, an official with the volunteer-based Appalachian Trail Conference credits the success of this organization in maintaining and administering the Trail to the willingness of government officials to delegate "real responsibility" to the volunteers (Sloan, 1986, p. 30). Not only does the approach help to inspire teamwork between volunteers and paid staff, but also it offers a forum to reconcile divergent goals, so that the parties work toward joint objectives.

The key element in this model of the volunteer program is the ability and willingness of staff to share power with the volunteers (Mausner, 1988). This relationship demands a foundation of trust between the parties. To the degree that mutual trust and an equitable balance of power are attained, volunteers and staff become "teammates," with joint responsibility for the implementation, operation, and evaluation of the program. "As a result, each partner on the team maintains a high level of commitment both to his/her participation and to the organization as a whole" (Mausner,

1988, p. 6). If government agencies can instill this sense of identification, they should be rewarded not only with more effective performance from their citizen partners but also greater accountability: The goals of the sponsoring organization are likely to guide the exercise of discretion and authority by volunteers. Thus, a central task before public managers must be to facilitate trust and power sharing between paid staff and volunteers.

Present Necessary Orientation and Training. Even a cursory review of the literature reveals, however, that trust does not come easily or naturally to these parties. Particularly during times of fiscal stringency, friction, more often than cooperation, may characterize their relationship. Orientation and training for both employees and volunteers is one means to develop the necessary basis for trust.

Although the advantages of volunteer participation are typically pitched at the agency level (for example, increased efficiency), training sessions for staff members should demonstrate the immediate benefits to them of working with volunteers. The advantages include relief from some tasks considered burdensome, assistance in areas where they feel deficient or lack requisite skills, and support from empathetic cohorts (see Chapter Six). In addition, staff should not overlook the ramifications of volunteer involvement for their own professional development, for example, the opportunity to gain managerial and supervisory experience. Agencies should be prepared to support (in whole or in part) advanced training in volunteer management for employees with a special interest or aptitude in this area. Above all, training must confirm that scholars and practitioners in the field of volunteerism, and volunteers themselves, intend a partnership with paid staff, not displacement of government personnel.

Orientation for volunteers should communicate the norms and philosophy of the sponsoring agency and the importance of its mission. Officials should take care to explain the foundation of public authority undergirding organizational goals, the need for accountability in using authority and discretion whether by paid or nonpaid staff, and the connection between documentation of action taken on the job and allocational decisions made elsewhere in the political system regarding funding, staffing, and other resources for the agency.

Successful volunteer programs match the skills, interests, and capabilities of volunteers with the demands of public organizations for productive labor and commitment. To that end, orientation meetings and materials, and organizational policies and procedures, should elaborate volunteer conduct, job activities, and responsibilities in service to the agency, even at the risk of losing potential participants. Informing citizens fully of the expectations for volunteering is essential, so that people can make reasoned choices about donating time, and public agencies can gain greater assurance that participants have some appreciation for the nature and constraints of the work environment. Establishing a mutual conception of volunteer service facilitates management of nonpaid personnel, retention of volunteers, and overall program performance (see Chapter Five).

Volunteer programs normally include training, even for jobs that seem relatively straightforward. Because many volunteers lack relevant background and competencies in the public sector, an educational component is imperative. As volunteers are thrust into direct service-delivery roles, training for them cannot remain "brief and focused" (Farr, 1983, p. 32), but must become more expansive in terms of transmitting both relevant job skills and values espoused in the public sector. In government organizations in which the investment of authority in volunteers is particularly strong, and the latitude for discretion apparent, the standards for training might approximate those for paid employees.

If volunteers are to assume positions of management and leadership for the volunteer program, as recommended above, the necessity for thorough training becomes even greater. For these roles, volunteers must acquire not only competencies in training, motivating, and directing a nonpaid workforce but also knowledge of the main practices, operations, and procedures in place at the sponsoring agency. Governmental institutions do not take lightly the delegation of managerial authority to public administrators, even when they have completed substantial formal education in the field. The same care should guide the assignment of program responsibilities to the volunteers, many of whom come to government with a far different set of perspectives and backgrounds. Public organizations must provide for volunteer training and support commensurate with this charge.

Increase Access to Volunteering. Many scholars and practitioners advocate the expansion of opportunities to volunteer because of the substantial benefits donating time yields participants. An equally compelling rationale for making this option more accessible to all citizens is to achieve greater diversity among volunteers in government organizations. As explicated in Chapter Four, volunteering opens avenues to exert influence over the missions of public agencies and the manner of their attainment. No more should this advantage be reserved to a select few than should the personal gratifications realized through volunteering, such as self-esteem, skill building, and social interaction.

Public administrators should facilitate the participation of disparate demographic and social groupings in volunteer programs not only to address the equity issues. They should do so as well for managerial reasons. As political scientists have argued, a public workforce broadly representative of all segments of society is instrumental to the achievement of significant goals (Krislov and Rosenbloom, 1981). The conclusion applies equally to volunteers. Ensuring heterogeneity among citizens in government volunteer programs promotes effective performance through: cementing ties to the community, imparting legitimacy to public institutions, serving as positive role models for agency constituents, showing greater understanding and empathy for clients in different circumstances, improving responsiveness to popular demands, capitalizing on a multiplicity of human resources, lessening bureaucratic procedures and mores, and raising the priority accorded social justice. Accountability is also enhanced. A narrowly homogeneous group of volunteers might be insulated from important needs, values, and expectations of clientele or the larger community, and stray, perhaps inadvertently, from program missions. In contrast, diversity among participants with respect to backgrounds, perspectives, and talents is a powerful catalyst to break the isolation and encourage a sense of responsibility to the populace for the delivery of government goods and services.

These advantages notwithstanding, extending the volunteer base will require the concerted efforts of government agencies. Although the trends have moderated somewhat over the past two decades, the rate of volunteer participation increases with income, home ownership, educational attainment, employment, and occupational status (Hodgkinson and Weitzman, 1988b). Married individuals and those with children in the household volunteer at higher rates. In addition, whites are more likely to volunteer, as are those of middle age. The demographic composition of volunteers can be expected to vary across public organizations (Sundeen, 1989), but a profile drawn from survey research would suggest that a "typical" volunteer might well be a member of a white middle- or upper-class family.

In order to broaden the pool of volunteers potentially available for service in government, officials must consider strategies aimed at facilitating their involvement (see Chapter Seven). The expenses incurred in volunteering, for example, for transportation, parking, meals, materials, child care, and so forth, can limit the participation of people with low income. Reimbursement by the sponsoring organization can bring this activity within the means of a wider audience. The conventional approach of restricting volunteer hours to the normal work day also precludes the involvement of large segments of the population. Greater flexibility on the part of public agencies in scheduling the time and location for volunteering can ameliorate this problem. Organizational policies that allow weekend and night hours for donating time, and job assignments that can be performed in the home, help to accommodate the schedules and constraints of more citizens and boost services to clients as well.

For these measures to succeed, government organizations must make citizens aware of opportunities for volunteering and the benefits individuals might realize through participation. While general calls for volunteers disseminated through the mass media should not be overlooked, they tend to be impersonal and to miss certain groups. Agency outreach in the community, including open meetings with the public and neighborhoods, visits to schools and churches, and presentations before clubs and civic associations, can both broaden and personalize the appeal for volunteers to disparate audiences. Recruitment efforts should also reach the workplace, for it is a highly potent source of volunteers, especially those organizations which endorse and support this activity for employees (Vizza, Allen, and Keller, 1986). Cooperative agreements with voluntary and nonprofit organizations, volunteer clearing houses, and voluntary action centers can also match citizens with desirable volunteer positions in the public sector.

Facilitation and outreach strategies lay the crucial groundwork for enriching the composition of volunteers. Yet, to be fully effective, the approaches require comparable attention to the quality of the volunteer experience once citizens have entered the agency. The most persuasive recruiters of volunteers are those who have found their involvement in an organization meaningful and rewarding. Unfortunately, volunteers who recount negative experiences can produce quite the opposite effect. Active recruitment can lead to a more diverse pool of citizens. Strategies that heighten the value of participation are just as important to retain them—and to attract new volunteers.

Obtain Feedback Regarding the Volunteer Program. Collecting reliable information about the delivery of public services is necessary to ensuring accountability. Feedback informs officials about the outcomes of government activity and helps fine-tune programs, objectives, and expectations. Public administrators need to gather two types of feedback concerning volunteer involvement.

First, volunteers should have every opportunity to communicate ideas and suggestions to agency personnel. Often, public managers are apprehensive about working with volunteers because the latter differ from paid employees. Yet that very distinctiveness holds advantages for obtaining novel and useful feedback. Volunteers are not bound as tightly to the organizational hierarchy and career structures; they assist governments for different motives and goals; they generally sustain stronger identification with clients and the community; they offer contrasting perspectives and insights. As "outsiders" within an agency, they can be a constructive force for innovation and betterment (see Chapter Three). Organizations that look to volunteers for labor only and ignore the possibilities for valuable feedback forego one of the primary benefits of the approach.

Encouraging feedback does not mean that all recommendations and advice should be implemented, but that volunteers should have input into the organizations to which they contribute their time and talents. Since this conception implies access to decision makers, once again, government officials have the responsibility to facilitate broad participation. Agencies that are receptive to feedback from volunteers can take advantage of numerous forums for productive interchange, including informal conferences, shared break periods, suggestion boxes, bulletin boards, newsletters, social events, formal meetings, orientation and training sessions, and so on.

Second, the volunteer program should undergo periodic formal evaluation to assess its operation and accomplishments. Like any project or undertaking supported by government, the volunteer component should be held accountable for the expenditure of funds, the exercise of public authority, and the realization of objectives. Fearing that this process may appear to question the worth of citizen efforts given freely to help others, however, public officials may be reluctant to subject the program to such scrutiny (Allen, 1987). Nevertheless, evaluation sends the right messages to volunteers: that they are valued members of the organization, their work and program are taken seriously, and their activities are expected to have a positive impact on clients and/or the agency. A lack of dedication to determining the results of volunteer involvement and how these might be improved is no compliment to the organization— or its citizen participants.

Effective volunteer programs emerge from a partnership between employees and volunteers (see above). Public personnel expected to collaborate with citizens should have these responsibilities written into job descriptions, and evaluations of their performance should encompass the requisite skills. In an analogous manner, organizational recognition activities so frequently endorsed for volunteers (banquets, awards, learning opportunities, and so forth) should extend equally to employees who have made valuable contributions to the volunteer program.

Summary and Implications

This chapter has presented recommendations for strengthening existing government volunteer programs and guiding new voluntary initiatives. The strategies center on adequate funding for the volunteer program, arrangements for power sharing, orientation and training for employees and volunteers, increased access to volunteer opportunities, and promotion of feedback from the program.

The success of these strategies rests with three groups. First, agency leadership must lend their full support to the volunteer operation. Their backing is vital to the development and financing of the program. Second, public administrators need to accept the involvement of volunteers and adjust to the demands of working with citizens. Government organizations can apply incentives to motivate their acceptance, but public personnel must decide to enrich their managerial skills to accommodate a nontraditional workforce.

The final group is the volunteers. As earlier chapters have explained, volunteers are less dependent on the sponsoring agency than are paid employees. Whether they use their increased autonomy to further, or frustrate, public values and goals is, of course, crucial. Formal structures and provisions for the volunteer program, such as those elaborated throughout this book, cannot guarantee effective and accountable performance unless those involved in delivering services possess an abiding commitment to public endeavors. Ultimately, volunteers must be not only good workers, but also good citizens.

Resource

~~~~~~

Survey Procedures and Questionnaires: Surveys of Chapter Chairpersons of the Service Corps of Retired Executives (SCORE) and Business Development Officers of the U.S. Small Business Administration (SBA)

Procedures

This book reports results from surveys of two groups: (1) chapter chairpersons of the Service Corps of Retired Executives, or the SCORE Association, and (2) business development officers at the U.S. Small Business Administration (SBA). The author conducted the surveys by mail. In both cases, respondents received a questionnaire, an explanatory cover letter, and a stamped, self-addressed envelope for return of the completed instrument.

The SCORE board of directors assisted in the development of the questionnaire for the chapter chairpersons, and the National SCORE Office provided a complete roster (with addresses) of these officials. The initial mailing of the survey took place in June 1985. To maximize response rate, after one month, the author sent chairpersons who had not returned the questionnaire a second instrument, envelope, and new cover letter requesting their participation. The last completed questionnaire was received in September 1985. Of the 391 chapter chairpersons surveyed, 333 returned the questionnaire, yielding an excellent response rate of 85.2 percent.

For purposes of its operations, the Small Business Administration divides the United States into ten geographic regions. Across these regions, the response rates to the SCORE survey ranged from a low of about 60 percent to a high nearing complete cooperation. The sample is very representative of SCORE chapters around the country.

The SBA Office of Business Development assisted in the early stages of the formulation of the second questionnaire, which was eventually administered to its staff members. The Office of Personnel provided a full listing of business development officers and assistant district directors for business development, and the location of their SBA field offices. For convenience in the research, this entire group is referred to simply as "business development officers" or "business development staff."

The SBA survey was first mailed in January 1986. As in the SCORE survey, to enhance response rate, the author sent a follow-up mailing (with questionnaire, stamped, self-addressed envelope, and new cover letter) one month after the initial survey to respondents who had not participated. Those who did not respond to this request after a reasonable passage of time received a second follow-up mailing. The last questionnaire was received in June 1986. Of the 202 business development staff surveyed, 103 returned the questionnaire, yielding an acceptable response rate of 51.0 percent. Across the SBA geographic regions, the rates of return varied between approximately 20 and 60 percent.

Questionnaires

SCORE Chapter Chairperson Questionnaire

SCORE Association Management Survey

Chapter Facilities

1. Does your SCORE chapter have a chapter office? _____ Yes; _____ No
   a. Is the chapter office located in a _____ SBA facility, _____ SBDC facility, _____ different government agency, _____ Chamber of Commerce, or _____ other facility?

b. How many hours per week is the chapter office open? _____Hours per week

2. Does this chapter have clerical support (aside from that provided by chapter members)?
_____Yes; _____No
a. Who provides the clerical support? _____SBA; _____SCORE Association;
_____From chapter-generated funds; _____Non-SCORE volunteers;
_____Other
b. How many hours per week does the office have clerical support?
_____Hours per week

3. Has this chapter had any difficulties obtaining adequate funding from SBA? _____Yes; _____No

4. Does this chapter currently have on hand (please check if "Yes"):
_____SCORE By-Laws?
_____Chapter Charter? _____Funds earned by the chapter?

Chapter Personnel: New Members

Please Note: FY84 means Fiscal Year 1984
(October 1, 1983 to September 30, 1984)

5. How many new members joined this chapter in FY84? _____New members

6. Who interviews and approves new members? _____Chapter Chairman; _____Chapter member;
_____Chapter committee; _____SBA official; _____No one

7. Are new members placed on probation? _____Yes; _____No ⟶ For how many months? _____Months

8. Are new members given training? _____Yes; _____No ⟶ For how many hours? _____Hours

9. Are new members systematically evaluated prior to final acceptance?
_____Yes; _____No

Chapter Personnel: All Members

10. How many members did this chapter have at the end of FY84?
_____Members

11. In a typical month, how many members participate in chapter activities? _____Members

12. How many chapter members filed claims for travel reimbursement in FY84? _____Members

13. How many members of this chapter are ACE members? _____ACE members

14. How many members left this chapter in FY84? _____ Members left chapter

15. Are chapter members evaluated for participation and quality of work? _____ Yes; _____ No
    a. How many members failed to meet standards in FY84? _____ Members
    b. What action was taken? _____ Members retrained; _____ Moved to inactive; _____ No action taken

Counseling Cases

16. Who assigns cases to chapter members for counseling? _____ Chapter Chairman; _____ Chapter member; _____ Chapter committee; _____ SBA official; _____ No one
    a. Do those assigning cases have a skills inventory of chapter members? _____ Yes; _____ No

17. Who evaluates the quality of counseling done by chapter members? _____ Chapter chairman; _____ Chapter member; _____ Chapter committee; _____ SBA official; _____ No one

18. How many cases were counseled by chapter members in FY84? _____ Cases counseled

19. How many actions did this chapter have in FY84? _____ Actions

20. In FY84 did this chapter refer cases to (please check if "Yes"): _____ SBA? _____ Small Business Development Center (SBDC)? _____ Small Business Institute (SBI)?
    a. Did chapter members serve on SBI teams or follow up on SBI cases? _____ Yes; _____ No

21. What percent of the total cases counseled by members of this chapter in FY84 were (please give your best estimate):
    a. Referred to the chapter by the SBA? _____ %
    b. Referred to the chapter by the SBDC? _____ %
    c. Came directly to the chapter without referral? _____ %
    Please note: Total = 100%

22. In addition to counseling cases, in FY84 did chapter members assist the SBA in screening applicants for loans? _____ Yes; _____ No

Workshops, Conferences, and Courses

23. How many workshops, conferences & courses did this chapter hold in FY84? _____ Number

24. In all, how many people attended the workshops, conferences & courses? _____ People

25. Did the workshops, conferences & courses generate revenue for the chapter? _____ Yes; _____ No

Frequency Information

26. Please answer the following questions in terms of frequency of occurrence. Your answers may range anywhere from *100%*, which • means "all the time," to *0%*, which means "none of the time." For example, an answer of *"60%"* means 60 percent of the time. Please give your best estimate of the frequency in each of the questions below.

    a. What percent of the time do chapter members complete the appropriate paperwork to record the progress of a case? _____% of the time

    b. What percent of the time do chapter members give clients "negative" counseling, for example, advising them *not* to go into business? _____% of the time

    c. What percent of the time do chapter members handle the clerical responsibilities of the chapter office? _____% of the time

    d. What percent of the time are the cases counseled by chapter members "Ma and Pa" businesses with little hope of success? _____% of the time

    e. What percent of the time are cases assigned more on the basis of geographic location of the member and client than on the member's business skills? _____% of the time

Chapter Meetings and Visitations

27. How many chapter meetings did this chapter hold in FY84? _____Meetings

28. How many of these chapter meetings did SBA personnel attend? _____Meetings

29. How many of the meetings did SBDC representatives attend? _____Meetings

30. What percent of chapter members regularly attended chapter meetings in FY84? _____%

31. How many times did the SCORE District Representative visit the chapter in FY84? _____Times

32. How many times did the SCORE Regional Representative visit the chapter in FY84? _____Times

33. How many times did SBA personnel visit the chapter in FY84? _____Times

    a. Were the results of the SBA visits productive for the chapter? _____Yes; _____No

Chapter Relationships with Other Officials

34. In terms of cooperation or conflict, how would you describe the relationship between this chapter and each of the following officials?

If the chapter does not interact with an official listed, please check "No Relation."

Official	Great Cooperation	Moderate Cooperation	Some Coop. & Some Conflict	Moderate Conflict	Great Conflict	No Relation
a. SBA mgmt. Assistance Officer (MAO).......	GC	MC	SS	MC	GC	NR
b. SBA Asst. DDist. Dir. for Mgmt. Asst. (ADD/MA)	GC	MC	SS	MC	GC	NR
c. SBA District Director.........	GC	MC	SS	MC	GC	NR
d. SBDC officials	GC	MC	SS	MC	GC	NR
e. SBI officials.....	GC	MC	SS	MC	GC	NR
f. SCORE District Rep..............	GC	MC	SS	MC	GC	NR
g. SCORE Regional Rep....	GC	MC	SS	MC	GC	NR
h. Natl. SCORE Office...........	GC	MC	SS	MC	GC	NR

Your Attitudes

35. Your attitudes are very important! Would you please rank the following in terms of their influence on chapter management (1 = highest influence):
    _____Chapter Chairman; _____Chapter Executive Committee; _____SBA; _____SBDC; _____SCORE District Representative; _____Chamber of Commerce

36. Please indicate whether you *strongly agree, agree, disagree,* or *strongly disagree* with each statement below.

Statement	Strongly Agree	Agree	Disagree	Strongly Disagree
a. SBA officials treat SCORE members the same as regular SBA employees.....	SA	A	D	SD
b. SBA funding for this chapter is adequate.........	SA	A	D	SD
c. The facilities of the chapter are adequate.......	SA	A	D	SD
d. Coordination between the chapter and SBA is adequate...................	SA	A	D	SD

e. The chapter offers members stimulating work........................	SA	A	D	SD
f. Chapter members' backgrounds are sufficiently diverse to handle any business need of a client..................	SA	A	D	SD
g. The morale of chapter members is high...........	SA	A	D	SD
h. Chapter members often bring in their friends to the chapter to join SCORE.....................	SA	A	D	SD
i. The SBA has too much control over SCORE........	SA	A	D	SD
j. SCORE receives proper recognition from the SBA for the services it provides	SA	A	D	SD
k. Most of the work of the chapter is done by a small number of members........	SA	A	D	SD
l. SBA officials do not know how to manage volunteers	SA	A	D	SD
m. Most of the cases assigned to the chapter for counseling are challenging and interesting................	SA	A	D	SD
n. The SBA treats SCORE as an equal partner in helping small business.....	SA	A	D	SD
o. SBDCs are not necessary to counsel small businesses..................	SA	A	D	SD
p. Transfer from the SBA to the Department of Commerce would improve the operation of SCORE	SA	A	D	SD
q. SBA officials look upon SCORE as a nuisance......	SA	A	D	SD

Information About You

37. How many years have you been a member of SCORE? _____ Years
38. In a typical month, how many hours do you work for SCORE? _____ Hours per month
39. How many years have you been the chairman of this chapter? _____ Years

40. Would you be willing to serve as the chairman of the chapter again?
    _____ Yes; _____ No
41. When you first joined SCORE, were your work responsibilities made
    clear? _____ Yes; _____ No
42. Has SCORE given you the personal satisfaction you expected when
    you joined? _____ Yes; _____ No
43. Do SCORE activities rate high on your list of things to do? _____ Yes;
    _____ No
44. If you had it to do all over again, would you join SCORE? _____ Yes;
    _____ No

PLEASE COMPLETE AND RETURN THIS QUESTIONNAIRE IN THE POSTAGE-PAID
ENVELOPE BY JUNE 21. YOUR RESPONSES WILL HELP THE SCORE ASSOCIATION.
THANK YOU FOR YOUR COOPERATION!!

SBA Business Development Officer Questionnaire

Working with BD Resources

1. With how many of each of the following resources do you work?

Resource	Number
a. SCORE Chapters.................................	_____
b. Small Business Development Centers (SBDCs).....	_____
c. Small Business Institute (SBI) Schools............	_____
d. Trade Associations...............................	_____

2. And, how frequently do you work with officials or members of each of the resources?

Resource		Work with Resource Once or More Every:					
a. SCORE..........Day	Week	2 Weeks	Month	3-6 Months	Year	Never
b. SBDC............Day	Week	2 Weeks	Month	3-6 Months	Year	Never
c. SBI..............Day	Week	2 Weeks	Month	3-6 Months	Year	Never
d. Trade Ass'ns......Day	Week	2 Weeks	Month	3-6 Months	Year	Never

3. Using the scale where *10 = Greatest or Highest* and *1 = Lowest or Least*, would you please rate the resources in your District on each of the Dimensions listed below.

Dimension	SCORE	SBDC	SBI	Trad'l Ass'n
a. Quantity of short-term cases counseled..................	_____	_____	_____	_____
b. Quality of short-term counseling.................	_____	_____	_____	_____
c. Quantity of long-term counseling.................	_____	_____	_____	_____
d. Quality of long-term counseling.................	_____	_____	_____	_____
e. Quantity of workshops, seminars..................	_____	_____	_____	_____
f. Quality of workshops, seminars & courses held....	_____	_____	_____	_____
g. Cooperation of resource with other resources.......	_____	_____	_____	_____
h. Your ability to work effectively with resource....	_____	_____	_____	_____

Work Attitudes and Activities

4. Of the cases you receive requiring Management Assistance counseling, what percent do you:

a. Counsel yourself?.............................._____%   Please give your
b. Refer to other SBA personnel for counseling? _____%   best estimate of
c. Refer to SCORE for counseling?.............._____%   these percentages
d. Refer to SBDC for counseling?................_____%

e. Refer to SBI for counseling?..................——%
f. Refer to trade associations for counseling?.....——%
Please Note: Total = 100%

5. The following questions ask about the percent of time certain things occur. Again, please give your best estimate.
   a. What percent of the time do the resources give clients "negative counseling," for example, advising them *not* to go into business? ——% of the time
   b. What percent of the time are cases assigned to resources more on the basis of geographic location of resource and client than on the expertise of the resource? ——% of time
   c. What percent of the time are the cases counseled "Ma and Pa" businesses with little hope of success? ——% of time

6. Your attitudes are very important! Please indicate whether you *strongly agree, agree, disagree,* or *strongly disagree* with each statement below.

Statement	Strongly Agree	Agree	Disagree	Strongly Disagree
a. I treat SCORE members the same as SBA employees..................	SA	A	D	SD
b. I would advise a friend to work for the SBA...........	SA	A	D	SD
c. I feel comfortable working with volunteers.............	SA	A	D	SD
d. I can rely on SCORE members to perform their SBA work...................	SA	A	D	SD
e. I am very satisfied with my job......................	SA	A	D	SD

7. Below, please find a list of activities that you may perform at work. In the first column ("Percent"), please indicate the percent of time that you spend on each activity. In the second column ("Satisfaction"), using the scale where *10 = Great Satisfaction* and *1 = No Satisfaction*, please indicate the level of satisfaction you receive from each activity.

Work Activity	Percent	Satisfaction
a. Providing services directly to clients (e.g., counseling cases).....................	——%	————
b. Working with SCORE.....................	——%	————
c. Working with other BD resources (e.g., SBDC, SBI, etc.)............................	——%	————
d. Performing tasks for non-BD units of SBA (e.g., Procurement)...................	——%	————
e. Performing special projects or assignments................................	——%	————

f. Other (Please specify):..................... _____% _____

Please note: Total = 100%

Rating SCORE in Your District

8. Please rate each of the following aspects of SCORE in your District
   on the scale: *very good, good, adequate, poor,* or *very poor.*

HOW WOULD YOU RATE...	Very Good	Good	Adequate	Poor	Very Poor
a. ...the level of coordination between SBA and SCORE?....	VG	G	A	P	VP
b. ...the diversity of expertise of SCORE members?............	VG	G	A	P	VP
c. ...the morale of SCORE members?......................	VG	G	A	P	VP
d. ...the business skills of SCORE members?............	VG	G	A	P	VP
e. ...SCORE chapter programs to train counselors?...........	VG	G	A	P	VP
f. ...Chapter programs to train counselors?....................	VG	G	A	P	VP
g. ...Chapter efforts to attract new clients?...................	VG	G	A	P	VP
h. ...Chapter efforts to become more self-sufficient?..........	VG	G	A	P	VP
i. ...the level of funding for SCORE?......................	VG	G	A	P	VP
j. ...the level of clerical support for SCORE?..................	VG	G	A	P	VP
k. ...the level of travel support for SCORE?...................	VG	G	A	P	VP
l. ...the image of SCORE among SBA officials?.........	VG	G	A	P	VP
m. ...the image of SCORE in the community?.............	VG	G	A	P	VP

9. Working with volunteers such as SCORE members can be different
   than working with regular SBA employees. For each of the following
   activities, how do SCORE members compare to regular SBA
   employees: *much better, somewhat better, about the same, somewhat
   worse,* or *much worse?* Please give your overall impression.

HOW DO SCORE MEMBERS COMPARE TO REGULAR SBA EMPLOYEES WITH RESPECT TO:	Much Better	Somewhat Better	About Same	Somewhat Worse	Much Worse
a. Knowledge of relevant SBA rules & procedures?.............	MB	SB	AS	SW	MW

Resource

213

HOW DO SCORE MEMBERS COMPARE TO REGULAR SBA EMPLOYEES WITH RESPECT TO:	Much Better	Somewhat Better	About Same	Somewhat Worse	Much Worse
b. Ability to counsel BD clients?	MB	SB	AS	SW	MW
c. Ability to counsel minority & women clients?	MB	SB	AS	SW	MW
d. Willingness to take directions?	MB	SB	AS	SW	MW
e. Completion of necessary paperwork?	MB	SB	AS	SW	MW
f. Dependability in fulfilling work commitments?	MB	SB	AS	SW	MW
g. Willingness to do any job task?	MB	SB	AS	SW	MW
h. Quality of work performed?	MB	SB	AS	SW	MW
i. On-time performance of work?	MB	SB	AS	SW	MW
j. Making efficient use of your time?	MB	SB	AS	SW	MW

General Attitudes

10. Once again, your attitudes are very important! Please indicate whether you *strongly agree, agree, disagree,* or *strongly disagree* with each statement below.

Statement	Strongly Agree	Agree	Disagree	Strongly Disagree
a. SCORE should take greater responsibility for managing its own affairs and operations	SA	A	D	SD
b. SBA funding and support for BD are adequate	SA	A	D	SD
c. Most of the cases assigned to SCORE for counseling are challenging and interesting	SA	A	D	SD
d. SBA National Office plays too great a role in work relationships between SBA and SBDC in the field	SA	A	D	SD
e. The reorganization of Management Assistance into BD will increase the				

effectiveness of the Division......................	SA	A	D	SD
f. The SBA has too much control over SCORE.........	SA	A	D	SD
g. SCORE receives proper recognition from the SBA for the services it provides	SA	A	D	SD
h. Nat'l. SCORE officials play too great a role in work relationships between SBA and SCORE in the field.................	SA	A	D	SD
i. Most of the work of SCORE chapters is done by a small number of members.....................	SA	A	D	SD
j. BD receives proper recognition from the SBA for the services it provides	SA	A	D	SD
k. The SBA treats SCORE as an equal partner in helping small business.....	SA	A	D	SD
l. SCORE more closely resembles a social club than an organization to help small business.........	SA	A	D	SD
m. SBDCs provide proper credit and recognition to SBA.......................	SA	A	D	SD
n. Nat'l SCORE officials are out of touch with SCORE needs at the local level.....	SA	A	D	SD
o. SBA places too much emphasis on loans and lending.....................	SA	A	D	SD
p. SCORE takes up too much of my time for the assistance it provides to small business..............	SA	A	D	SD
q. Transfer from the SBA to the Department of Commerce would improve the operation of SCORE	SA	A	D	SD

Information About You

11. How many years have you worked for the SBA? _____Years

12. How many years have you worked in Management Assistance (or BD)? _____Years

13. How many years have you worked in this District of the SBA?
    _____Years

14. How many years have you held your present position in the SBA?
    _____Years

15. Have you had formal training or education in the management of volunteers? _____Yes; _____No
    a. How many hours of such training/education have you completed?
       _____Hours
    b. Was this training/education _____very useful, _____somewhat useful, or _____not useful?

16. Have you had college training or education in Business or Management? _____Yes; _____No
    a. How many hours of such training/education have you completed?
       _____Hours

17. Please indicate the highest level of formal education you have completed:
    _____High School; _____Some College; _____College Grad;
    _____Some Post-Grad; _____Masters Deg.; _____Doctoral Deg.

18. Would you like to receive a copy of the results of this survey?
    _____Yes; _____No

PLEASE COMPLETE AND RETURN THIS QUESTIONNAIRE IN THE
POSTAGE-PAID ENVELOPE WITHIN TWO WEEKS.
THANK YOU VERY MUCH FOR YOUR COOPERATION!!

Please use this space for comments:

References

ACTION. *Americans Volunteer, 1974.* Washington, D.C.: ACTION.

Adams, D. S. "Ronald Reagan's 'Revival': Voluntarism as a Theme in Reagan's Civil Religion." *Sociological Analysis,* 1987, *48* (1), 17–29.

Adams, N. "Smithsonian Horizons." *Smithsonian,* 1988, *19* (1), 10.

Agranoff, R., and Pattakos, A. N. "Intergovernmental Management: Federal Changes, State Responses, and New State Initiatives." *Publius,* 1984, *14* (Summer), 49–84.

Ahlbrandt, R. S., Jr., and Sumka, H. J. "Neighborhood Organization and the Coproduction of Public Services." *Journal of Urban Affairs,* 1983, *5* (3), 211–220.

Allen, J. W., and others. *The Private Sector in State Service Delivery: Examples of Innovative Practices.* Washington, D.C.: Urban Institute, 1989.

Allen, K. K., and Schindler, A. "Is Volunteerism in Trouble? NCVA's Response to the *Psychology Today* Article." *Voluntary Action Leadership,* 1978 (Summer), 35–36.

Allen, N. J. "The Role of Social and Organizational Factors in the Evaluation of Volunteer Programs." *Evaluation and Program Planning,* 1987, *10* (3), 257–262.

217

Anderson, J., and Clary, B. "Coproduction in Emergency Medical Services." *Journal of Voluntary Action Research,* 1987, *16* (3), 33-42.

Appel, M. A., Jimmerson, R. M., Macduff, N., and Long, J. S. "Northwest Volunteer Managers: Their Characteristics, Jobs, Volunteer Organizations, and Perceived Training Needs." *Journal of Volunteer Administration,* 1988, *7* (1), 1-8.

Beck, P. A., Rainey, H. G., Nicholls, K., and Traut, C. "Citizen Views of Taxes and Services: A Tale of Three Cities." *Social Science Quarterly,* 1987, *68* (2), 223-243.

Becker, D. G. "Exit Lady Bountiful: The Volunteer and the Professional Social Worker." *Social Service Review,* 1964, *38* (1), 57-72.

Bendick, M., Jr., and Levinson, P. M. "Private-Sector Initiatives or Public-Private Partnerships?" In L. M. Salamon and M. S. Lund (eds.), *The Reagan Presidency and the Governing of America.* Washington, D.C.: Urban Institute, 1984.

Bjur, W. E., and Siegel, G. B. "Voluntary Citizen Participation in Local Government: Quality, Cost, and Commitment." *Midwest Review of Public Administration,* 1977, *11* (2), 135-149.

Bocklet, R. "Volunteers Aid to Better Policing." *Law and Order,* 1988, *36* (1), 180-184.

Borkman, T. "A Study of the Mismatch Between Volunteer Availability and the Needs of Community Agencies in Northern Virginia: A Report." Department of Sociology, George Mason University, 1986.

Braithwaite, J. "Role of Volunteers in Corrections." *Proceedings of the 104th Annual Congress of Corrections.* Houston, Tex.: American Correctional Association, 1974.

Bratt, R. G. "The Role of Citizen-Initiated Programs in the Formulation of National Housing Policies." In J. DeSario and S. Langton (eds.), *Citizen Participation in Public Decision Making.* New York: Greenwood Press, 1987.

Brown, J. "Government Volunteers: Why and How?" *Journal of Volunteer Administration,* 1983, *2* (Fall), 9-18.

Brown, K. M. "What Goes Wrong and What Can We Do About It?" *Voluntary Action Leadership,* 1981 (Spring), 22-23.

Brudney, J. L. "Local Coproduction of Services and the Analysis of Municipal Productivity." *Urban Affairs Quarterly,* 1984, *19* (4), 465-484.

Brudney, J. L. "The SBA and SCORE: Coproducing Management Assistance Services." *Public Productivity Review,* 1986, no. 40 (Winter), 57-67.

Brudney, J. L. "The Use of Volunteers by Local Governments as an Approach to Fiscal Stress." In T. N. Clark, W. Lyons, and M. R. Fitzgerald (eds.), *Research in Urban Policy.* Vol. 3. Greenwich, Conn.: JAI Press, 1989a.

Brudney, J. L. "Using Coproduction to Deliver Services." In J. L. Perry (ed.), *Handbook of Public Administration.* San Francisco: Jossey-Bass, 1989b.

Brudney, J. L. "The Availability of Volunteers: Implications for Local Governments." *Administration and Society, 21* (4), Feb. 1990, pp. 413-424.

Brudney, J. L., and England, R. E. "Toward a Definition of the Coproduction Concept." *Public Administration Review,* 1983, *43* (1), 59-65.

Butler, S. M. " 'People Power' Can Rid Housing Projects of Longstanding Woes." *Atlanta Journal and Constitution,* Feb. 12, 1989, pp. 1-D, 3-D.

Byrne, R. A., and Caskey, F. "For Love or Money? What Motivates Volunteers?" *Journal of Extension,* 1985, *23* (Fall), 4-7.

Caldwell, W. E. "Middle Management Volunteers Fill Needed Roles, Gain Skills, Satisfaction." *Voluntary Action Leadership,* 1988 (Spring), 18-21.

Caraway, J., and Van Gilder, J. "The Role of Lay Volunteers in a Community Hypertension Control Program." *Journal of Voluntary Action Research,* 1985, *14* (2-3), 133-141.

Chambré, S. M. "Kindling Points of Light: Volunteering as Public Policy." *Nonprofit and Voluntary Sector Quarterly,* 1989, *18* (3), 249-268.

Choate, P., and Walter, S. *America in Ruins: The Decaying Infrastructure.* Durham, N.C.: Duke University Press, 1983.

Cigler, B. A. "Redefined Challenges for Local Administrators." In J. L. Perry (ed.), *Handbook of Public Administration*. San Francisco: Jossey-Bass, 1989.

Clary, B. B. "Designing Urban Bureaucracies for Coproduction." *State and Local Government Review*, 1985, *17* (3), 265–272.

Clary, E. G. "Social Support as a Unifying Concept in Voluntary Action." *Journal of Voluntary Action Research*, 1987, *16* (4), 58–68.

Clotfelter, C. T. *Federal Tax Policy and Charitable Giving*. Chicago: University of Chicago Press, 1985.

Connors, T. D. (ed.). *The Nonprofit Organization Handbook*. (2nd ed.) New York: McGraw-Hill, 1988.

Corporate Volunteer Coordinators Council. "The Virtues of Volunteering." *Personnel Journal*, 1984, *63* (8), 42–48.

Dailey, R. C. "Understanding Organizational Commitment for Volunteers: Empirical and Managerial Implications." *Journal of Voluntary Action Research*, 1986, *15* (1), 19–31.

Danzig, R., and Szanton, P. *National Service: What Would It Mean?* Lexington, Mass.: Heath, 1986.

David, I. T. "Public vs. Private: States and Localities Cash In on Privatization." *Touche Ross Public Sector Review*, 1987 (Apr.), 1–6.

DeHoog, R. H. "Theoretical Perspectives on Contracting Out for Services: Implementation Problems and Possibilities of Privatizing Public Services." In G. C. Edwards, III (ed.), *Public Policy Implementation*. Greenwich, Conn.: JAI Press, 1984.

Deitch, L. I., and Thompson, L. N. "The Reserve Police Officer: One Alternative to the Need for Manpower." *Police Chief*, 1985, *52* (5), 59–61.

DeLaat, J. "Volunteering as Linkage in the Three Sectors." *Journal of Voluntary Action Research*, 1987, *16* (1, 2), 97–111.

Democratic Leadership Council. *Citizenship and National Service: A Blueprint for Civic Enterprise*. Washington, D.C.: Democratic Leadership Council, 1988.

DeMott, B. "The Day the Volunteers Didn't." *Psychology Today*, 1978, *11* (10), 23–34, 131–132.

Diana, J., Lawrence, J., and Draine, N. "A Richmond Experiment." *Journal of Extension*, 1985, *23* (Fall), 16.

Dorwaldt, A. L., Solomon, L. J., and Worden, J. K. "Why Volunteers Helped to Promote a Community Breast Self-Exam Program." *Journal of Volunteer Administration*, 1988, *6* (4), 23-30.

Drucker, P. F. "The Non-Profits' Quiet Revolution." *Wall Street Journal*, Sept. 8, 1988, p. 30.

Duncombe, S. "Volunteers in City Government: Advantages, Disadvantages, and Uses." *National Civic Review*, 1985, *74* (9), 356-364.

Duncombe, S. "Volunteers in City Government: Getting More Than Your Money's Worth." *National Civic Review*, 1986, *75* (5), 291-301.

Durant, D. "Volunteers and the Food Stamp Program." *Food and Nutrition*, 1985, *15* (3), 4-6.

"Editorial: The Essential Need for Volunteers." *National Civic Review*, 1983, *72* (1), 4-5.

Ellis, S. J. "Daytime Volunteers: An Endangered Species?" *Journal of Volunteer Administration*, 1985a, *3* (3), 30-33.

Ellis, S. J. "Research on Volunteerism: What Needs to Be Done." *Journal of Voluntary Action Research*, 1985b, *14* (2-3), 11-14.

Ellis, S. J. *From the Top Down: The Executive Role in Volunteer Program Success.* Philadelphia: Energize Associates, 1986.

Ellis, S. J., and Noyes, K. H. *By the People: A History of Americans as Volunteers.* Philadelphia: Energize Associates, 1978.

Farr, C. A. *Volunteers: Managing Volunteer Personnel in Local Government.* Washington, D.C.: International City Management Association, 1983.

Farynowski, D. "The Poem Approach to a Volunteer Program." *The Book Report*, 1987, *6* (3), 11-12.

Ferris, J. M. "Coprovision: Citizen Time and Money Donations in Public Service Provision." *Public Administration Review*, 1984, *44* (4), 324-333.

Ferris, J. M. "The Use of Volunteers in Public Service Production: Some Demand and Supply Considerations." *Social Science Quarterly*, 1988, *69* (1), 3-23.

Fixler, P. E., and Poole, R. W. "Status of State and Local Privatization." *Proceedings of the Academy of Political Science*, 1987, *36* (3), 164–178.

Forrister, A. G. "McKenna House: In Seeking a Service, They Began to Serve Themselves." *Public Management*, 1987, *69* (5), 22–24.

Gallup Organization. *Americans Volunteer, 1981.* Princeton, N.J.: Gallup Organization, 1981.

Gallup Organization. "32% of U.S. Public Reports Being Involved in Charitable Activities." *Gallup Report*, nos. 201–202 (June–July). Princeton, N.J.: Gallup Organization, 1982.

Gallup Organization. *Americans Volunteer, 1985.* Princeton, N.J.: Gallup Organization, 1986.

Gamm, L., and Kassab, C. "Productivity Assessment of Volunteer Programs in Not-for-Profit Human Services Organizations." *Journal of Voluntary Action Research*, 1983, *12* (3), 23–38.

Gidron, B. "Volunteer Workers: A Labour Economy Perspective." *Labour and Society*, 1980, *5* (4), 355–365.

Gidron, B. "Sources of Job Satisfaction Among Service Volunteers." *Journal of Voluntary Action Research*, 1983, *12* (1), 20–35.

Glazer, N. "Towards a Self-Service Society?" *The Public Interest*, 1983, no. 70 (Winter), 66–90.

Goetcheus, V. M. "Voluntarism . . . and Reagan." *Journal of the Institute for Socioeconomic Studies*, 1984, *9* (Summer), 40–48.

Goetter, W.G.J. "When You Create Ideal Conditions, Your Fledgling Volunteer Program Will Fly." *American School Board Journal*, 1987, *194* (6), 34–37.

Gora, J. G., and Nemerowicz, G. M. *Emergency Squad Volunteers: Professionalism in Unpaid Work.* New York: Praeger, 1985.

Gotbaum, V., and Barr, E. "On Volunteerism." *Social Policy*, 1976, *7* (3), 50–51.

Graff, L. L. "Considering the Many Facets of Volunteer/ Union Relations." *Voluntary Action Leadership*, 1984 (Summer), 16–20.

Greer, J. D. "Volunteers in Resource Management: A Forest Service Perspective." *Journal of Volunteer Administration,* 1985, *3* (4), 1-9.

Haberek, J. "The Volunteer Protection Act of 1987: Getting H.R. 911 Passed." *Voluntary Action Leadership,* 1987 (Spring/Summer), 15-17.

Haeuser, A. A., and Schwartz, F. S. "Developing Social Work Skills for Work with Volunteers." In F. S. Schwartz (ed.), *Voluntarism and Social Work Practice: A Growing Collaboration.* Lanham, Md.: University Press of America, 1984.

Hall, P. D. "Abandoning the Rhetoric of Independence: Reflections on the Nonprofit Sector in the Post-Liberal Era." *Journal of Voluntary Action Research,* 1987, *16* (1-2), 11-28.

Hanley, R. "A Jersey Town Searches for Vanishing Volunteers." *New York Times,* Jan. 4, 1988, pp. B-1, B-3.

Harman, J. D. (ed.). *Volunteerism in the Eighties: Fundamental Issues in Voluntary Action.* New York: University Press of America, 1982.

Hart, J. L. "LIVE from Central Park." *Parks and Recreation,* 1986, *21* (2), 34-39.

Hatry, H. P. *A Review of Private Approaches for Delivery of Public Services.* Washington, D.C.: Urban Institute, 1983.

Hill, M. *Understanding Social Policy.* Oxford: Blackwell, 1980.

Hodgkinson, V. A. *Academic Centers and Research Institutes Focusing on the Study of Philanthropy, Voluntarism, and Not-for-Profit Activity: A Progress Report.* Washington, D.C.: Independent Sector, 1988.

Hodgkinson, V. A., and Weitzman, M. S. *The Charitable Behavior of Americans: A National Survey.* Washington, D.C.: Independent Sector, 1986.

Hodgkinson, V. A., and Weitzman, M. S. *Dimensions of the Independent Sector: A Statistical Profile.* Washington, D.C.: Independent Sector, 1988a.

Hodgkinson, V. A., and Weitzman, M. S. *Giving and Volunteering in the United States: Findings from a National Survey.* Washington, D.C.: Independent Sector, 1988b.

Hoetmer, G. J., and Paul, A. C. "Municipalities and the Volunteer Fire Service." In *The Municipal Year Book, 1981*, pp. 178–187. Washington, D.C.: International City Management Association, 1981.

Holme, A., and Maizels, J. *Social Workers and Volunteers.* London: Allen and Unwin, 1978.

Ilsley, P. J., and Niemi, J. A. *Recruiting and Training Volunteers.* New York: McGraw-Hill, 1981.

Independent Sector. *Americans Volunteer 1985: Summary Report.* Washington, D.C.: Independent Sector, 1986.

Independent Sector. "A Blueprint for Increasing Volunteering and Giving." *Voluntary Action Leadership*, 1987 (Winter), 20–22.

Kahn, J. D. "Legal Issues Survey Results." *Journal of Volunteer Administration*, 1985–86, *4* (2), 28–34.

Kantrowitz, B. "The New Volunteers." *Newsweek*, July 10, 1989, pp. 36–38.

Karn, G. N. "Money Talks: A Guide to Establishing the True Dollar Value of Volunteer Time, Part I." *Journal of Volunteer Administration*, 1982–83, *1* (Winter), 1–17.

Karn, G. N. "Money Talks: A Guide to Establishing the True Dollar Value of Volunteer Time, Part II." *Journal of Volunteer Administration*, 1983, *1.*(Spring), 1–19.

Karn, G. N. "The No-Apologies Budget: How to Justify the Financial Support a Volunteer Program Deserves." *Voluntary Action Leadership*, 1984 (Spring), 29–31.

Kettl, D. F. *Government by Proxy: (Mis?)Managing Federal Programs.* Washington, D.C.: CQ Press, 1988a.

Kettl, D. F. "Performance and Accountability: The Challenge of Government by Proxy for Public Administration." *American Review of Public Administration*, 1988b, *18* (1), 9–28.

Knoke, D. "Commitment and Detachment in Voluntary Associations." *American Sociological Review*, 1981, *46* (April), 141–158.

Kramer, R. M. *Voluntary Agencies in the Welfare State.* Berkeley, Calif.: University of California Press, 1981.

Krislov, S., and Rosenbloom, D. H. *Representative Bureaucracy and the American Political System.* New York: Praeger, 1981.

Kuntz, P. "Bush Outlines His Proposal for Volunteer Service." *Congressional Quarterly Weekly Report*, 1989, *47* (25), 1555-1556.

Kweit, M. G., and Kweit, R. W. *Implementing Citizen Participation in a Bureaucratic Society: A Contingency Approach.* New York: Praeger, 1981.

Landau, L. J. M. "Volunteers in Rape Prevention . . . It Works." *The Police Chief*, 1980, *47* (3), 32-33, 69.

Langbein, L. I. *Discovering Whether Programs Work: A Guide to Statistical Methods for Program Evaluation.* Santa Monica, Calif.: Goodyear, 1980.

Langton, S. "Volunteering and the Future of Community." *Voluntary Action Leadership*, 1986 (Fall), 2, 30-31.

Langton, S. "Lincoln Filene Center Conducting Opinion Surveys About Volunteering." Association of Voluntary Action Scholars *Newsletter*, 1988a, *16* (1-2), 6.

Langton, S. *Volunteer Needs, Contributions, and Opportunities in Eastern Massachusetts: A Study of Experiences and Opinions of Nonprofit Organizations and Government Agencies.* Medford, Mass.: Lincoln Filene Center for Citizenship and Public Affairs, Tufts University, 1988b.

Levine, C. H. "Citizenship and Service Delivery: The Promise of Coproduction." *Public Administration Review*, 1984, *44* (special issue), 178-189.

Lipsky, M. *Street-Level Bureaucracy: Dilemmas of the Individual in Public Services.* New York: Russell Sage Foundation, 1980.

Lotz, A. R. "Alternatives in Health and Human Services." *Public Management*, 1982, *64* (10), 10-12.

Manchester, L. D., and Bogart, G. S. *Contracting and Volunteerism in Local Government: A Self-Help Guide.* Washington, D.C.: International City Management Association, 1988.

Manser, G. "Volunteers." In A. Minahan (ed.), *Encyclopedia of Social Work.* Vol. 2. Silver Spring, Md.: National Association of Social Workers, 1987.

Marando, V. L. "Local Service Delivery: Volunteers and Recreation Councils." *Journal of Volunteer Administration*, 1986, *4* (4), 16-24.

Martin, S. "The Arvada Volunteer Story." *Public Management,* 1982, *64* (10), 13-14.

Mausner, C. "The Underlying Dynamics of Staff-Volunteer Relationships." *Journal of Volunteer Administration,* 1988, *6* (4), 5-9.

McChesney, F. S. "Government Prohibitions on Volunteer Fire Fighting in Nineteenth-Century America: A Property Rights Perspective." *Journal of Legal Studies,* 1986, *15* (1), 69-92.

McCroskey, J., Brown, D., and Greene, S. R. "Are Volunteers Worth the Effort?" *Public Welfare,* 1983, *41* (1), 5-8.

McCurley, S. H. "Should Paid Staff Replace Volunteers?" *Voluntary Action Leadership,* 1981 (Spring), 20.

McCurley, S. H. "State Volunteer Liability Legislation." *Voluntary Action Leadership,* 1987 (Summer/Fall), 15-17.

McHenry, C. A. "Library Volunteers: Recruiting, Motivating, Keeping Them." *School Library Journal,* 1988, *35* (8), 44-47.

Millard, S. "Voluntary Action and the States: The Other Alternative." *National Civic Review,* 1983, *72* (5), 262-269.

Minnesota Office of Volunteer Services. *Volunteers—the Best of Minnesota: A Report on the State of Volunteerism in Minnesota.* St. Paul, Minn.: Minnesota Office of Volunteer Services, 1987.

Moen, M. C. "The Political Agenda of Ronald Reagan: A Content Analysis of the State of the Union Messages." *Presidential Studies Quarterly,* 1988, *28* (4), 775-785.

Moore, L. F. (ed.). *Motivating Volunteers: How the Rewards of Unpaid Work Can Meet People's Needs.* Vancouver, B.C.: Vancouver Volunteer Centre, 1985.

Moore, N. A. "The Application of Cost-Benefit Analysis to Volunteer Programs." *Volunteer Administration,* 1978, *11* (1), 13-22.

Morgan, D. R., and England, R. E. "The Two Faces of Privatization." *Public Administration Review,* 1988, *48* (6), 979-987.

Morley, E. "Patterns in the Use of Alternative Service Delivery Approaches." In *Municipal Year Book, 1989.* Washington, D.C.: International City Management Association, 1989.

Morner, A. L. "Junk Aid for Small Business." *Fortune*, 1977, *96* (5), 204-207, 210, 212, 214.

Moskos, C. C. *A Call to Civic Service: National Service for Country and Community*. New York: Free Press, 1988.

Musselwhite, J. C., Jr. "The Impacts of New Federalism on Public/Private Partnerships." *Publius*, 1986, *16* (1), 113-131.

Myers, P., and Reid, A. C. *State Parks in a New Era: A Survey of Issues and Innovations*. Washington, D.C.: Conservation Foundation, 1986.

Nagel, J., Cimbolic, P., and Newlin, M. "Efficacy of Elderly and Adolescent Volunteer Counselors in a Nursing Home Setting." *Journal of Counseling Psychology*, 1988, *35* (1), 81-86.

Nalbandian, J. "The Evolution of Local Governance: A New Democracy." *Public Management*, 1987, *69* (6), 2-5.

Navaratnam, K. K. "Volunteers Training Volunteers: A Model for Human Service Organizations." *Journal of Volunteer Administration*, 1986, *5* (1), 19-25.

Naylor, H. H. *Volunteers Today—Finding, Training, and Working with Them*. Dryden, N.Y.: Dryden Associates, 1973.

Naylor, H. H. "Beyond Managing Volunteers." *Journal of Voluntary Action Research*, 1985, *14* (2, 3), 25-30.

Netting, F. E. "Ethical Issues in Volunteer Management and Accountability." *Social Work*, 1987, *32* (3), 250-252.

Newland, C. A. "Response to Redburn and Cho." *Public Administration Review*, 1984, *44* (special issue), 161-163.

"The New Volunteers: America's Unsung Heroes." *Newsweek*, July 10, 1989, pp. 36-66.

O'Connell, B. "What Colleges Ought to Do to Instill a Voluntary Spirit in Young Adults." *Chronicle of Higher Education*, Apr. 15, 1987, p. 104.

O'Connell, B. "What Voluntary Activity Can and Cannot Do for America." *Public Administration Review*, 1989, *49* (5), 486-491.

Old, D. "Volunteers in Public Service: A Canadian Model for the Support of Volunteerism in Government." *Journal of Volunteer Administration*, 1986-87, *5* (2), 42-48.

Park, J. M. *Meaning Well Is Not Enough: Perspectives on Volunteering*. South Plainfield, N.J.: Groupwork Today, 1983.

Parker, M. A. "Student Volunteers: An Endangered Species?" *Campus Activities Programming*, 1988, *20* (Mar.), 49–51.

Parks, R. B., and others. "Consumers as Coproducers of Public Services: Some Economic and Institutional Considerations." *Policy Studies Review*, 1981, *9* (7), 1001–1011.

Parkum, K. H. "Instrumental and Expressive Dimensions of the Impact of Volunteers on Hospital Patients." *Journal of Voluntary Action Research*, 1985, *14* (2–3), 123–132.

Pattakos, A. N. *Volunteers and the Provision of Local Government Services: A Preliminary Issue Paper.* Washington, D.C.: International City Management Association, 1982.

Pearce, J. L. "Something for Nothing: An Empirical Examination of the Structures and Norms of Volunteer Organizations." Unpublished doctoral dissertation, School of Organization and Management, Yale University, 1978.

Pearce, J. L. "Leading and Following Volunteers: Implications for a Changing Society." *Journal of Applied Behavioral Science*, 1982, *18* (3), 385–394.

Pearce, J. L. "Job Attitude and Motivation Differences Between Volunteers and Employees from Comparable Organizations." *Journal of Applied Psychology*, 1983a, *68* (4), 646–652.

Pearce, J. L. "Participation in Voluntary Associations: How Membership in a Formal Organization Changes the Rewards of Participation." In D. H. Smith and J. Van Til (eds.), *International Perspectives on Voluntary Action Research.* Washington, D.C.: University Press of America, 1983b.

Pearce, J. L. "Managing Volunteers: The Role of Ambiguity in Volunteer Motivation." *Proceedings of the Fifteenth Annual Meeting of the Association of Voluntary Action Scholars.* Kansas City, Mo.: Cookingham Institute of Public Affairs, University of Missouri–Kansas City, 1987, 323–339.

Peat, Marwick, and Mitchell. *Directors' and Officers' Liability: A Crisis in the Making.* Chicago: Peat, Marwick, and Mitchell, 1987.

Pecorella, R. F. "Coping with Crises: The Politics of Urban Retrenchment." *Polity*, 1984, *17* (2), 298–316.

Peirce, N. R.. "Tax Revolt, Ten Years Later: A Dangerous Cure." *PA Times,* 1988, *11* (8), 2.

Percy, S. L. "Conceptualizing and Measuring Citizen Coproduction of Community Safety." *Policy Studies Journal,* 1978, *7* (special issue), 486–492.

Percy, S. L. "Citizen Coproduction: Prospects for Improving Service Delivery." *Journal of Urban Affairs,* 1983, *5* (3), 203–210.

Percy, S. L. "Citizen Participation in the Coproduction of Urban Services." *Urban Affairs Quarterly,* 1984, *19* (4), 431–446.

Percy, S. L. "Citizen Involvement in Coproducing Safety and Security in the Community." *Public Productivity Review,* 1987, *10* (Summer), 83–93.

Perkins, K. B. "Volunteer Fire Departments: Community Integration, Autonomy, and Survival." *Human Organization,* 1987, *46* (4), 342–348.

Peterson, G. E. "The State and Local Sector." In J. L. Palmer and I. V. Sawhill (eds.), *The Reagan Experiment: An Examination of Economic and Social Policies Under the Reagan Administration.* Washington, D.C.: Urban Institute, 1982.

Peterson, R. D. "The Anatomy of Cost-Effectiveness Analysis." *Evaluation Review,* 1986, *10* (1), 29–44.

Pierucci, J., and Noel, R. D. "Duration of Participation of Correctional Volunteers as a Function of Personal and Situational Variables." *Journal of Community Psychology,* 1980, *8* (1), 245–250.

Plant, J., and Thompson, F. J. "Deregulation, the Bureaucracy, and Employment Discrimination: The Case of the EEOC." In M. W. Combs and J. Gruhl (eds.), *Affirmative Action: Theory, Analysis, and Prospects.* Jefferson, N.C.: McFarland, 1986.

Powell, B. "Volunteers in the Schools: A Positive Approach to Schooling." *NASSP Bulletin,* 1986, *70* (Dec.), 32–34.

"Quincy Auxiliary Police Unit More Welcome in Braintree." *New York Times,* Sept. 13, 1987, p. 70.

Rastikis, L. "Kettering Fire Department Breaks with Tradition." *Public Management,* 1986, *68* (12), 26–28.

230   References

Redburn, F. S., and Cho, Y. H. "Government's Responsibility for Citizenship and the Quality of Community Life." *Public Administration Review*, 1984, *44* (special issue), 158–161.

Reeves, T. Z. *The Politics of the Peace Corps and Vista.* Tuscaloosa, Ala.: University of Alabama Press, 1988.

Rehm, P. T. "Volunteers: Another Endangered Species?" *Graduate Woman*, 1980, *75* (May/June), 21–24.

Rosentraub, M. S., and Warren, R. "Citizen Participation in the Production of Urban Services." *Public Productivity Review*, 1987, *11* (Spring), 75–89.

Rutter, L. *The Essential Community: Local Government in the Year 2000.* Washington, D.C.: International City Management Association, 1980.

Rydberg, W. D., and Peterson, L. J. (eds.). *A Look at the Eighties: Crucial Environmental Factors Affecting Volunteerism.* Appleton, Wis.: Aid Association for Lutherans, 1980.

Salamon, L. M. "Rethinking Public Management: Third-Party Government and the Changing Forms of Government Action." *Public Policy*, 1981, *29* (3), 255–275.

Salamon, L. M. "Nonprofit Organizations: The Lost Opportunity." In J. L. Palmer and I. V. Sawhill (eds.), *The Reagan Record.* Cambridge, Mass.: Ballinger, 1984.

Salamon, L. M. "Partners in Public Service: The Scope and Theory of Government-Nonprofit Relations." In W. W. Powell (ed.), *The Nonprofit Sector: A Research Handbook.* New Haven, Conn.: Yale University Press, 1987.

Salamon, L. M. (ed., assisted by M. S. Lund). *Beyond Privatization: The Tools of Government Action.* Washington, D.C.: Urban Institute, 1989.

Salamon, L. M., Musselwhite, J. C., Jr., and Abramson, A. J. "Voluntary Organizations and the Crisis of the Welfare State." *New England Journal of Human Services*, 1984, *4* (Winter), 25–36.

Salmon, R. "The Use of Aged Volunteers: Individual and Organizational Considerations." *Journal of Gerontological Social Work*, 1985, *8* (3-4), 211–223.

Samuelson, R. J. "Playing the Numbers Game." *Newsweek*, June 1, 1987, p. 49.

Savas, E. S. *Privatization: The Key to Better Government.* Chatham, N.J.: Chatham House, 1987.

Scheier, I. H. "Staff Nonsupport of Volunteers: A New Look at an Old Failure." *Voluntary Action Leadership,* 1977 (Fall), 32–36.

Scheier, I. H. "Positive Staff Attitude Can Ease Volunteer Recruiting Pinch." *Hospitals,* 1981, *55* (3), 61–63.

Scheier, I. H. "Empowering a Profession: Seeing Ourselves as More Than Subsidiary." *Journal of Volunteer Administration,* 1988a, *7* (1), 29–34.

Scheier, I. H. "Empowering a Profession: What's in Our Name?" *Journal of Volunteer Administration,* 1988b, *6* (4), 31–36.

Scheier, I. H. "Empowering a Profession: Leverage Points and Process." *Journal of Volunteer Administration,* 1988–89, *7* (2), 50–57.

Schiff, J. A. "Charitable Contributions of Money and Time: The Role of Government Policies." Unpublished doctoral dissertation, Department of Economics, University of Wisconsin–Madison, 1984.

Schiff, J. A., and Weisbrod, B. A. "Tax Policy and Volunteering." In *Working Papers for the Spring Research Forum.* Washington, D.C.: Independent Sector, 1986.

Schindler-Rainman, E. "Volunteer Administration: New Roles for the Profession to 'Make a Difference.' " *Journal of Volunteer Administration,* 1986–87, *5* (2), 13–17.

Schindler-Rainman, E. "Administration of Volunteer Programs." In T. D. Connors (ed.), *The Nonprofit Organization Handbook.* (2nd ed.) New York: McGraw-Hill, 1988.

Schneider, A. L. "Coproduction of Public and Private Safety: An Analysis of Bystander Intervention, 'Protective Neighboring,' and Personal Protection." *Western Political Quarterly,* 1987, *40* (4), 611–630.

Schwartz, F. S. "The Professional Staff and the Direct Service Volunteer: Issues and Problems." *Journal of Jewish Communal Service,* 1977, *54* (2), 147–154.

Schwartz, F. S. (ed.). *Voluntarism and Social Work Practice: A Growing Collaboration.* Lanham, Md.: University Press of America, 1984.

Schwartz, M. I. *The State Office of Volunteerism Manual.* Washington, D.C.: ACTION, 1989.

SCORE Association. *A Report of Accomplishments, 1987.* Washington, D.C.: 1988.

Scott, K. M., and Sontheimer, H. G. "Road Map to Volunteerism in Justice Agencies." *Juvenile and Family Court Journal,* 1985, *36* (1), 23-29.

Seidman, H., and Gilmour, R. *Politics, Position, and Power: From the Positive to the Regulatory State.* (4th ed.) New York: Oxford University Press, 1986.

Sharp, E. B. "Toward a New Understanding of Urban Services and Citizen Participation: The Coproduction Concept." *Midwest Review of Public Administration,* 1980, *14* (2), 105-118.

Shulman, M. A. *Alternative Approaches for Delivering Public Services.* Urban Data Service Reports, no. 14. Washington, D.C.: International City Management Association, 1982.

Siegel, G. B. "Voluntarism in Local Government Central Personnel Agencies in California." *Public Personnel Management Journal,* 1983, *12,* 129:145.

Siegel, G. B., and Sundeen, R. A. "Volunteering in Municipal Police Departments: Some Hypotheses on Performance Impacts." *Public Productivity Review,* 1986, *10* (Winter), 77-91.

Sigler, R. T., and Leenhouts, K. J. *Management of Volunteer Programs in Criminal Justice.* Denver, Colo.: Yellowfire Press, 1985.

Sills, D. L. *The Volunteers.* Glencoe, Ill.: Free Press, 1957.

Silverman, M., Hepner, B., Ricci, E., and Wick, R. "The Importance of *Staff* Involvement in Volunteer Program Planning." *Voluntary Action Leadership,* 1984 (Summer), 25-29.

Sloan, C. "Trail Blazers." *National Parks,* 1986, *60* (11-12), 24-30.

Smith, D. H. "Types of Volunteers and Voluntarism." *Volunteer Administration,* 1972, *6* (3), 3-10.

Smith, D. H. "Altruism, Volunteers, and Volunteerism." *Journal of Voluntary Action Research,* 1981, *10* (1), 21-36.

Smith, D. H. "A National Endowment for Volunteerism: Concept Paper." *Proceedings of the Fifteenth Annual Meeting of the Association of Voluntary Action Scholars.* Kansas City, Mo.: Cookingham Institute of Public Affairs, University of Missouri-Kansas City, 1987, 101-116.

Snider, A. "The Dynamic Tension: Professionals and Volunteers." *Journal of Extension,* 1985, *23* (Fall), 7-10.

Stenzel, A. K., and Feeney, H. M. *Volunteer Training and Development: A Manual.* rev. ed. New York: Seabury Press, 1976.

Strickler, G. "The Social Work Profession's Attitude Towards Volunteerism." *Journal of Volunteer Administration,* 1987, *5* (4), 24-31.

Sundeen, R. A. "Explaining Participation in Coproduction: A Study of Volunteers." *Social Science Quarterly,* 1988, *69* (3), 547-568.

Sundeen, R. A. "Citizens Serving Government: Volunteer Participation in Local Public Agencies." In *Working Papers for the Spring Research Forum.* Washington, D.C.: Independent Sector, 1989.

Sundeen, R. A., and Siegel, G. B. "The Uses of Volunteers by Police." *Journal of Police Science and Administration,* 1986, *14* (1), 49-61.

Sundeen, R. A., and Siegel, G. B. "The Community and Departmental Contexts of Volunteer Use by Police." *Journal of Voluntary Action Research,* 1987, *16* (3), 43-53.

Susskind, L., and Elliott, M. *Paternalism, Conflict, and Coproduction: Learning from Citizen Action and Citizen Participation in Western Europe.* New York: Plenum Press, 1983.

Task Force on Critical Problems. *Bolstering New York State's Human Services . . . Any Volunteers? A Report on Promoting Volunteerism.* Albany, N.Y.: New York State Senate, 1982.

Tedrick, T., Davis, W. W., and Coutant, G. J. "Effective Management of a Volunteer Corps." *Parks and Recreation,* 1984, *19* (2), 55-59, 70.

Thomas, J. C. *Between Citizen and City: Neighborhood Organizations and Urban Politics in Cincinnati.* Lawrence, Kans.: University Press of Kansas, 1986.

234   References

Thomas, J. C. "Neighborhood Coproduction and Municipal Productivity." *Public Productivity Review*, 1987, *11* (Summer), 95–105.

Tierce, J. W., and Seelbach, W. C. "Elders as School Volunteers: An Untapped Resource." *Educational Gerontology*, 1987, *13* (1), 33–41.

Touche Ross. *Privatization in America*. Washington, D.C.: Touche Ross, 1987.

Traut, C. A. "Toward a Political Theory of Volunteerism." *Proceedings of the Fifteenth Annual Meeting of the Association of Voluntary Action Scholars*. Kansas City, Mo.: Cookingham Institute of Public Affairs, University of Missouri–Kansas City, 1987, 85–99.

U.S. Department of Agriculture. Cooperative Extension Service. *The Value of Extension-Volunteer Partnerships*. Washington, D.C.: Cooperative Extension System, 1988.

U.S. Department of Labor. *Americans Volunteer, 1969*. Washington, D.C.: U.S. Department of Labor, 1969.

U.S. General Accounting Office. *Changes Needed for a Better Peace Corps*. Washington, D.C.: U.S. General Accounting Office, Feb. 6, 1979.

U.S. Small Business Administration. *Small Business Administration Program Costs, Fiscal Years 1982 and 1983*. Washington, D.C.: U.S. Small Business Administration, Office of the Comptroller, 1984.

U.S. Small Business Administration. *SBA Budget Estimate, Fiscal Year 1990*. Washington, D.C.: U.S. Small Business Administration, Office of the Comptroller, 1989.

Utterback, J., and Heyman, S. R. "An Examination of Methods in the Evaluation of Volunteer Programs." *Evaluation and Program Planning*, 1984, 7 (3), 229–235.

Valente, M. G. "Volunteers Help Stretch Local Budgets." *Rural Development Perspectives*, 1985, 2 (1), 30–34.

Valente, C. F., and Manchester, L. D. *Rethinking Local Services: Examining Alternative Delivery Approaches*. Information Service Special Report, no. 12. Washington, D.C.: International City Management Association, 1984.

Van Til, J. *Mapping the Third Sector: Voluntarism in a Changing Social Economy.* New York: Foundation Center, 1988.

Vizza, C., Allen, K., and Keller, S. *A New Competitive Edge: Volunteers from the Workplace.* Arlington, Va.: VOLUNTEER-The National Center, 1986.

VOLUNTEER-The National Center. *Volunteering: A National Profile.* Arlington, Va.: VOLUNTEER-The National Center, 1988.

VOLUNTEER-The National Center. *Insurance for Volunteers.* Arlington, Va.: VOLUNTEER-The National Center, 1989.

Walter, V. "Volunteers and Bureaucrats: Clarifying Roles and Creating Meaning." *Journal of Voluntary Action Research,* 1987, *16* (3), 22-32.

Warren, R. "Introduction to the Special Issue: Coproduction, Volunteerism, Privatization, and the Public Interest." *Journal of Voluntary Action Research,* 1987, *16* (3), 5-10.

Warren, R., Rosentraub, M. S., and Harlow, K. S. "Citizen Participation in the Production of Services: Methodological and Policy Issues in Coproduction Research." *Southwestern Review of Management and Economics,* 1983, *2* (1), 41-55.

Warren, R., Rosentraub, M. S., and Harlow, K. S. "Coproduction, Equity, and the Distribution of Safety." *Urban Affairs Quarterly,* 1984, *19* (4), 447-464.

Watts, A. D., and Edwards, P. K. "Recruiting and Retaining Human Service Volunteers: An Empirical Analysis." *Journal of Voluntary Action Research,* 1983, *12* (3), 9-22.

Weisbrod, B. A. *The Nonprofit Economy.* Cambridge, Mass.: Harvard University Press, 1988.

Weitzman, M. S. "Measuring the Number, Hours Spent, and Dollar Value of Volunteer Activity of Americans." In *Working Papers for the Spring Research Forum.* Washington, D.C.: Independent Sector, 1983.

Weschler, L. E., and Mushkatel, A. H. "The Developer's Role in Coprovision, Cofinancing, and Coproduction of Urban Infrastructure and Services." *Journal of Voluntary Action Research,* 1987, *16* (3), 62-69.

Wheeler, C. M. "Facing Realities: The Need to Develop a Political Agenda for Volunteerism." *Journal of Volunteer Administration,* 1986-87, *5* (2), 1-12.

Whelan, R., and Dupont, R. "Some Political Costs of Coprovision: The Case of the New Orleans Zoo." *Public Productivity Review,* 1986, no. 40 (Winter), 69-75.

Whitaker, G. P. "Coproduction: Citizen Participation in Service Delivery." *Public Administration Review,* 1980, *40* (3), 240-246.

Willing, P. R. *A History of Management Assistance and Educational Programs of the Small Business Administration from 1953 to 1978.* Unpublished doctoral dissertation, School of Education, Health, Nursing, and Arts Professions, New York University, 1982.

Wilson, M. *The Effective Management of Volunteer Programs.* Boulder, Colo.: Johnson, 1976.

Wilson, M. "Reversing the Resistance of Staff to Volunteers." *Voluntary Action Leadership,* 1981 (Spring), 21.

Wilson, M. "The New Frontier: Volunteer Management Training." *Training and Development Journal,* 1984, *38* (7), 50-52.

Wineburg, C. R., and Wineburg, R. J. "Local Human Service Development: Institutional Utilization of Volunteers to Solve Community Problems." *Journal of Volunteer Administration,* 1987, *5* (4), 9-14.

Wolf, J. H. " 'Professionalizing' Volunteer Work in a Black Neighborhood." *Social Service Review,* 1985, *59* (3), 423-434.

Wolozin, H. "The Economic Role and Value of Volunteer Work in the United States: An Exploratory Study." *Journal of Voluntary Action Research,* 1975, *4* (1), 19-34.

Young, C. L., Goughler, D. H., and Larson, P. J. "Organizational Volunteers for the Rural Frail Elderly: Outreach, Casefinding, and Service Delivery." *Gerontologist,* 1986, *26* (4), 342-344.

Young, D. *The Nonprofit Sector and NASPAA's Redefinition of Public Service.* Washington, D.C.: National Association of Schools of Public Affairs and Administration, 1987.

Index

237

Q

Questionnaires, 203–215

R

Rastikis, L., 150
Reagan, R., 7–8, 12–13, 14, 41, 71, 123, 141
Recognition, 164
Record keeping, 84
Recreation services, volunteer assistance in, 4
Recruiting, 105, 142, 153–161, 198
Reeves, T. Z., 86, 153–154, 175
Rehm, P. T., 153
Reimbursement expenses, 30
Religious organizations, and volunteers, 147–148
Reorganization Plan Number 1 of 1971, 5
Research, 181–189
Retired Senior Volunteer program, 5
Rydberg, W. D., 33

S

Salamon, L. M., 6, 76, 84, 87
Samuelson, R. J., 141, 142
Scheier, I. H., 2, 119, 137, 151, 187
Schiff, J. A., 85, 152–153
Schindler-Rainman, E., 191
Schools, volunteer assistance in, 63
Schwartz, F. S., 24, 25, 34, 181
SCORE. See Service Corps of Retired Executives
Scott, K. M., 164
Screening, 105–106
Senior Companion program, 5
Service Corps of Retired Executives (SCORE), 6, 21: assessing cost-effectiveness of, 40–48; assessing job performance of, 54, 57–60; benefits of volunteers in, 68, 71; client counseling function in, 129; fund-raising by, 31; influence of volunteers in, 86–87; insurance costs of, 29; job design

at, 156; management of, 65, 112–114; office costs of, 27–28; organizing of, 98–99, 125; recruitment for, 159, 160–161; survey procedures and guidelines of, 202–215; value disagreements in, 82–83
Service volunteers: defined, 3; in government, 4–6. See also Volunteers
Sharp, E. B., 16
Shulman, M. A., 155
Siegel, G. B., 62, 71
Sigler, R. T., 56
Simon, J. G., 177
Sloan, C., 193
Small Business Act of 1953, 29, 42, 123
Small Business Development Centers (SBDC), 57, 58, 59, 71–72
Small Business Institutes (SBI), 57, 58, 59
Smith, D. H., 3, 144
Social Service Block Grant, 174
Social Workers and Volunteers (Holme and Maizels), 124
Solomon, L. J., 69
Sontheimer, H. G., 164
Staff. See Paid staff; Volunteers
State Offices of Volunteerism (SOV), 5, 177, 181, 182
"Street-level bureaucrats," 76, 78
Strickler, G., 121
Sumka, H. J., 36
Sundeen, R. A., 62, 71, 77, 182, 184, 197
Survey procedures and guidelines, 202–215

T

Task allocation, 132–134
Task Force on Private Sector Initiatives, 12, 123
Tax assistance programs, 6
Tax Counseling for the Elderly (TCE), 6
Tax Reform Act of 1986, 152–153
Tax revolt, 8–9
Termination, 111

Thomas, J. C., 13
Thompson, F. J., 16
Thompson, L. N., 16
Tocqueville, A. de, 1
Trade associations, job performance of, 57, 58, 59
Training: cost of, 27, 28, 31; orientation and, 107–109, 194–196; in volunteer management and supervision, 109–114

U

U.S. Department of Agriculture, 5, 32, 39. *See also* Cooperative Extension Service
U.S. Department of Health and Human Services, 6
U.S. Department of Housing and Urban Development, 6
U.S. Department of Justice, 6
U.S. Department of the Interior, 6
U.S. Department of Transportation, 6
U.S. Department of Treasury, 6
U.S. Forest Service, 6, 39, 85, 137
U.S. Small Business Administration (SBA), 6, 21, 29, 40, 54, 65, 79, 125, 156, 184, 202–215. *See also* Service Corps of Retired Executives
Urban Affairs Quarterly, 15
Utterback, J., 63, 117, 123, 171

V

Values, differences in, 81–84, 86
Van Til, J., 18, 66–67, 144, 155, 156
Veterans Administration, 6
Virginia Department of Volunteerism, 39
Virginia State Government Volunteers Act of 1977, 123
VISTA. *See* Volunteers in Service to America
Vizza, C., 160, 198
Voluntary Action Leadership, 20, 127, 181
Volunteer Income Tax Assistance (VITA) programs, 6

Volunteerism: education on, 177–181; fiscal climate and, 7–9; need for, 11–14; renewed interest in, 7–14, 77, 78; research on, 181–189
Volunteer management: cost of, 26–27; director of volunteer services, 101–102; importance of, 20–21; lack of, 78–80; staff effectiveness and, 64–65; training in, 109–114; volunteers in, 31
Volunteer positions: job descriptions for, 104–105; job design for, 155–157; matching volunteers with, 60–61, 102–106
Volunteer programs: calculating cost of, 46–47; centralized vs. decentralized, 100–101; designing, 92–97; evaluating, 116–117, 186–188; feedback on, 198–200; funding for, 192; guidelines for, 191–201; housing, 98–101; increasing access to, 196–198; legislation and, 122–123; organizational policy and, 123–124; organizing, 97–102; planning for, 125–128; reasons for, 121–122; shared power in, 192–194
Volunteer Protection Act, 174
Volunteers: adapting public organizations to, 157–158; areas of involvement of, 4, 77–78; assessing organizational needs for, 103–104; autonomy of, 79–80; availability of, 142–153; benefits of, 66–72, 134–138; competition for, 150–153; cost savings and, 32–36; dependence on, 84–85; dollar value of contributions of, 2, 41–45; evaluation of, 114–116; influence of, 84–87; job performance of, 53–61; matching with positions, 60–61, 102–106, 195; motivation of, 66–67, 93–95; nontraditional, 161; number of, 2, 10–11, 77, 145–148; orientation and training of, 107–109, 194–196; paid employees vs., 32–36, 113; placing, 106; profile